THE
WEST WING
S C R I P T   B O O K

THE
WEST WING
S C R I P T B O O K

JOHN WELLS PRODUCTIONS

NEWMARKET PRESS • NEW YORK

The West Wing Script Book Production Team:

Randall Warner, Television Executive, John Wells Productions

Melanie O'Brien, Manager of Sales
Skye Van Raalte-Herzog, Manager of Book Production
Warner Bros. Worldwide Publishing

Aaron Sorkin photos by Ron Jaffe

The West Wing Created by Aaron Sorkin

This book is published in the United States of America.

First Edition

10 9 8 7 6 5 4 3 2 1

ISBN 1-55704-499-6

Library of Congress Cataloging-in-Publication Data
Sorkin, Aaron.
    The West Wing script book / introductions by Aaron Sorkin. – 1ˢᵗ ed.
        p. cm.
    "John Wells Productions."
    "All scripts by Aaron Sorkin" —T.P. verso.
    ISBN 1-55704-499-6
West Wing (Television program) I. Sorkin, Aaron. II. Title.

PN1992.77.W44 S67 2002
791.45'72—dc21   2002023538

QUANTITY PURCHASES
Companies, professional groups, clubs, and other organizations may qualify for
special terms when ordering quantities of this title. For information, write Special
Sales Department, Newmarket Press, 18 East 48th Street, New York, NY 10017; call
(212) 832-3575; fax (212) 832-3629; or e-mail mailbox@newmarketpress.com.

www.newmarketpress.com

Manufactured in the United States of America.

CONTENTS

ACKNOWLEDGMENTS

"If you're dumb, surround yourself with smart people. If you're smart, surround yourself with smart people who disagree with you."

—Isaac Jaffee in *Sports Night*

Here are just a few of the smart people without whom these and all the other episodes couldn't have been written: Allison Abner, Eli Attie, Aeden Babish, Patrick H. Caddell, Lauren Carpenter, Nanda Chitre, Rick Cleveland, Julia Dahl, Marlin Fitzwater, Laura Glasser, Dee Dee Myers, Peggy Noonan, Lawrence O'Donnell, Jr., Peter Parnell, Lauren Schmidt, Diana Son, Gene Sperling, Felicia Willson, the incredible Paul Redford, and the amazing Kevin Falls.

Additional thanks to: John Eakin, Ron Jaffe, Mindy Kanaskie, Brandon Lu, Mike Neilson, W.J. Rinier, Jr., and Andrew Stearn.

And Tommy did some things.

—Aaron Sorkin

THE
WEST WING
SEASON ONE

INTRODUCTION

"I'd like to write a show about senior staffers at the White House."
I was lying.

A lunch meeting had been set up with John Wells, Executive Producer of such modest hits as *China Beach* and *E.R.* The idea was that we were going to talk about my creating a TV series. We were going to talk about it, I wasn't actually going to do it.

I'd spent the last year and a half doing day work. I was asked to write some quips for Sean Connery and Nicolas Cage in *The Rock* and I did it. I was asked to work on some of Will Smith's scenes in *Enemy of the State* and I did it. I pitched in on *Bulworth*.

I didn't want to start writing something of my own because to do that I'd have to start writing something. I love writing but hate starting. The page is awfully white and it says, "You may have fooled some of the people some of the time but those days are over, *giftless*. I'm not your agent and I'm not your mommy, I'm a white piece of paper, you wanna dance with me?" and I really, really don't. I don't want any trouble. I'll go peaceable-like.

My first play, *A Few Good Men*, opened on Broadway when I was 28 and didn't close for another 497 performances. I followed that with an off-Broadway disaster called *Making Movies*. I followed that with the screen adaptation of *A Few Good Men* and then *Malice* and then *The American President*. I followed *The American President* with a 28 day stay at the Hazelden Center in Minnesota to kick a cocaine habit. And I followed Hazelden with day work. It saved me from having to come up with an idea. And the nights. And the white piece of paper.

David Lonner was my agent at CAA. I was sitting in his office and he was telling me about all the great directors who wanted to work with me and I was trying to think of a way to work with them back without having to write anything when Judith Krantz's son walked in.

Tony Krantz was the biggest TV agent at the agency and as he shook my hand he said, "You know what rhymes with superstar? Aaron Sorkin." I'm a professional writer so I knew he was mistaken but I liked the sound of it and I told him sure I'd have lunch with his client, John Wells.

The night before the lunch some friends came over for dinner, including Brad Whitford and his wife, Jane Kaczmarek and the writer Akiva Goldsman, who'd not yet written *A Beautiful Mind* which would win him the Academy Award. The third game of the '96 World Series was on but it held little interest for me since the Yankees had already dropped the first two games in the Bronx. You don't come back to win the World Series after losing the first two games at home. Ever. (The Yankees would come back to win the World Series after losing the first two games at home and not lose another World Series game for five years. I'm wrong about almost everything.) So with Game 3 and the World Series safely in the back pocket of the Atlanta Braves, Akiva and I went downstairs where I had a small office and lit cigarettes.

"You know what would make a good TV series?" he said. "That." He was pointing at the framed poster of *The American President*. "If you concentrated on the senior staffers. Senior staffers at the White House, you'd be good writing that series."

"I'm just having lunch," I said.

"You sure?" he asked me.

"I'm certain," I answered. "I'm sure." And that's when Whitford shouted downstairs that Darryl Strawberry had just parked one over the left field fence to put the Yankees ahead.

As I walked into Ca' del Sole the next day I immediately saw that I was screwed. There were three agents at the table. John hadn't come to schmooze.

"What's your idea," he asked me.

Okay, an idea was what he was expecting.

"I'd like to write a show about senior staffers at the White House."

"Great," he said, "we've got a deal."

Super.

Following my usual routine, I thought about the pilot for six months and wrote it in four days. John liked it. Warner Bros. liked it. Then I finally caught a break. NBC didn't want to do it.

- Washington shows don't work.
- Shows about politics don't work.
- You can't have Jewish people on TV.
- You can't have divorced people on TV.
- You can't have people from New York on TV.
- You can't have people with mustaches on TV.

The first two were sentiments expressed about *The West Wing* pilot script, the last four were uttered in 1970 by an executive at CBS. People who don't know anything tend to make up fake rules, the real rules being considerably more difficult to learn.

Little matter. Because after the John Wells meeting, Judith Krantz's son had left CAA to run the TV department at Ron Howard's company, Imagine. He called me and said, "Remember that movie idea you were talking about? Behind the scenes at a national cable sports show? Remember that? Don't you think it'd make a good TV series?"

I did, and I wrote *Sports Night*. Stu Bloomberg, chairman of ABC, read the pilot and said he wished it was more like *Frasier*. I said I wished it was more like *Birth of a Nation* but life's full of disappointments and he ordered 13 episodes and then nine more after that and then another season after that.

I'd never met Tommy Schlamme but I'd heard his name and when you hear his name you don't forget it. When you see his work you don't forget it either. When he came in to meet me for the job of directing the *Sports Night* pilot, I asked him what he might do, as director, to make *Sports Night* more like *Frasier*. He said, "Nothing. I want to direct <u>this</u>."

Tommy directed the pilot, about a dozen episodes after that, was an Executive Producer on the show and won an Emmy for it. The downside for him was that he would become my closest collaborator and confidant.

In the meantime, NBC lost *Seinfeld* and the NFL in the same week and they hadn't developed a new half-hour to equal or come close to the success of *Friends* and it was time for a changing of the guard. Scott

Sassa replaced Don Ohlmeyer, Warren Littlefield was replaced by Garth Ancier (who would later be replaced by Jeff Zucker) and the unthinkable happened: Somebody forgot to tell Scott and Garth you can't do a show about Washington and politics. They ordered *The West Wing*.

John Wells Productions was our production company with John Wells serving as Executive Producer along with Tommy, who was also serving as principal director, with me doing the typing. Warner Bros. was our studio and NBC our network. We began casting in January, about a month before the other pilots, to get a jump on the best actors. For Leo McGarry, the Chief of Staff, I wanted someone like John Spencer. Casting asked me, "How 'bout John Spencer?" I said, "We'll never get John Spencer." So we got John Spencer. Richard Schiff beat out Eugene Levy and I don't know how many other people for Toby Ziegler. Rob Lowe left our jaws on the floor after performing Sam Seaborn's Act IV speech to his boss's daughter without knowing it's his boss's daughter. Brad Whitford, whom I'd known and loved for the ten years since he appeared on stage in *A Few Good Men*, gave simply the best audition for anything I'd ever seen. Moira Kelly was tapped to play Mandy Hampton. For the Press Secretary there was a problem. We'd all fallen in love with Allison Janney. Married men were ready to leave their wives. The problem was that Allison's Caucasian and so was the rest of the cast so far. This was making us nervous. The network too. It also wasn't right. There was a wonderfully talented Jamaican actress who was reading very well for it. Still, when we closed our eyes at night we wanted Allison.

So we cast Allison.

There was a one scene part, Josh's assistant, Donna. We cast Janel Moloney, an actress Tommy and I had used for one scene on *Sports Night*. The idea was that Donna would be in a few episodes here and there. Janel so knocked our socks off in the pilot that I just kept writing Donna in every episode. By the second season we officially made Janel what she already unofficially was in the first season: a series regular.

All we needed was the President. We had an idea list that went from Alan Alda to Jason Robards to Sidney Poitier. Then one afternoon my assistant, Lauren Carpenter, stepped into my office--

LAUREN

Charlie Sheen is on the phone.

ME

Probably not.

LAUREN

Martin Sheen?

ME

There you go.

Martin Sheen has lived an extraordinary life. One of the results being that the less extraordinary things in his life tend to get pushed to the back burner. John Wells had set up the call.

ME

Martin, hello, this is Aaron.

MARTIN

Aaron, it's Martin Sheen.

ME

It's good to talk to you, thanks
for calling.

MARTIN

You remember me?

ME

Of course I remember you.

MARTIN

I played the Chief of Staff in *The
American President*, you remember me
from that movie?

ME

Yes, also from *Badlands* and *Apocalypse
Now*.

MARTIN

Badlands was a good movie.

ME

Yes it was.

MARTIN

A.J. McInerny, the Chief of Staff.

ME

Martin, I know exactly who you are and
so does everyone else in the Western
world.

And then we got to talking about *The West Wing*.

"Come with me, I wanna show you this shot."

It's easy to love Tommy Schlamme, even when he's not excited about a shot he's just choreographed, but on this occasion he'd just mapped out what would be the first big camera move of the series, the shot that would take us inside the West Wing of the White House. We started on the bronze Seal of the President that's embedded in the floor and flowed effortlessly through the Northwest Lobby and past security and down corridors and into offices and out of offices and we got teased by the biggest office of them all before settling in and the whole thing was gonna last five minutes but seem like five seconds and it would stamp a visual style that the show would adhere to forever. Tommy hadn't just directed the pilot, he'd just written the series in directors' language.

I'm mentioning this because when the publishers came to me with the idea of putting out a volume of *The West Wing* scripts, I thought, "Oh good, a chance for me to turn a solo without all the annoying frou-frou of actors and directors and designers and technicians. Cameras and whatnot. People." But now that I think about it, the only thing I'm not going to miss are the commercials. So as you read these, I urge you to remember the power that Martin Sheen and John Spencer bring to a scene, the dignity of Dulé Hill, the intensity of Richard Schiff and the passion of Brad Whitford, the humor of Rob Lowe and the ungodly elegance of Allison Janney and Janel Moloney.

And how Tommy can make a camera dance.

Here's the pilot.

Pilot

<u>TEASER</u>

FADE IN:

1   **INT. FOUR SEASONS HOTEL/GEORGETOWN — NIGHT**   1

The well-dressed and powerful are having after-dinner drinks
in the crowded hotel lounge. We hear snippets of
conversations as the camera finds its way around the room.

A woman we'll know later as LAURIE, dressed sexy and having a
drink with a girlfriend, whispers an order to a WAITER, who in
turn makes his way over to the bar.

>   WAITER
> Two Absolut martinis up, and another
> Dewars rocks.

We find SAM SEABORN at the bar with a REPORTER (BILLY).

>   SAM
> I don't think we're gonna run the table,
> if that's what you're asking.

>   BILLY
> It's not.

>   BILLY
> Deep background. I'm not gonna come
> close to using your name.

>   SAM
> You're not gonna come close to getting a
> quote, either.

>   BILLY
> Why are we sitting here?

>   SAM
> You sat down.

>   BILLY
> Is Josh on his way out?

>   SAM
> No.

>   BILLY
> Is he?

                    SAM
No.

                    BILLY
I know he's your friend.

                    SAM
He is.

                    BILLY
Did Caldwell say--

                    SAM
Billy, I'm not talkin' about this.

                    BILLY
Who do I call?

                    SAM
No one.

                    BILLY
Just tell me who to call.

                    SAM
Well you could call 1-800 BITE ME.

                    BILLY
Sam--

                    SAM
He's not going anywhere, Billy, it's a
non-story.

                    BILLY
Okay. You're lying now, aren't you.

                    SAM
That hurts, Billy. Why would I lie to a
journalist of all people.

                    BILLY
Why do you keep looking over my shoulder?

                    SAM
Why?

                    BILLY
Yes.

                    SAM
'Cause Alger Hiss just walked in with my
secret pumpkin.

> BILLY
> What the--

> SAM
> There's a woman over there. I think
> she's looking at me.

> BILLY
> Really?

> SAM
> I don't know. I never know if they're
> looking or not.

BILLY turns 180 degrees in his seat to look at LAURIE.

> BILLY
> Yeah, I think she was.

> SAM
> I wanna thank you for the casual way that
> you did that just now. She probably
> didn't notice that.

CUT TO:

2   **EXT. AFFLUENT STREET IN CHEVY CHASE - DAWN**   2

The sun is just beginning to rise over a large Tudor.

> RADIO ANNOUNCER (V.O.)
> Also in the news this morning. Twenty-
> five cars jumped the tracks spilling
> twenty thousand gallons of sodium
> hydroxide...

CUT TO:

3   **INT. LEO MCGARRY'S DINING ROOM — CONTINUOUS**   3

LEO MCGARRY is eating breakfast and working on the crossword.
His coffee cup is re-filled by a MAID. We hear a telephone
ringing.

> LEO
> Seventeen across is wrong. It's just
> <u>wrong</u>. You believe that, Ruth?

> MAID
> You should call them.

> LEO
> I <u>will</u> call them.

Leo's wife calls from the kitchen--

                    MRS. MCGARRY (O.S.)
          Telephone, Leo.

                    LEO
          I'm in the shower.

                    MRS. MCGARRY (O.S.)
          It's Potus.

LEO puts down the coffee cup and heads to the phone.

                    LEO
               (into phone)
          Yeah?

                                        CUT TO:

4   **INT. HEALTH CLUB — DAWN**   4

C.J. CREGG is running on a treadmill while doing her best to
have a pleasant conversation with a nice-looking MAN.

                    C.J.
          You can have a normal life. You'd be
          amazed at how normal I can be. See, it's
          all about budgeting your time. This
          time, this hour, this is my time. Five
          a.m. to six a.m. I can workout, as you
          see. I can think about personal matters.
          I can meet an interesting man.

C.J.'s beeper goes off--

                    C.J.
          The trick is--

                    MAN
          Your beeper's going.

                    C.J.
          What?

                    MAN
          I think your beeper's going.

C.J. checks her beeper, something she hasn't quite mastered
doing while running on a tread mill, and goes flying off the
tread mill.

5   **INT. JOSH LYMAN'S OFFICE — PRE-DAWN**   5

JOSH sleeps at his desk and is awaken by something. Beeping.
He picks his pager up off his desk, hits a button and looks at
the message. He punches some numbers into his phone and waits
a moment.

                    JOSH
               (into phone)
          Yeah. This is Josh Lyman. What's going
          on...

6   **INT. THE REDEYE — DAWN**   6

All the shades are down and all the lights are off in the
cabin except the one over the coach seat occupied by TOBY
ZIEGLER. He's got a lap-top, some papers and a cup of coffee
spread out in front of him as he works away.

                    FLIGHT ATTENDANT (V.O.)
          We ask at this time that you turn off all
          electronic devices, stow your tray tables
          and return your seat backs to the full
          and upright position. We will be landing
          shortly at Washington Dulles Airport.
               (over dialogue)
          ...and we'd like to thank you for flying
          with us today...

A FLIGHT ATTENDANT (a different one) stops at TOBY's seat.

                    FLIGHT ATTENDANT #2
          Sir, I need you to turn off your
          computer.

                    TOBY
          I'm just about done.

                    FLIGHT ATTENDANT #2
          I need you to turn off your laptop, sir,
          it interferes with our navigational
          systems.

                    TOBY
          You know, when you guys say that it
          sounds pretty ridiculous to most people,
          right?

                    FLIGHT ATTENDANT #2
          Sir--

Another FLIGHT ATTENDANT walks up--

                    FLIGHT ATTENDANT #3
          Mr. Ziegler? A message was just patched
          up to the cockpit for you. I'm not sure
          I've got it right. "Potus in a bicycle
          accident"?

                    TOBY
          You got it right.

TOBY takes out his cell phone--

                    FLIGHT ATTENDANT #2
          You can't use your phone until we land,
          sir.

                    TOBY
          We're flying in a Lockheed Eagle series
          L1011. It came off the line 20 months ago
          and carries a Sim5 Transponder tracking
          system. Are you telling me I can still
          flummox this thing with something I
          bought at Radio Shack?

                    FLIGHT ATTENDANT #3
          You can call when we land, sir.

The FLIGHT ATTENDANTS move on--

                    TOBY
              (raising his voice a little)
          Also, I never got my peanuts.

                                              CUT TO:

7   **INT. LAURIE'S BEDROOM — DAWN**   7

The digital clock on the night table turns over to 5:20 a.m.
as we pull back to reveal LAURIE, the woman at the hotel bar,
sitting up in bed and smoking a joint. SAM steps out of the
bathroom having just taken a shower.

                    LAURIE
          How're you doing, Sam?

                    SAM
          Let me tell you something. The water
          pressure in here is really impressive.

                    LAURIE
          I know.

                    SAM
          You could run hydraulics in there.

>   LAURIE
>   (re: the pot)
>   You want some?

>   SAM
>   I'm fine.

>   LAURIE
>   I'm wasted.

>   SAM
>   And probably free of cataracts.

>   LAURIE
>   I get that. That's funny.

>   SAM
>   Thank you.

>   LAURIE
>   (remembering)
>   Oh wait. I'm sorry--your message--your
>   pager went off while you were in the
>   shower. I hit the button because I
>   thought it was mine.

SAM takes a look at the message as LAURIE recites it--

>   LAURIE
>   "Potus in a bicycle accident. Come to
>   the office."

SAM starts getting dressed.

>   LAURIE
>   I memorized it just in case I erased it
>   by accident. These things look exactly
>   alike. Anyway, like I said, I'm totally
>   baked. But, uh, no, it's not like I'm a
>   drug person. I just love pot.

>   SAM
>   Uh... Laurie, I have to go.

>   LAURIE
>   You're kidding me. It's 5:30 in the
>   morning.

SAM is throwing on his shirt and jacket.

>   SAM
>   I know this doesn't look good.

> LAURIE
> Not that good, no.

> SAM
> You know what? I really like you and if
> you give me your number, I'd like to call
> you.

> LAURIE
> Stay right here and save yourself a call.

> SAM
> It's not that I don't see the logic in
> that, but I really gotta go.

> LAURIE
> 'Cause Potus was in a bicycle accident?

> SAM
> Yep.

LAURIE picks up the pad and pen from the night table and
scratches out her number. She stands up and places it in
SAM's hip pocket as she plants a kiss on him.

> LAURIE
> Tell your friend Potus he's got a funny
> name and he should learn how to ride a
> bicycle.

> SAM
> I would, but he's not my friend, he's my
> boss. It's not his name, it's his title.

> LAURIE
> "Potus"?

> SAM
> President of the United States. I'll
> call you.

SMASH CUT TO:

MAIN TITLES

END OF TEASER

ACT ONE

FADE IN:

8   **EXT. THE WHITE HOUSE/NORTHWEST EXECUTIVE ENTRANCE — MORNING**   8

As LEO approaches the entrance, a MARINE GUARD at parade rest comes to attention and opens the door. LEO breezes by and into--

9   **INT. THE WHITE HOUSE/NORTHWEST LOBBY — CONTINUOUS**   9

LEO passes through a metal detector--

                    SECURITY OFFICER
          It's a nice morning, Mr. McGarry.

                    LEO
          We'll take care of that in a hurry, won't
          we, Mike?

                    SECURITY OFFICER
          Yes sir.

LEO's immediately met by an aide (BONNIE) with some papers.

                    BONNIE
          Don't kill the messenger, Leo.

                    LEO
          Oh why the hell not, Bonnie.

                    BONNIE
          Five minutes?

                    LEO
          Please.

LEO starts walking through the corridors of the West Wing of the White House. Office doors are open along the hallways and staffers walk in and out. CNN and C-SPAN are on monitors.

                    LEO
          Hey, Emma.

                    EMMA
          Good morning.

                    LEO
          Wilson?

                    WILSON
          Hey, Leo.

                LEO
Joe.

                JEFFREY
Jeffrey.

                LEO
Whatever.

LEO pops his head into an outer office and calls to the back.

                LEO
            (calling)
Josh!

10   **INT. BULLPEN — CONTINUOUS**   **10**

DONNATELLA MOSS, Josh's assistant, sits at her computer behind LEO. Donna is devoted to Josh and hates admitting it.

                DONNA
Good morning, Leo.

                LEO
Hey, Donna. Is he in yet?

                DONNA
Yeah.

                LEO
Can you get him?

                DONNA
            (shouting)
Josh!

                LEO
Thanks.

JOSH shows himself in the office doorway and indicates that he's on the phone and he'll be just a second.

                DONNA
I heard it's broken.

                LEO
You heard wrong.

                DONNA
I heard--

                    LEO
It's a mild sprain, he'll be back later
today.

                    DONNA
And what was the cause of the accident?

                    LEO
What are you, from State Farm? Go do a
job, would you.

                    DONNA
I'm just--

                    LEO
He was swerving to avoid a tree.

                    DONNA
And what happened?

                    LEO
He was unsuccessful.

11   **INT. JOSH LYMAN'S OFFICE - CONTINUOUS**   11

                    JOSH
          (into phone)
Yeah, that's fine. Just don't do
anything until you talk to justice.
Okay. 'Bye.
          (hangs up)
Hey.

                    LEO
How many Cubans exactly have crammed
themselves into these fishing boats?

                    JOSH
It's important to understand, Leo, that
by and large they're not fishing boats.
You hear fishing boats, you conjure the
image of, well, a <u>boat</u>, first of all.
What the Cubans are on would charitably
be described as <u>rafts</u>. Okay? They're
making the hop from Havana to Miami in
fruit baskets basically, let's just be
clear on that.

                    LEO
We are.

12   **INT. PRESS BULLPEN — CONTINUOUS**   12

                    JOSH
Donna's desk, if it could float, would
look good to them right now.

                    LEO
I get it. How many are there?

                    JOSH
We don't know.

                    LEO
What time exactly did they leave?

                    JOSH
We don't know.

                    LEO
Do we know when they get here?

                    JOSH
No.

                    LEO
     (pause)
True or False: If I were to stand on
high ground in Key West with a good pair
of binoculars, I'd be as informed as I am
right now.

                    JOSH
That's true.

                    LEO
The intelligence budget's money well-
spent, isn't it?

                    JOSH
Tell him to send in the Coast Guard, Leo,
come on. I understand, but they're never
gonna make it to our territorial waters.

                    LEO
Thank you.

                    JOSH
What if the DEA suspected they had drugs?

                    LEO
Does the DEA suspect there were drugs?

> JOSH
> We can make a phone call.

13   **INT. LOBBY - CONTINUOUS**   13

> LEO
> Josh--

> JOSH
> If the DEA or Navy-Intel thought the
> Cubans were bringing in drugs, wouldn't
> we have to go out there and search those
> rafts with, you know, guns and blankets?

> LEO
> You look like hell. You know that, don't
> you?

> JOSH
> Yes, I do. Listen, Leo, did he say
> anything?

14   **INT. CORRIDOR — CONTINUOUS**   14

> LEO
> Did he say anything? The President's
> pissed as hell at you, Josh, and so am I.

> JOSH
> I know.

> LEO
> We gotta work with these people. And
> where the hell do you get off struttin'
> your--

> JOSH
> I know.

> LEO
> Al Caldwell's a good man.

> JOSH
> Al Caldwell wasn't there.

> LEO
> I'm saying you take everyone on the
> Christian right, dump `em into one big
> pile and label `em stupid. We need these
> people.

> JOSH
> We do not need these people.

                    LEO
Josh--

                    JOSH
We need Al Caldwell, we <u>want</u> Al Caldwell,
we do <u>not</u> need John van Dyke and we do
not need Mary Marsh.

                    LEO
And I think there shouldn't be instant
replay in football but that's not my
call, now is it.

                    JOSH
It was stupid.

                    LEO
Damn straight.

LEO takes off down the hallway--

                    JOSH
I was right, though.

                    LEO
          (over his shoulder)
Like I don't know that.

                                        CUT TO:

15   **INT. OVAL OFFICE — CONTINUOUS**   15

Leo steps into the outer office where MRS. LANDINGHAM, the
President's secretary, is at work with BONNIE.

                    MRS. LANDINGHAM
Oh, Mr. McGarry, have they done an x-ray?

                    LEO
Yep.

                    MRS. LANDINGHAM
Is anything broken?

                    LEO
A four-thousand dollar Lynex Titanium
touring bike that I swore I'd never lend
anyone.

                    MRS. LANDINGHAM
I don't understand, how did he--

                    LEO
He's a klutz, Mrs. Landingham, your
President's a geek.

              MRS. LANDINGHAM
Mr. McGarry, you know how I feel about
that kind of talk in the Oval Office.

                    LEO
I apologize.

              MRS. LANDINGHAM
Just in this <u>room</u>, Mr. McGarry, is all
I'm asking.

                    LEO
Yes. Oh, Bonnie, call OEOB and set up a
briefing for the Vice-President... let's
coordinate with Katy Simons' office on
the appointments.

                 BONNIE
Should I get everybody in?

                    LEO
Yeah.
        (to his secretary)
Margaret, please call the editor of the
New York Times crossword and tell him
that Khaddafi is spelled with an "H" and
two "D"s' and isn't a seven letter word
for anything.

                 MARGARET
Is this for real or is this just funny?

                    LEO
Apparently it's neither.

16   **INT. LEO'S OFFICE — CONTINUOUS**   16

The Chief of Staff gets a nice office. A platter of pastry
and coffee is on the table as the Senior Staff members start
to filter in for their morning meeting.

Eight or 10 staffers sit around the room with a few aides
standing nearby. From time to time, a secretary will slip in
and hand someone a written message to be glanced over.

C.J., who we met earlier at the health club, is the White
House Press Secretary and enters with TOBY ZIEGLER, a rumpled
and sleepless Communications Director. They join SAM, the
Deputy Communications Director.

Throughout this scene, LEO will drift in and out of full
participation as his attention is from time to time taken by
some papers in front of him or an item in the newspaper.   In
other words, nothing going on here is an emergency.

> C.J.
> Is there anything I can say other than
> the President rode his bicycle into a
> tree?

> LEO
> He hopes never to do it again.

JOSH enters with DONNA...

> C.J.
> Seriously, they're laughing pretty hard.

> LEO
> He rode his bicycle into a tree, C.J.,
> what do you want me--"The President,
> while riding a bicycle on his vacation in
> Jackson Hole, came to a sudden arboreal
> stop."--What do you want from me?

> C.J.
> A little love, Leo.

> LEO
> (to SAM)
> What do you know about the Cubans?

> SAM
> I don't know any more than Josh.
> Somewhere between twelve hundred and two
> thousand Cubans began embarking from a
> fishing village 30 miles south of Havana.

> STAFFER
> Where are they headed.

> JOSH
> Vegas.

> SAM
> Miami, though it's not clear how
> sophisticated their navigational
> equipment--

> JOSH
> Navigational equipment--"That way is
> North" I think is pretty--

                    C.J.
Josh--

                    JOSH
C.J. if one of those guys could throw a
split-fingered fast-ball we'd send in the
U.S.S. Eisenhower.

                    C.J.
That's not entirely true.

                    TOBY
Oh for God's sake forget the journey,
okay. The voyage is not our problem.

                    C.J.
What's our problem?

                    TOBY
What to do when the Nina, the Pinta, and
the Get Me the Hell Out Of Here hit
Miami.

                    LEO
Sam?

                    SAM
We can't send `em back. They'll go to
jail if they're lucky.

                    TORY
We'll get whacked in--what--at least--

                    SAM
--three Congressional districts. Dade
County--

                    TOBY
--those seats are gone.

                    JOSH
Not to mention the fact that it's wrong.

                    SAM
Plus that.

                    JOSH
What about Texas?

                    SAM
I wouldn't worry about it.

>   LEO
>   (to SAM)
>   Keep Josh in the loop on this throughout
>   the day.

>   SAM
>   Me?

>   LEO
>   Yeah.

>   SAM
>   The thing is, my day's a little tight--

>   TOBY
>   Deal with it.

>   SAM
>   And I'm happy to, it's just that--

>   LEO
>   Sam--

>   SAM
>   I'm just saying isn't this more of a
>   military area?

>   LEO
>   Military?

>   SAM
>   Yeah.

>   TOBY
>   You think the United States is under
>   attack from twelve hundred Cubans in
>   rowboats?

>   SAM
>   I'm not saying I don't like our chances.

>   TOBY
>   It's mindboggling to me that we ever won
>   an election.

>   LEO
>   Pat Thomas wants to call up the Guard.

>   JOSH
>   He shouldn't.

>   SAM
>   He's right.

                    C.J.
You send in the Guard and you create a
panic situation.

                    TOBY
I agree with Josh and I agree with C.J.
and I agree with Sam. And you know how
that makes me crazy.

                    LEO
Yeah, I do.

                    TOBY
They're running for their lives. You
don't have to start a game of Red Rover
with Castro, but you don't send in the
National Guard. You send food. And you
send doctors.

                    JOSH
Sam, see that INS is working with the Red
Cross and the Centers for Disease
Control.

                    SAM
I got my guy from CDC on the phone right
now--

                    LEO
Go talk to him.

                    SAM
    (over)
Talk to him.

SAM exits down the hallway--

                    LEO
Moving on. Let's talk about Josh...

                                        CUT TO:

17   **INT. PRESS BRIEFING ROOM — DAY**   17

A dozen or so REPORTERS are standing and sitting about, mostly
talking to each other. A few are in the back on laptops and
cell phones. BILLY is holding court with three of them.

                    BILLY
Al Caldwell scares the hell out of the
President and Josh knows it.

                    REPORTER #1
He's not gonna fire him.

                    BILLY
He's got no choice.

                    REPORTER #1
Billy, the President's not gonna fire
Josh Lyman.

                    BILLY
He doesn't have a choice. Listen, I had
drinks with Sam Seaborn last night.

                    REPORTER #1
And Sam said that the President was gonna
fire Josh?

                    BILLY
He needs these people. He's gonna have
to give `em Josh.

C.J. steps up to the podium with some papers.

                    C.J.
          (calling for them to sit)
Folks. Folks.

Two AIDES begin passing out press packets--

                    REPORTER #1
Billy what do you--

                    BILLY
He doesn't have a choice.

                    C.J.
Good morning. Dr. Randal Haymen,
H-A-Y-M-E-N, Chief of Orthopedics at St.
Johns' Hospital, has diagnosed the
President with a mild sprain in his left
ankle, sustained while cycling into a
large Cypress tree. The details can be
found in the pool report that Linda and
Suzanne are distributing, along with pool
photographs of the President resisting
the help of a Secret Service agent and
then falling down again. By all means,
enjoy yourselves. Item number 2--

                    REPORTER
C.J., has the President--

> C.J.
> It's a light day, Chris, let's just get
> through this and then I'll take a couple
> of questions. Item number 2: The
> Association of Retired--

18   **INT. JOSH'S OFFICE — DAY**   18

JOSH is at his desk, playing the same videotape back and
forth, only now we can see what he's watching. He's on a
Sunday morning roundtable show called Capital Beat with a
moderator and well-groomed woman named MARY MARSH.

> JOSH (ON TV)
> None of your business. Look, if thirty-
> eight states--

> MARY MARSH (ON TV)
> No. Well, I can tell you that you don't
> believe in any God that I pray to, Mr.
> Lyman. Not any God that I pray to.

> JOSH (ON TV)
> Lady, the God you pray to is too busy
> being indicted for tax fraud.

And just as MARY MARSH starts to explode, JOSH stops the tape,
rewinds it and starts to play it again.

> MARY MARSH (ON TV)
> No. Well, I can tell you that you don't
> believe in any God that I pray to, Mr.
> Lyman. Not any God that I pray to.

> JOSH (ON TV)
> Lady, the God you pray to is too busy
> being indicted for tax fraud.

JOSH stops the tape, rewinds it and starts to play it again.

> JOSH (ON TV)
> Lady, the God you pray to is too busy
> being indicted for--

JOSH looks up. DONNA's standing in the doorway with a cup of
coffee. JOSH stops the tape.

> DONNA
> You shouldn't have worn that tie on
> television. It bleeds.

                    JOSH
          I don't think it was the tie that got me
          in trouble.

                    DONNA
          Yeah, but I've told you a zillion times.

                    JOSH
          What's that?

                    DONNA
          It's coffee.

                    JOSH
          I thought so.

                    DONNA
          I brought you some coffee.

                    JOSH
          What's goin' on, Donna?

                    DONNA
          Nothing's going on--

                    JOSH
          Donna--

                    DONNA
          I brought you some coffee.

                    JOSH
          Close the door.

DONNA closes the inner office door.

                    JOSH
          Donnatella Moss. When did you start
          working for me?

                    DONNA
          Mmm, during the campaign.

                    JOSH
          And how long have you been my assistant?

                    DONNA
          A year and a half.

                    JOSH
          And when was the last time you brought me
          a cup of coffee?

DONNA thinks...

                    JOSH
          It was never. You've never brought me a
          cup of coffee.

                    DONNA
               (picking up the mug)
          Well, if you're gonna make a big deal out
          of--

                    JOSH
          Donna, if I get fired I get fired.

                    DONNA
          Do you think he's gonna do it?

                    JOSH
               (beat)
          No.

There's a knock at the door--

                    TOBY (O.S.)
          It's Toby.

                    DONNA
               (quietly)
          You won that election for him. You and
          Leo and C.J. and Sam.

                    TOBY (O.S.)
          Open the damn door.

                    DONNA
          And him.

DONNA opens the door.

                    JOSH
          Thanks for the coffee.

                    DONNA
          You're welcome.

She goes back to her desk.

                    TOBY
          Donna brought you coffee?

                    DONNA
               (over her shoulder)
          Shut up.

TOBY steps into the office.

> JOSH
> What's up?

> TOBY
> What'd I tell you before you went on the
> air yesterday?

> JOSH
> You said don't get cute with Mary Marsh.

> TOBY
> I said don't get cute with Mary Marsh. I
> said Al Caldwell is not to be treated
> like some revival tent clown.

> JOSH
> Al Caldwell wasn't there.

> TOBY
> He sure as hell was watching.

> JOSH
> Look, I already took Leo's morning
> beating, what do you want from me?

> TOBY
> I want you to keep your job.

> JOSH
> How?

> TOBY
> I'm gonna make a suggestion which might
> help you out. But I don't want this
> gesture to be mistaken for an indication
> that I like you.

> JOSH
> I understand.

> TOBY
> (carefully)
> In preparation for the Sunday morning
> radio address on family values--

> JOSH
> When did _that_ get on the schedule?

> TOBY
> Listen to me for one sec.

JOSH
When did it get on the schedule?

TOBY
It's the regular Sunday morning--

JOSH
Yeah, but when did we schedule family
values?

TOBY
We scheduled it, Josh, after your smug,
taunting, you know, <u>calamitous</u>
performance on *Capital Beat*.
　　(beat)
America for Better Families, the AAF and
Al Caldwell, Mary Marsh, I invited them
all for coffee this afternoon along with
a couple of speech writers to talk about--

JOSH
What they want to hear.

TOBY
Yes.

JOSH
Yes, sir. Yeah, if you listen carefully,
you can hear two centuries of presidents
rolling over in their--

TOBY
Come to the meeting.

JOSH
No.

TOBY
Come to the meeting and be nice.

JOSH
Why?

TOBY
So C.J. can put it in the papers.

JOSH
Al Caldwell's friends with bad people. I
think he should say so for the common
good, screw politics, how `bout that.

               TOBY
You don't run social policy for this
Government, how 'bout <u>that</u>.

               JOSH
Toby--

               TOBY
I'm in charge of the message around here.
It's my job to tell the President that
the best thing he can do from a p.r.
standpoint is to show you the door.
    (pause)
Come to the meeting. Be nice. Keep your
job.

               JOSH
    (pause)
Yeah, I'll be there.

TOBY turns to leave--

               TOBY
Oh, take a look at this.

TOBY takes out a small newspaper clipping--

               JOSH
What's that?

               TOBY
One of the kids from the newsroom clipped
that from the *Journal* this morning.
Guess who's leaving Lennox/Chase to start
consulting in town?

JOSH looks over the article...

               TOBY
She's leasing offices downtown. She
starts today.

               JOSH
Who is she working for?

               TOBY
I'm checking it out.

JOSH looks at the picture a moment longer...smiles...

                    JOSH
          That's a good picture of her.

                                        FADE OUT.

                  <u>END OF ACT ONE</u>

ACT TWO

FADE IN:

19   **EXT. WASHINGTON STREET — DAY**   19

MANDY is driving, a little too fast, in her BMW convertible
and talking on her cell phone. She cruises through a red
light.

> MANDY
> (into phone)
> Bruce... Bruce... Bruce, I may have just
> gotten back into the business this
> morning, but I didn't come by way of a
> turnip truck, you know what I'm saying?
> You phaff me around on this and I'm gonna
> get cranky right in your face. Now I was
> your source on 443--big fat by-line <u>above</u>
> the fold--I think it's time we play
> what've you done for <u>me</u> lately.

MANDY sees the flashing red LIGHTS of a POLICE CAR in her rear
view mirror. She doesn't register a reaction, but simply
pulls to the side and keeps talking on the phone.

> MANDY
> (into phone)
> I don't want to hear that you're gonna
> <u>try</u>, Bruce, this isn't gym class. I
> said, gym class... gym class. Bruce...
> Bruce... Bruce. Because it's important
> in gym to try, but it is not necessarily--
> Look. Bruce, it was a simple metaphor.

A POLICE OFFICER gets out of the cruiser and starts toward
Mandy's car.

> MANDY
> Now listen up! You're misinterpreting me
> and you're misinterpreting the Senator
> and bush-league reporting is beneath even
> <u>your</u> newspaper.

> POLICE OFFICER
> You know you ran a red light back there.

> MANDY
> (to the OFFICER)
> Hold on.
> (to BRUCE)
> Bruce, please. You huckle me around like
> this, I'm gonna make you cry like a girl.

                    POLICE OFFICER
          License and registration, please.

                    MANDY
               (to Officer)
          Just a second.
               (to Bruce)
          I'm telling you--

                    POLICE OFFICER
          License and registration now, please.

                    MANDY
               (into phone)
          Listen, I'm under arrest. I'm gonna have
          to call you back, Bruce.

                                              CUT TO:

20   **EXT. THE WHITE HOUSE/ESTABLISHING — DAY**   20

                                              CUT TO:

21   **INT. ROOSEVELT ROOM — DAY**   21

     A meeting among LEO and two ECONOMIC ADVISERS is just breaking
     up.

                    ECONOMIST #1
          Uh, they're two and a half percent in the
          third quarter at the end of the fiscal
          year.

                    LEO
          That's fine, but the President's gonna
          look at the WBO revenue analysis and say
          that economists were put on this planet
          to make astrologers look good.

     JOSH slips into the room--

                    ECONOMIST #1
          Leo.

                    LEO
          Luther. Ballpark. One year from today.
          Where's the Dow?

                    ECONOMIST #2
          Tremendous. Up a thousand.

                    LEO
          Fred. One year from today.

> ECONOMIST #1
>
> Not good. Down a thousand.

> LEO
>
> A year from today at least one of you is
> gonna look pretty stupid.

> ECONOMIST #2
>
> Can we go now?

> LEO
>
> (ushering them out the door)
> Oh, go. Get out.

The ECONOMISTS say their good-byes and leave as SAM slips
in...

> SAM
>
> We have a storm system moving into South
> Florida.

> LEO
>
> See, with any luck the Cubans'll turn
> around and live to defect another day.

> JOSH
>
> Yeah, `cause they're probably all tuned
> to the National Weather Service, but
> that's not what I'm here for.

> LEO
>
> What's on your mind?

> JOSH
>
> We've gotta look at the whole field for a
> minute, `cause I think we're about to get
> tagged.

> LEO
>
> With regard to what?

> JOSH
>
> Reelection.

> LEO
>
> Oh, we're not there yet.

> JOSH
>
> Don't let Lloyd Russell push us around on
> Medicare or medium range missiles.

                    LEO
You're taking Lloyd Russell too
seriously.

                    SAM
His numbers are starting to get
interesting.

                    JOSH
Hollywood likes him.   He can raise money.

                    LEO
We're not there yet.

                    JOSII
30 second hypothetical: You're Lloyd
Russell, newly-crowned prince of the
white suburban woman, the upper-middle
class black man, the teacher's union...
you're no friend of the sitting
President.   What do you do?

                    LEO
Put together an exploratory committee.

                    JOSH
Who do you get to run it?

                    LEO
You.

                    JOSH
I already got a job.

                    LEO
For the moment.

                    JOSH
Who do you get?

                    LEO
Well, if I could get Mandy to leave nine
hundred thousand dollars a year at
Lennox/Chase, I'd get Mandy.

                    JOSH
You'd be smart.

                    LEO
Hey, come to think of it, you think she'd
be interested in his job?

                    JOSH
          You're in luck.

                    LEO
          She in town?

                    JOSH
          Just got here today.

                    LEO
          What's she doing?

                    JOSH
          Working for Lloyd Russell.

It takes LEO about two seconds to take this in...

                    LEO
              (calling)
          Margaret! Get me Senator Russell's
          office on the phone.

JOSH and SAM stand there.

                    SAM
          Is that the same suit you wore yesterday?

                    JOSH
          Yeah.
              (beat)
          You?

                    SAM
          Yeah.

                                        CUT TO:

22   **INT. DINER — DAY**   22

A real joint. The lunchtime crowd has thinned out. At one
table, two female COLLEGE STUDENTS are gazing over at a table
off-screen.

                    STUDENT #1
          I think it's him.

                    STUDENT #2
          It is.

                    STUDENT #1
          Okay, I'm going over there.

The two students grab a magazine from their table as we FOLLOW them over to where JOSH and MANDY are sitting.

                    STUDENT #2
Excuse me.

                    STUDENT #1
We're sorry to interrupt your lunch--

                    STUDENT #2
We're juniors at Florida State--

                    STUDENT #1
We're with this poly-sci group--

                    STUDENT #2
Anyway--

                    STUDENT #1
Anyway, we just wanted to say that we think you're excellent, and could we have your autograph.

She puts down a copy of *George* magazine, featuring Josh on the cover.

                    JOSH
Sure.
        (nodding over with his head as
        he writes)
Oh, this is Mandy Hampton. She's excellent, too.

                    STUDENT #1
From the campaign.

                    STUDENT #2
Didn't you guys used to be a thing?

                    STUDENT #1
Jennifer!

                    STUDENT #2
Sorry.

                    JOSH
She used to steal money from me.

                    STUDENT #1
Really?

                    JOSH
Yeah. Thanks for stopping by.

                    STUDENTS #1 AND #2
          Thanks.

                         JOSH
          Sure.

As the STUDENTS go back to their table they ad lib good-byes.

                         JOSH
          See 'ya.

                         MANDY
          Listen. You called me. What do you
          wanna know? Is Lloyd gonna run?

                         JOSH
          I really don't care one way or the other,
          he's a lightweight. I just--

                         MANDY
          You don't like him.

                         JOSH
          Not when I can't use him, no. I just
          wanna know how much trouble he's gonna be
          on the budget surplus.

                         MANDY
          You should get to know him.

                         JOSH
          I have enough friends.

                         MANDY
          Not these days you don't.

                         JOSH
          Jeez, Mandy, it's not like these people
          were in our camp to begin with.

                         MANDY
          Right, Josh, and they've been waiting for
          you to trip over your mouth and you
          handed it to them. It's Christmas morning
          for Mary Marsh.
                  (pause)
          You're a Fulbright Scholar, are you
          honestly the only adult in America who
          doesn't think you're about to be fired?
          Do what Toby's telling you to do.

                         JOSH
          Did you just call him Lloyd?

                MANDY
Who?

                JOSH
Senator Russell.

                MANDY
When?

                JOSH
Just now. You said "What do you wanna
know? Is Lloyd gonna run?"

                MANDY
I don't remember. What does it--

                JOSH
It's unusual for you that you'd call a
Senator by his first name to a third
party.

                MANDY
A third party?

                JOSH
You know what I'm saying.

                MANDY
No, but as long as one of us does--

                JOSH
You're dating Lloyd Russell.

                MANDY
        (beat)
Yes.

                JOSH
        (pause)
Wow. That's great.

                MANDY
Are you gonna freak out?

                JOSH
No, no, no, not at all.
        (pause)
It's just I always thought he was gay.

                MANDY
No you didn't.

> JOSH

I did.

> MANDY

He's not gay.

> JOSH

Are you sure?

> MANDY

Very sure.

> JOSH

He always seemed effeminate to me.

> MANDY

He happens to be very athletic. Plenty
masculine.

> JOSH

I think he's a woman.

> MANDY

Josh, take me seriously.

> JOSH

I do.

> MANDY

The *New York Times* is gonna release a
poll in the next few days that brings
your unfavorables up to 48%.

> JOSH
>   (beat)

This is the first I'm hearing of it.

> MANDY

You'll have it in about an hour.

> JOSH

Where'd you get this?

> MANDY

We don't play for the same team anymore.

> JOSH

Wait a minute. One minute you're giving
me career advice, the next minute you're
telling me we don't play for the same
team.

              MANDY
I'm just gonna be here a while. And I
want you at your fighting weight when I
start bitch-slapping you guys around the
beltway.

The waitress brings their food...

              JOSH
You and Lloyd Russell, huh?

              MANDY
     (beat)
Yeah.

                             CUT TO:

23   **INT. LEO'S OFFICE — DAY**   23

As LEO speaks on the phone, a few STAFFERS will come in and
out to leave something on the desk.

              LEO
     (into phone)
Seventeen across.
     (beat)
Yes, seventeen across is wrong.

C.J. comes in...

              LEO
     (into phone)
You're spelling his name wrong... What's
my name? My name doesn't matter. I'm
just an ordinary citizen who relies on
the *Times* crossword for stimulation. And
I'm telling you that I met the man twice.
And I recommended a pre-empted Exocet
Missile strike against his Air Force. So,
I think I know how to--

              C.J.
Leo.

              LEO
They hang up on me every time.

              C.J.
That's almost hard to believe.

LEO's begun gathering up some things--

                    LEO
What do you need?

                    C.J.
Nightline needs someone for the East
Asia--

                    LEO
Send Naomi. What else?

                    C.J.
There might be a press leak on A-3-C-3.

                    LEO
That was Hutchinson. What else?

                    C.J.
Leo...

                    LEO
Please don't ask me about Josh.

                    C.J.
I was gonna ask--

                    LEO
I honestly don't know anything.

                    C.J.
You know the President.

                    LEO
So do you.

                    C.J.
You know him better.

                    LEO
I've known him 40 years, C.J. And all I
can promise you is, on any given day
there's really no predicting what he's
gonna choose to care about.

                    C.J.
Yeah.

                    LEO
I'm sorry. I'm late.

LEO exits, leaving C.J. for a moment before we:

                                        CUT TO:

24   **INT. BULLPEN — DAY**   24

SAM is walking along a corridor with his lunch tray, being
followed by two STAFFERS.

> STAFFER #1
>
> You can't use those stats.

> STAFFER #2
>
> The assault stats.

> STAFFER #1
>
> The assault stats are wrong.

> SAM
>
> We got 'em from your office.

> STAFFER #2
>
> We got them from HUD.

> SAM
>
> And they're wrong?

> STAFFER #2
>
> Even if they were right, don't use them.

> SAM
>
> Well, A) Let's make `em right. B) Why
> can't I use `em?

> STAFFER #2
>
> The 76-year-old grandmother.

> STAFFER #1
>
> Every time we use those assault stats
> Carr and Gilmore come back--

> SAM
>
> Who's the 76-year-old grandmother?

> STAFFER #2
>
> Every day, 17,000 Americans defend
> themselves with a gun--

> SAM
>
> That's flatly untrue.

> STAFFER #2
>
> --including a 76-year-old grandmother in
> Chicago who defended herself against an
> intruder in the middle of the night.

SAM's secretary, CATHY, slips in during the following...

                    STAFFER #1
          Just don't use the stat.

                    SAM
          The 76-year-old grandmother doesn't
          defend herself with a modified AK47
          Assault Rifle, Larry. Unless she's
          defending herself against Turkish rebels.

                    CATHY
          Excuse me.

                    SAM
          Oh, you guys know my assistant Cathy?

                    STAFFER #1
          We talk a lot on the phone.

                    CATHY
          Yeah hi.
               (to SAM)
          I need you for just a second.

                    SAM
          Uh, right.
               (to the STAFFERS)
          Call me at the end of the day.

     SAM and CATHY talk on the way to SAM's office...

25   **INT. WEST WING HALLWAYS - CONTINUOUS**   25

                    CATHY
          Leo's wife called.

                    SAM
          That woman hates me.

                    CATHY
          Yes.

                    SAM
          What'd I do?

                    CATHY
          You tried to hit on her at a party fund
          raiser.

                    SAM
          Yes. I meant <u>recently</u>. I meant why did
          she call.

                    CATHY
          She wants you to--

                    SAM
          For the hundredth time, I didn't know who
          she was. How much longer am I gonna be
          crucified for that?

                    CATHY
          Well, a little while longer. Anyway--

                    SAM
          I, I, I would think most women would be
          flattered--

                    CATHY
          Yeah, I think Leo was especially touched
          that you--

                    SAM
          What'd she want?

                    CATHY
          She was supposed to give a tour to some
          students from her daughter's fourth grade
          class. She can't make it and she wants
          you to do it.

                    SAM
          I can't.

They walk into the offices of the White House communications
staff--

                    CATHY
          You have to. They wrote essays.

                    SAM
          No really, I can't. I'm not a good tour
          guide. I don't know anything about the
          White House.

                    CATHY
          You wanna call Mrs. McGarry and tell her
          that?

SAM's pager BEEPS--

                    SAM
          Oh God, please let this be a national
          emergency.

SAM picks up a phone and punches in a number off his pager.

A WOMAN picks up...

                    WOMAN (V.O.)
          Cashmere Escorts.

                    SAM
               (beat)
          Hi. You paged me?

                    WOMAN (V.O.)
          Who is this?

                    SAM
          This is Sam Seaborn.

                    WOMAN (V.O.)
          I'm sorry. There's been a mistake.

                    SAM
          Who's this?

                    WOMAN (V.O.)
          Cashmere Escort Service.

                    SAM
               (a little worried)
          Okeydoke.

SAM hangs up...

                    SAM
               (to CATHY)
          Page me.

                    CATHY
          Where you going?

                    SAM
          I'm standing right here. Page me and
          punch in the number.

CATHY does as she's told. SAM watches his pager. Nothing.

                    CATHY
          You switched pagers with someone.

                    SAM
          A woman's about to call me. She's not
          gonna know why. Put her through.

SAM goes into his office and closes the door.

26   **INT. SAM'S OFFICE — CONTINUOUS**   26

The phone BEEPS. SAM picks it up--

                    SAM
              (into phone)
          Hello?

                    LAURIE (V.O.)
          Hello? You paged me?

                    SAM
              (into phone)
          Laurie?

                                              INTERCUT WITH:

27   **INT. LAURIE'S APARTMENT — SAME TIME**   27

                    LAURIE (V.O.)
          Who's this?

                    SAM
              (into phone)
          It's Sam.

                    LAURIE (V.O.)
          Hiii.

                    SAM
          Sam Seaborn.

                    LAURIE (V.O.)
              (happy)
          Yeah, you called me.

                    SAM
              (into phone)
          Yeah. Uh, actually, you called me. And
          that's because, uh, you have my pager.
          And I have yours.

                    LAURIE (V.O.)
              (beat)
          Oh.

                    SAM
              (into phone)
          Yeah. Look. Listen, can I come by and
          see you real quick?

                    LAURIE (V.O.)
          Yes.

             SAM
Thanks, good, okay.

CUT TO:

28   **INT. A WEST WING LOBBY — DAY**   28

A few REPORTERS are waiting around for C.J., who turns a corner and approaches.

        MALE REPORTER
--A full four columns above the fold.

        FEMALE REPORTER
You better be wrong.

        C.J.
Guys, I don't have a lot of time to answer questions right now.

        CHRIS
C.J., has--

        C.J.
But that shouldn't stop you from asking them anyway. Chris?

        CHRIS
Has the President had any reaction to Josh on the show?

        C.J.
None that I'm aware of.

        CHRIS
Do you know--

        C.J.
Seriously, that's it. I'll get you wheels-down time when I've got it.

C.J. walks past Toby's office and is intercepted.

        TOBY
They're picking up the scent.

        C.J.
Billy is. The rest of `em are picking up Billy's scent.

        TOBY
Josh is gonna come to the coffee.

45.

                    C.J.
Keep him cool.

                                        FADE OUT.

                    <u>END OF ACT TWO</u>

ACT THREE

FADE IN:

29   **EXT. LAFAYETTE PARK — DAY**   29

LEO is walking along with AL CALDWELL.

> LEO
> This President is a deeply religious man,
> Reverend, I don't need to tell you that.

> CALDWELL
> No.

> LEO
> His work with the Southern Baptist
> Leadership Conference, his work with the
> Catholic League--

> CALDWELL
> He's spoken at my church.

> LEO
> Yes, he has, and he also spent eight
> months traveling around the country
> discouraging young women from having
> abortions.

> CALDWELL
> Hang on, he never said any--

> LEO
> He does not believe that it's the
> Government's place to legislate this
> issue, but that's never stopped him from
> playing his role as a moral leader,
> something which cost him dearly in the
> campaign and you know that.

> CALDWELL
> Why does he insist on demonizing us as a
> group?

> LEO
> Because your group has plenty of demons.

> CALDWELL
> Every group has plenty of demons.

                    LEO
You don't have to tell me about it,
Reverend. I'm a member of the Democratic
Party.

                    CALDWELL
Then why does the White House suddenly
talk like everyone in the Christian right
is the same?

                    LEO
Forgive me, Al, but when you stand that
close to Mary Marsh and John Van Dyke,
it's sometimes hard not to paint you all
with the same brush.

                    CALDWELL
I need John and Mary for political
muscle.

                    LEO
I don't think you do, but I recognize
you're in a tough spot.

                    CALDWELL
I'm not looking for a Holy War, Leo.

                    LEO
I know you're not, Al. And I think that
you and I can keep this from escalating
beyond a petulant woman being angry about
getting her hair a little messed up on
TV.

                    CALDWELL
There you go again.

                    LEO
What?

                    CALDWELL
It was not a little deal.

                    LEO
No one's saying--

                    CALDWELL
If I make sure of nothing else, I wanna
make sure you take this seriously.

                    LEO
You don't think we're taking this
seriously?
                    (MORE)

LEO (cont'd)
24 hours ago, the President ordered me to
fire Josh Lyman. I've been trying to
talk him down from it ever since. He's
getting off the plane in ten minutes,
it's 6-to-5 and pick `em whether Josh
still has a job, now I don't know how
much more seriously we can take it.

CALDWELL
Well, it's regrettable.

LEO
Yes, it is.
  (beat)
Anyway, I'm glad Toby organized your
meeting this afternoon.

CALDWELL
So am I.

The two men stroll a little farther in silence, the Northwest
Executive Entrance of the White House coming INTO VIEW, as we:

CUT TO:

30   **INT. LAURIE'S APARTMENT — DAY**   30

As LAURIE, in jeans and a sweatshirt, answers the KNOCKING at
the door. SAM is standing there in his overcoat.

SAM
Hi.

LAURIE
Hi.

SAM
Can I come in?

LAURIE
Sure.

LAURIE lets SAM in the door. SAM stands there awkwardly for a
moment.

SAM
This is a nice apartment.

LAURIE
You saw it last night.

SAM
Yeah, and I really like it. It makes
very good use of space.

LAURIE
Thanks.

SAM
The way the ladle hangs from peg boards.

LAURIE
The ladle didn't actually come with the
apartment. It's mine.

SAM
Right.

LAURIE
Yes.

SAM
Uh, can I ask you something?

LAURIE
Am I a hooker?

SAM
No, no. What I was gonna say is this: Is
it possible, that in addition to being a
law student and part-time bartender, that
you are what I'm certain would have to be
a very high-priced call girl? I, by the
way am making no judgments. The thing
is, with my job--

LAURIE
Yes.

SAM
Yes?

LAURIE
Yes. I'm sorry. I shoulda told you. I
wanted you to like me.

SAM
I do.
     (pause)
I have to go.

He waits a moment, then moves to the door...

LAURIE
Sam?

SAM
Yeah?

>   LAURIE
>   My pager.

>   SAM
>   Oh. Right.

They exchange pagers...

>   LAURIE
>   Thanks.

>   SAM
>   Listen, I don't know how often you get
>   up--

>   LAURIE
>   Sam. Go. You don't know who I am.

>   SAM
>   It's just that there are people who'd pay
>   a lot of money to try--

>   LAURIE
>   I know.
>   (beat)
>   Go. It's okay.

SAM turns and goes. LAURIE closes the door behind him as we

>   CUT TO:

31   **INT. WEST WING CORRIDOR — DAY**   31

A group of visitors, AL CALDWELL, MARY MARSH, JOHN VAN DYKE
and several of their assistants and staff people are walking
briskly toward a STAFFER who's waiting at the door.

>   STAFFER
>   Reverend Caldwell, if you all would just
>   step in here.

The group goes into the mural room as CATHY passes by and
looks into the Roosevelt Room. Several nine-year-olds are
waiting patiently with their teacher, MALLORY O'BRIAN.

>   CATHY
>   Excuse me. Hi. We're gonna be just a
>   minute so why doesn't everybody have a
>   seat.

>   MALLORY
>   Alright, everybody. Nicely and quietly
>   take a seat.

CATHY continues on as we

CUT TO:

32   **INT. JOSH'S OFFICE/CORRIDOR/LOBBY — DAY**   32

DONNA is standing in front of Josh, holding out a fresh shirt and tie.

>   JOSH
> No.

>   DONNA
> Put it on.

>   JOSH
> No.

>   DONNA
> Put it on.

>   JOSH
> No.

>   DONNA
> You've been wearing the same clothes for
> 31 hours now, Josh.

>   JOSH
> I am not gettin' spruced up for these
> people, Donna.

>   DONNA
> All the girls think you look really hot
> in this shirt.

Josh looks skeptical, but he's not taking any chances. Josh grabs the shirt and tie. We FOLLOW DONNA out into the corridor--

>   DONNA
>   (calling out)
> Bonnie?

>   BONNIE
> Yeah?

>   DONNA
> Tell Toby he's changing his shirt.

>   BONNIE
> Right.

As DONNA peels off, we continue to the lobby where CATHY meets
SAM as he enters--

> CATHY
> You're late.

> SAM
> I'm having kind of a weird day.

SAM and CATHY begin walking to the Roosevelt Room.

> CATHY
> Leo's daughter's class is waiting with
> their teacher and a couple of parents in
> the Roosevelt Room.

> SAM
> I don't know what to say to them.

> CATHY
> You're supposed to tell them about the
> building and its history. Do you need
> anything?

> SAM
> I need someone to tell me about the
> building and its history.

> CATHY
> Just fake it.

> SAM
> I can't fake it.

> CATHY
> Of course you can fake it.

CUT TO:

33   **INT. ROOSEVELT ROOM — DAY**   33

A dozen fourth-graders, dressed in their White House best, are
sitting patiently along with their teacher, MALLORY O'BRIAN,
and two parent-chaperones.

SAM and CATHY pull around the corner and stop outside the
door.

> SAM
> Which one is Leo's daughter?

> CATHY
> What does it matter?

                    SAM
I want to make a good impression. What
does she look like?

                    CATHY
I don't know.

                    SAM
Okay, I'd just like to thank you for all
your help.

                    CATHY
Sure.

SAM goes inside--

                    SAM
Hi, I'm sorry to be late.

                    MALLORY
Mr. Seaborn, Mallory O'Brian.

                    SAM
Hi.

                    MALLORY
And these are the fourth graders at
Clearlakc Elementary School who wrote the
best essays on why they wanted to visit
the White House.

                    SAM
Well that's just great, why don't we get
started.

Throughout this, the nine year-olds will be transfixed by Sam,
without actually understanding a word that he's saying.
Mallory and the parents will grow slightly concerned.

                    SAM
My name is Sam Seaborn and I'm the Deputy
Communications Director. What does that
<u>mean</u> exactly? Well, to begin with, I'm a
counselor to the President. Mostly on
domestic matters, though generally not
security related. I work with Toby
Ziegler, the Communications Director, and
C.J. Cregg, the Press Secretary, on
crafting our message and getting it out
through the electronic and print media.
                    (MORE)

SAM (cont'd)
And while my functions here are generally
perceived to be politically skewed, it's
important to remember that it's not the
DNC, but rather your tax dollars that pay
my salary. So I work for you whether you
voted for us or not.

There's an awkward silence in the room before--

MALLORY
(pause)
Mr. Seaborn, maybe you could give us some
history.

SAM
Sure. I graduated law school eight years
ago and started working at
Dewey/Ballantine--

MALLORY
Actually, I'm sorry to interrupt,
actually I meant a history of the
building.

SAM
The White House.

MALLORY
Yes.

SAM
Sure. The White House, as you know, was
built several years ago. Mostly, if I'm
not mistaken, out of cement. The room
we're in right now, the Roosevelt Room,
is very famous. It is named after our
18th president, Franklin Delano
Roosevelt. The chairs that you're
sitting on today are fashioned from the
lumber of a pirate ship captured during
the Spanish-American--

MALLORY
All right. Kids, I need to speak to Mr.
Seaborn. Sit tight for a second.

SAM follows MALLORY into the corridor--

34   **INT. CORRIDOR - CONTINUOUS**   34

MALLORY
Hi.

                    SAM
          How ya doin'.

                    MALLORY
          I'm sorry to be rude, but are you a
          moron?

                    SAM
          In this <u>particular</u> area, yes.

                    MALLORY
          The 18th president was Ulysses S. Grant,
          and the Roosevelt room was named for
          Theodore.

                    SAM
          Really?

                    MALLORY
          There's like a six foot painting on the
          wall of Teddy Roosevelt.

                    SAM
          I shoulda put two and two together.

                    MALLORY
          Yes.

                    SAM
          Look. The thing is, while there really
          are a great many things on which I can
          speak with authority, I'm not good at
          talking about the White House.

                    MALLORY
          You're the White House Deputy
          Communications Director and you're not
          good at talking about the White House?

                    SAM
          Ironic, isn't it.

                    MALLORY
          I don't believe this--

MALLORY starts to go back in--

                    SAM
          Wait a minute. Please. Could you do me
          a favor. Could you tell me which one of
          those kids is Leo McGarry's daughter?

                    MALLORY
Why?

                    SAM
Well, if I could make eye contact with
her, make her laugh, you know, just see
that she's having a good time, it might
go a long way to making my life easier.

                    MALLORY
These children worked hard. All of them.
And I'm not inclined at this moment to
make your life easier.

                    SAM
Ms. O'Brian, I understand your feelings,
but please believe me when I tell you
that I'm a nice guy having a bad day. I
just found out the *Times* is publishing a
poll that says a considerable portion of
Americans feel that the White House has
lost energy and focus. A perception
that's not likely to be altered by the
video footage of the President riding his
bicycle into a tree. As we speak, the
Coast Guard are fishing Cubans out of the
Atlantic Ocean while the Governor of
Florida wants to blockade the Port of
Miami. A good friend of mine is about to
get fired for going on television and
making sense, and it turns out that I
accidentally slept with a prostitute last
night. Now would you please, in the name
of compassion, tell me which one of those
kids is my boss's daughter.

                    MALLORY
That would be me.

                    SAM
You?

                    MALLORY
Yes.

                    SAM
Leo's daughter's fourth grade class.

                    MALLORY
Yes.

                    SAM
             (pause)
Well this is bad on so many levels.

                                          FADE OUT.

                  END OF ACT THREE

ACT FOUR

FADE IN:

JOSH, C.J., TOBY, DONNA and a few AIDES walk briskly through a
doorway and into--

36   **INT. WEST WING CORRIDORS — CONTINUOUS**   36

As the group makes its way toward the Mural Room.

>   C.J.
> She's gonna try and bait you, Josh, you
> understand what I'm saying?

>   JOSH
> Lloyd Russell. Yeah that'll last.

>   C.J.
> Are you listening to me?

>   JOSH
>   (repeating)
> They're gonna try and bait me.

>   C.J.
> They want you to say something arrogant.

>   JOSH
> Well I don't need baiting for <u>that</u>.

This is said as they turn into the open doors of

37   **INT. THE MURAL ROOM — CONTINUOUS**   37

CALDWELL, MARSH, VAN DYKE and the AIDES have already been at
the coffee and whatnot.

>   TOBY
> Hi. Hi. Good afternoon. We apologize,
> we're running a bit late today.

>   CALDWELL
> Good afternoon... How's the President's
> health?

>   C.J.
> It's a mild sprain--Everyone greet each
> other.

They all say their hellos...

                    TOBY
Everybody sit, sit, sit. We're happy you
all could come talk with us today. As
you know, the President makes a usual
Sunday morning radio address, and in a
few weeks he's scheduled--

                    CALDWELL
Toby, if I can interrupt for just a
moment. Uh, the goals and spirit of
Christian and Family oriented
organizations, while embraced by a great
and growing number of Americans, have
been met with hostility and contempt by
their Government. Now, yesterday
morning, on the television program
Capital Beat, that contempt was given a
voice and a face and a name.
        (to JOSH)
I'm referring of course to you, sir.

                    JOSH
Yes, I know, and I'm glad you brought
that up.

                    CALDWELL
I'm surprised at you, Josh. I've always
counted you as a friend.

                    JOSH
And I'm honored by that, Reverend.
First, let me say that when I spoke on
the program yesterday, I was not speaking
for the President or this administration.
That's important to know. Second, please
allow me to apologize. My remarks were
glib and insulting. I was going for the
cheap laugh, and anybody willing to step
up and debate ideas deserves better than
a political punch line. Mary, I
apologize.

                    MARY MARSH
        (beat)
Good then. Let's deal.

                    TOBY
I'm sorry?

                    MARY MARSH
What do we get?

                    TOBY
For what?

                    MARY MARSH
Insulting millions of Americans.

                    TOBY
Well, like Josh said--

                    MARY MARSH
I heard what Josh said, Toby, what do we
get?

                    TOBY
An apology.

                    MARY MARSH
Sunday morning radio address. Public
morals. School prayer or pornography,
take your pick.

                    TOBY
School prayer or pornography?

                    JOHN VAN DYKE
It's on every street corner.

                    TOBY
I've seen it Mary--

                    MARY MARSH
Condoms in the schools.

                    TOBY
What?

                    MARY MARSH
Condoms in the schools.

                    TOBY
Well, that's a problem.

                    MARY MARSH
What?

                    TOBY
We have a Surgeon General who says they
dramatically reduce the risk of teen
pregnancy and AIDS.

                    MARY MARSH
So does abstinence.

JOHN VAN DYKE
Show the average American teenage male a
condom and his mind will turn to thoughts
of lust.

TOBY
Show the average American teenage male a
lug wrench and his mind'll turn--

C.J.
Toby--

MARY MARSH
School prayer, pornography, condoms.
What's it gonna be?

TOBY
We're not prepared to make any sort of a
deal right now.

JOSH
Sure we are. Mary, I--

MARY MARSH
(to Josh)
My read of the landscape is that you're
cleaning out your desk before the end of
business today, so I'd just as soon
negotiate with Toby if it's all the same
to you.

CALDWELL
Mary--

MARY MARSH
(to CALDWELL)
Please allow me to work. It was only a
matter of time with you, Josh.

JOSH
Yes.

MARY MARSH
That New York sense of humor was just--

CALDWELL
Mary, there's no need--

MARY MARSH
Reverend, please, they think they're so
much smarter. They think it's smart talk.
But nobody else does.

> JOSH
> I'm actually from Connecticut, but that's
> neither here nor there. The--the point
> is, Mary, I--

> TOBY
> She meant Jewish.

A stunned silence. Everyone stares at Toby.

> TOBY
> When she said "New York sense of humor,"
> she was talking about you and me.

> JOSH
> You know what, Toby, let's not even go
> there.

> CALDWELL
> There's been an apology, let's move on.

> JOHN VAN DYKE
> I'd like to discuss why we hear so much
> talk about the First Amendment coming out
> of this building, but no talk at all
> about the First Commandment.

> MARY MARSH
> I don't like what I've just been accused
> of.

> TOBY
> I'm afraid that's just tough, Mrs. Marsh.

> JOHN VAN DYKE
> The First Commandment says "Honor thy
> Father."

> TOBY
> No it doesn't.

> JOSH
> Toby--

> TOBY
> It doesn't.

> JOSH
> Listen--

                    TOBY
        No, if I'm gonna make you sit through
        this preposterous exercise, we're gonna
        get the names of the damn commandments
        right.

                    MARY MARSH
        Okay, here we go.

                    TOBY
        "Honor thy Father" is the Third
        Commandment.

                    JOHN VAN DYKE
        Then what's the First Commandment?

And from the doorway, a MAN, standing with the help of a cane,
speaks.

                    MAN
        "I am the Lord your God. Thou shalt
        worship no other God before me."

The man is PRESIDENT JOSIAH (JED) BARTLET, Democrat of New
Hampshire, and a direct descendant of one of the signers of
the Declaration. A few paces behind the Bartlet is his
personal aide, CHARLIE. A few SECRET SERVICE can be seen out
in the corridor.

                    BARTLET
        Boy, those were the days, huh?

EVERYONE is standing--

                    CALDWELL
        Good afternoon, Mr. President.

                    BARTLET
        Al. What have we got here, C.J.?

                    C.J.
        Well, we've got some hot tempers, Mr.
        President.

                    BARTLET
        Mary.

                    JOHN VAN DYKE
        Mr. President, I'm, uh, John van Dyke.

                    BARTLET
        Yes. Reverend.

                    JOHN VAN DYKE
May I ask you a question, sir?

          BARTLET
Of course.

          JOHN VAN DYKE
If our children can buy pornography on
any street corner for five dollars, isn't
that too high a price to pay for free
speech?

          BARTLET
No.

          JOHN VAN DYKE
Really?

          BARTLET
On the other hand, I do think that five
dollars is too high a price to pay for
pornography.

          C.J.
Why don't we all sit down.

          BARTLET
No, let's not, C.J. These people won't
be staying that long. May I have some
coffee, Mr. Lewis? Al, how many times
have I asked you to denounce the
practices of a fringe group that calls
itself The Lambs of God?

          CALDWELL
Sir, that's not up to me--

          BARTLET
Crap. It is up to you, Al.

LEO and SAM, with CATHY in tow, appear in the doorway and slip
quietly into the room.

          BARTLET
You know, my wife, Abbey, she never wants
me to do anything while I'm upset. Thank
you, Mr. Lewis. Twenty-eight years ago,
I came home from a very bad day at the
State House. I tell Abbey I'm going out
for a drive. I get in the station wagon,
put it in reverse and pull out of the
garage full speed. Except I forgot to
open the garage door.
          (MORE)

> BARTLET (cont'd)
> (beat)
> Abbey told me not to drive while I was
> upset and she was right. She was right
> yesterday when she told me not to get on
> that damn bicycle when I was upset, but I
> did it anyway, and I guess I was just
> about as angry as I've ever been in my
> life. It seems my granddaughter, Annie,
> had given an interview in one of those
> teen magazines and somewhere between
> movie stars and makeup tips, she talked
> about her feelings on a woman's right to
> choose. Now Annie, all of 12, has always
> been precocious, but she's got a good
> head on her shoulders and I like it when
> she uses it, so I couldn't understand it
> when her mother called me in tears
> yesterday. I said "Elizabeth, what's
> wrong"? She said, "It's Annie." Now I
> love my family and I've read my Bible
> from cover to cover so I want you to tell
> me: From what part of Holy Scripture do
> you suppose the Lambs of God drew their
> divine inspiration when they sent my 12
> year-old granddaughter a Raggedy Ann doll
> with a knife stuck through its throat?
> (pause)
> You'll denounce these people, Al. You'll
> do it publicly. And until you do, you
> can all get your fat asses out of my
> White House.

Everyone is frozen.

> BARTLET
> C.J., show these people out.

> MARY MARSH
> I believe we can find the door.

> BARTLET
> Find it now.

The group exits the room in a slow, quiet and awful manner.

> CALDWELL
> (quietly to LEO)
> We'll fix this, Leo.

> LEO
> See that you do.

They're gone. BARTLET has gone out the side door, through an adjoining room and into the Oval Office. The staff begins recovering from this last moment and following the President.

>   JOSH
> Okay, can I just say that, as it turned
> out, I was the calmest person in the
> room.

>   C.J.
> Way to stay cool.

>   TOBY
> I'm not in power to auction off the Bill
> of Rights.

>   JOSH
> I thought you were gonna take a swing at
> her there.

>   TOBY
> She was calling us New York Jews, Josh.

>   JOSH
> Yes, but being from Connecticut, I didn't
> mind so much.

We follow them into

38   **INT. OVAL OFFICE - CONTINUOUS**   38

>   JOSH
> You, C.J., on the other hand... you were
> brilliant. I particularly liked the part
> where you said nothing at all.

>   C.J.
> I'm sorry, Josh, I was distracted. All I
> could really think about was Lloyd
> Russell and your girlfriend.

>   SAM
> Mandy and Lloyd Russell.

>   JOSH
> I'm puttin' an end to that.

>   BARTLET
> "Hello, Mr. President. Did you have a
> nice trip, sir? How's the ankle, sir?"

During this, MARGARET, LEO's secretary, brings him a note which he'll read over.

>   BARTLET
>   It seems to me we've all been taking a
>   little break. Thinking about our
>   personal lives or thinking about keeping
>   our jobs. Breaks are good. It's not a
>   bad idea to take a break every now and
>   then. I know how hard you all work.

LEO slips BARTLET the note.

>   BARLET
>   There was this time that Annie came to me
>   with this press clipping. It seems that
>   these theologians down in South America
>   were all excited because this little girl
>   from Chile had sliced open a tomato, and
>   the inside flesh of the tomato had
>   actually formed a perfect Rosary. The
>   theologians commented that they thought
>   this was a very impressive girl. Annie
>   commented that she thought it was a very
>   impressive tomato. I don't know what
>   made me think of that.

During that story, BARTLET glances at the note he was handed
and now tells the rest of the group about it.

>   BARTLET
>   (matter-of-fact)
>   Naval Intelligence reports approximately
>   twelve hundred Cubans left Havana this
>   morning. Approximately 700 turned back
>   due to severe weather, some 350 are
>   missing and are presumed dead, 137 have
>   been taken into custody in Miami and are
>   seeking asylum.
>   (beat)
>   With the clothes on their back, they came
>   through a storm. And the ones that didn't
>   die want a better life. And they want it
>   here. Talk about impressive. My point
>   is this: Break's over.

>   LEO
>   Thank you, Mr. President.

>   SAM
>   Thank you, sir.

The meeting's over too. Impressed by their boss, perhaps in a
way they haven't been for a while, the group extend a simple
"Thank you, Mr. President./Thank you/Thank you, sir/etc."...

and disperses through various doors. BARTLET calls to Josh
who's almost out the door--

> BARTLET
> Josh.

JOSH turns around...

> BARTLET
> "...too busy being indicted for tax
> fraud"?
>   (beat)
> Don't ever do it again.

> JOSH
>   (quietly)
> Yes, sir.

JOSH exits the Oval Office as BARTLET calls out--

> BARTLET
> Mrs. Landingham. What's next?

We PULL BACK on this scene as MRS. LANDINGHAM begins to run
through the President's schedule...

> MRS. LANDINGHAM
> Governor Thomas and the Majority Leader
> have asked to be conferenced in and the
> group from NASA is assembling for their
> photo-op. At seven o'clock you have, uh,
> cocktails...

This scene continues MOS for a moment before we

> FADE TO BLACK.

END OF SHOW

A PROPORTIONAL
RESPONSE

Directed by Marc Buckland

Something happened, I can't remember what. Khaddafi bombed one of our airfields, I think, but I could be off by three countries and two dictators.

Whatever. It was early in Clinton's first term and he was with his national security advisors and they were discussing various options for a proportional response and Clinton asked, "What's the virtue of a proportional response?" and I really liked the question. So much so that I had two different people ask it, Michael Douglas and then Martin Sheen. Pat Caddell helped me with the answer. Pat was a very young uber-pollster for Jimmy Carter and has been active in Democratic politics and women's gymnastics his entire life. Pat's a genius and I'm lucky that he's one of our advisors. Pat's also a lunatic but that's a different book.

I like the scene at the end with Martin and John. I like any scene with Martin and John. But what I'll always remember and love about the episode is this:

It's when we first met Dulé Hill.

A Proportional Response

<u>TEASER</u>

FADE IN:

1   **EXT./EST. - THE WHITE HOUSE - MORNING**   1

A grey day. There might be a light drizzle outside.

CUT TO:

2   **INT. WEST WING/MAIN LOBBY/CORRIDOR/BULLPEN/JOSH'S OFFICE -** 2
    SAME TIME

As JOSH punches in his I.D., DONNA crosses to meet him.

> DONNA
> C.J.'s looking for you.

> JOSH
> Hm?

> DONNA
> C.J.'s looking for you.

We FOLLOW JOSH and DONNA as they head toward JOSH's office --

> JOSH
> Donna?

> DONNA
> Yeah?

> JOSH
> "Good morning, Josh" is a pretty good way
> to start the day.

> DONNA
> Good morning.

> JOSH
> What's up?

> DONNA
> C.J.'s looking for you.

> JOSH
> Tell her I'm in the office.

> DONNA
> Josh, I'm saying C.J. is <u>looking</u> for you.

(CONTINUED)

2   CONTINUED:

JOSH knows what this means and stops walking, holding onto
DONNA's arm to get her to stop walking as well. They speak
in hushed tones.

> JOSH
> What did I do?

> DONNA
> How would I know?

> JOSH
> Because you know everything.

> DONNA
> I <u>do</u> know everything.

> JOSH
> Donna--

> DONNA
> I'm saying you say that now, but anytime
> I want to make a substantive
> contribution--

> JOSH
> You make plenty of substantive
> contributions.

> DONNA
> Like what?

> JOSH
> <u>This</u>. This could be a substantive
> contribution.

> DONNA
> I need a raise.

> JOSH
> So do I.

> DONNA
> You're my boss.

> JOSH
> I'm not the one who pays you.

> DONNA
> Yes, but you could <u>recommend</u> that I got a
> raise.

(CONTINUED)

2   CONTINUED: (2)

> JOSH
> Donna, she's looking for me. Do you
> think this is a really good time to talk
> about a raise?

> DONNA
> Mmm. I think it's the <u>best</u> time to talk
> about a raise.

> JOSH
> Donna, you're not a very nice person.

> DONNA
> You gotta get to know me.

> JOSH
> Donna--

> DONNA
> The best I can cobble together from the
> small shards of information I've been
> able to overhear in the restroom and at
> the Danish cart--

> JOSH
> (frustrated)
> Donna --

> DONNA
> Is it possible that there's a situation
> involving Sam, a woman and C.J. being
> denied information about something?

It only takes a moment for the penny to drop--

> JOSH
> Okay. Here's what I'm gonna do:

> DONNA
> Hide in your office?

> JOSH
> No. I'm not gonna hide in my office. I
> am gonna <u>go</u> into my office. And devise a
> strategy. That's what I do.

They continue on the short distance to the office--

> JOSH (CONT'D)
> I'm a professional. I'm not a little boy.

> DONNA
> That's the spirit.

                                        (CONTINUED)

2   CONTINUED: (3)

> JOSH
> But if she calls, I'm at the dentist,
> I'll be back in an hour.

> DONNA
> Got it.

JOSH opens his office door and--

> JOSH
> *Aaghh*!

C.J.'s sitting in Josh's chair, her feet up on the desk...

> C.J.
> Wow, are <u>you</u> stupid.

SMASH CUT TO:

MAIN TITLES

<u>END OF TEASER</u>

<u>ACT ONE</u>

FADE IN:

3   **INT. JOSH'S OFFICE - A SECOND LATER**   3

Josh is standing at the doorway. C.J.'s sitting behind the
desk.

> JOSH
> You can't be mad at me for this,
> C.J.

> C.J.
> Really?

> JOSH
> Listen--

> C.J.
> Let's see if I can. Let's see if I
> can find it <u>in</u> me.

DONNA pops in--

> DONNA
> Wait, she was here?

> JOSH
> Yes.

> C.J.
> Would you excuse us, Donna?

> DONNA
> How did I miss that?

> JOSH
> I don't know, but you can kiss that raise
> goodbye.

> DONNA
> Senior staff in five minutes.

> JOSH
> Thanks.

DONNA closes the door behind her.

> C.J.
> A call girl?

> JOSH
> Here's the thing:

(CONTINUED)

3   CONTINUED:

> C.J.
> A call girl, Josh?

> JOSH
> (pause)
> You're not <u>asking</u> me if I'd like a call
> girl right now, are you?

> C.J.
> Do you have any idea how serious
> this is?

> JOSH
> See, the thing is, I really don't think
> it <u>is</u> that serious.

> C.J.
> Why not?

> JOSH
> A couple of things for you to bear in
> mind: First of all, he didn't know that
> she was a call girl when he slept with
> her. He did not pay her money. He didn't
> participate in, have knowledge of, or
> witness anything illegal. Or for that
> matter unethical, immoral or suspect.

> C.J.
> Okay. A couple of things for <u>you</u> to
> bear in mind: None of that matters on
> *Hard Copy.*

> JOSH
> You're overreacting.

> C.J.
> Am I?

> JOSH
> Yes.

> C.J.
> As women are prone to do?

> JOSH
> That's not what I meant.

> C.J.
> Yes, it is.

> JOSH
> No, it isn't.

(CONTINUED)

3   CONTINUED: (2)   3

                         C.J.
               It's always what you mean.

                         JOSH
               You know what, C.J., I really think I'm
               the best judge of what I mean, you
               paranoid Berkeley shiksa femin*ista*.
                    (beat)
               Whoa, that was <u>way</u> too far.

                         C.J.
               No, no.
                    (beat)
               Well, I've got a staff meeting to go to
               and so do you, you elitist Harvard
               fascist missed-the-Dean's-list-two-
               semesters-in-a-row Yankee jackass.

                         JOSH
               Feel better getting that off your chest
               there, C.J.

                         C.J.
               I'm a whole new woman.

      C.J.'s out the door and JOSH follows into:

4   INT. CORRIDORS - CONTINUOUS   4

                         JOSH
               You look like a million bucks, by the
               way.

                         C.J.
               Don't try and make up with me.

                         JOSH
               I'll talk to Sam.

                         C.J.
               <u>I'll</u> talk to Sam.

      They walk into--

5   INT. LOBBY - CONTINUOUS   5

      TOBY is entering the building as they cross the lobby --

                         JOSH
               Toby.

                         TOBY
               Hey.

                                                   (CONTINUED)

5   CONTINUED: 5

As they walk, the volume of their voice tells us this
conversation isn't for everyone.

                    JOSH
          How was last night?

                    TOBY
          It was the longest dinner of my life. The
          President was up from the table every
          five minutes, teeing off on Cashman and
          Berryhill. He's barking at the Secretary
          of State, he's scaring the hell out of
          Fitzwallace, which I didn't think was
          possible, he's snapping at the First
          Lady, he's talking about blowing up half
          of North Africa--

They walk into--

6   **INT. WEST WING CORRIDORS - CONTINUOUS**   6

                    C.J.
          He's snapping at Mrs. Bartlet?

                    JOSH
               (lowering his voice)
          C.J., this may be a good time to tell the
          President about Sam and the call girl.

                    TOBY
          She knows?

                    JOSH
          Yeah.

                    C.J.
          Yes, I'm afraid I have that
          information now, and I'll be in to
          see you, my friend, very shortly.

                    TOBY
          How the hell did I get into trouble?

                    JOSH
          Today? All you had to do was get outa
          bed.

They walk into Leo's office as we:

                                            CUT TO:

7   **EXT. SOUTH PORTICO - MORNING**   7

The drizzle has turned into rain. Nothing hard yet. That'll
come later. A DRESS MARINE is standing at parade rest by the
door and a SECRET SERVICE AGENT is standing halfway down the
portico. Bartlet and Leo round the corner.

                         BARTLET
               This is crap, Leo, it's been three days.
               This is amateur hour.

                         LEO
               Cashman and Berryhill have to revise the
               response scenarios so that they speak to
               State's concern over--

                         BARTLET
               Cashman and Berryhill are dragging their
               feet. Cashman and Berryhill are trying to
               make me look like a clown, and State
               should concern itself with what I damn
               well <u>tell</u> them to be concerned with.

As they approach the MARINE, he snaps to attention and opens
the door.

                         LEO
               It doesn't work like that.

They walk into:

8   **INT. THE WEST WING - CONTINUOUS**   8

                         BARTLET
               So I've discovered.

A STAFFER passes--

                         STAFFER
               Good morning, Mr. President.

                         BARTLET
               Good morning.

                         LEO
               Moreover, you <u>know</u> that's not the way it
               works. The Chiefs are moving as swiftly
               as they can even though, frankly, time
               isn't a factor.

They enter--

9   **INT. OVAL OFFICE - CONTINUOUS**   9

                    MRS. LANDINGHAM
          Good morning, Mr. President.

                    BARTLET
          Good morning.

                    LEO
          Not to pile on, but Cashman and Berryhill
          have a reasonable point with respect to
          the security council.

                    BARTLET
          Uh, Mrs. Landingham, I can't seem to find
          my glasses anywhere, could you please do
          whatever it is you do when I can't find
          my glasses?

                    MRS. LANDINGHAM
          Certainly, Sir.

                    BARTLET
          It's been 72 hours, Leo. That's more
          than three days since they blew him out
          of the sky. And I'm tired of waiting,
          dammit. This is <u>candy</u> ass. We're gonna
          draw up a response scenario today. I'm
          gonna give the order today. We're gonna
          strike back today.

                    LEO
               (pause)
          I wish you wouldn't say "him," Mr.
          President.

                    BARTLET
               (beat)
          What?

                    LEO
          Three days since they blew him out of the
          sky. Of course that's fine while it's
          just you and me, sir. But in there, with
          Fitzwallace and the Chiefs, I hope you
          say "it" or "the airplane." Not "him."

                    BARTLET
          You think I'm taking this personally?

                    LEO
          I think--

                              (CONTINUED)

9   CONTINUED: 9

                    BARTLET
          And why the hell shouldn't I take it
          <u>personally</u>?

                    LEO
          I think the fact that Morris was on the
          plane--

                    BARTLET
          <u>Americans</u> were on that plane.

                    LEO
          Mr. President--

                    BARTLET
          I met Morris four or five times. Let's
          not do this like he was my son.

                    LEO
          Yes.

                    BARTLET
               (calling)
          Mrs. Landingham--

                    LEO
          Mr. President, I still think we need to
          talk about--

MRS. LANDINGHAM appears--

                    BARTLET
          I can't find my glasses anywhere.

                    MRS. LANDINGHAM
          Yes sir, we're on it.

                    BARTLET
          Thank you.

                    MRS. LANDINGHAM
          The Director is waiting.

                    BARTLET
          Yeah, let's have 'em.
               (to LEO)
          What'd you want to say?

                    LEO
          Nothing.

                                        (CONTINUED)

9   CONTINUED: (2)   9

                              BARTLET
                    You sure.

                              LEO
                    Yeah. I've got staff.

                              BARTLET
                    I'll see you in an hour.

                              LEO
                    Thank you, sir.

                              BARTLET
                    Thank you.

          MRS. LANDINGHAM is leading in the CIA DIRECTOR and his small
          team for the President's morning intelligence briefing as Leo
          exits through the side door. We FOLLOW him into:

11   **INT. LEO'S OFFICE - CONTINUOUS**   11

          JOSH, TOBY, C.J. and a few Aides are sitting or standing
          around the office, waiting for the meeting to start as LEO
          walks in.

                              LEO
                    Good morning.

                              C.J.
                    Morning, Leo.

                              JOSH
                    How's his mood?

                              LEO
                    How's his mood?

                              JOSH
                    Yeah.

                              LEO
                    Don't worry about it.

                              C.J.
                    Toby said he was--

                              LEO
                    And I said don't worry about it.

          SAM enters--

                                                              (CONTINUED)

                         LEO (CONT'D)
          Hey, Sam, what do you know?

                         SAM
          It's true.

                         LEO
          You're kidding.

                         SAM
          I have the transcript from the broadcast.

                         TOBY
          What broadcast?

                         LEO
          Listen to this:

                         SAM
          Congressman Bertram Cole is appearing on
          a radio program in his home district--

                         JOSH
          Right.

                         LEO
          The 5th.

                         JOSH
          Yes.

                         SAM
          Eastchester County and part of Lofton.

                         LEO
          Where we just recommended cuts in funding
          for the M-6 Beacon.

                         TOBY
          What'd he say?

                         SAM
          He was on the broadcast along with
          several officers from Cromwell Air Force
          Base when he said--regarding the
          President being weak on defense--
                    (reading)
          "Folks down here are patriotic. Fiercely
          patriotic. The President better not be
          planning on making any visits to this
          base. If he does, he may not get out
          alive."

                                              (CONTINUED)

11   CONTINUED: (2)

                        TOBY
           He said that?

                        LEO
           You believe it?

                        TOBY
           Sitting with military officers?

                        SAM
           Yeah.

                        JOSH
           Don't take the bait.

                        TOBY
           Josh--

                        JOSH
           Don't take the bait.

                        TOBY
           You better believe I'm gonna take the
           bait.

                        JOSH
           Toby--

                        LEO
           There oughta be a law against it.

                        TOBY
           There _is_ a law against it.

                        JOSH
           Why did you get him started?

                        TOBY
           How 'bout Threatening the Life of the
           President. He's talking to other people,
           how 'bout Conspiracy. They were military
           officers, how 'bout Treason.

                        JOSH
           Toby--

                        TOBY
           That was a member of our own party, Leo,
           that was a Democrat who said that.

                        LEO
           It's bad, I know.

                                            (CONTINUED)

                    TOBY
That's it?

                    LEO
What're you gonna do?

                    TOBY
Have the Justice Department bring him in
for questioning pending felony charges.

                    JOSH
Toby's right. What's the good of being in
power if you're not gonna haul your
enemies in for questioning.

                    TOBY
We're really not gonna do anything about
this?

                    LEO
Yeah, Toby. 'Cause what we really need to
do is to arrest people for being mean to
the President.

                    TOBY
There is no law. There is no decency.

                    JOSH
He's just gettin' that now.

                    LEO
Listen up. In the event an attack order's
given today, we'll need a half-hour on
the networks. Uh, when do they need to
be told?

                    C.J.
Ninety minutes notice.

                    LEO
Wait 'til the last minute. Toby start
working on a draft for the President.

                    TOBY
I need to know what we're hitting.

                    LEO
Yeah. You and me both.

                    TOBY
Leo--

                                        (CONTINUED)

11   CONTINUED: (4)   11

                         LEO
              It's military, Toby, you'll know when you
              know.

                         TOBY
              Sam, coordinate with the State Department
              guy--

                         SAM
              Beach.

                         TOBY
              --and whoever the spokesperson is--

                         SAM
              Hutchinson.

                         LEO
              Let's do this right.

                         JOSH
              Not much chance of that.

                                                      CUT TO:

12   **INT. CORRIDOR - A FEW MOMENTS LATER**   12

      As the meeting begins to break up and spill out.

                         C.J.
              We need to be fully stocked. State
              Department officials, Pentagon, we'll
              need the Embassy office--

                         JOSH
              We should get McMartin on board.

                         C.J.
              He's standing by.

                         JOSH
              And Adam Lee at the Pentagon.

                         C.J.
              Got him.

                         JOSH
              So you're all set? Good. So how do we
              tell 'em what we know without telling 'em
              what we know?

                                                      (CONTINUED)

>   C.J.
>   Well we don't know anything, so that
>   shouldn't be hard. Oh, Samuel?

>   SAM
>   Yeah.

>   C.J.
>   Could you stop by my office around
>   lunch time, please.

>   SAM
>   Sure.

C.J. and JOSH head off. Toby's spying something with interest
at the end of the corridor: It's a small group of REPORTERS.

>   SAM (CONT'D)
>   Think she knows?

>   TOBY
>   (more interested in the
>   REPORTERS)
>   Yeah.

>   SAM
>   Why?

>   TOBY
>   She told me she knows.

>   SAM
>   Should you and I talk for a minute?

>   TOBY
>   Yeah. In my office. I'll be right back.

TOBY walks intently in the direction of the REPORTERS as if
he's trying to get by without being asked a question.

>   REPORTER #1
>   Toby.

>   TOBY
>   (stopping)
>   Yeah.

>   REPORTER #1
>   Did you guys hear what Bertram Cole said
>   on the radio?

>   TOBY
>   Yeah.

                                                    (CONTINUED)

12   CONTINUED: (2)   12

                              REPORTER #2
                    And?

                              TOBY
                    The Secret Service investigates all
                    threats made against the President. It's
                    White House policy not to comment on
                    those investigations.

                              REPORTER #1
                    Are you telling me there's gonna be a
                    criminal investigation?

                              TOBY
                    I really can't comment on that right now.
                         ("remembering")
                    Damn, I gotta get back to my office.

          TOBY turns away from the REPORTERS and heads back, perhaps a
          slight smile creeping through.

                                                          FADE OUT.

                              <u>END OF ACT ONE</u>

ACT TWO

FADE IN:

13   **INT. C.J.'S OFFICE - DAY**   13

C.J's meeting with two AIDES who take notes.

> C.J.
> I think the thing to say is that we don't
> think anybody here would be disappointed
> if no one paid attention to the process.
> So maybe the thing'll wear itself out.

> AIDE #1
> This is on Agriculture?

> C.J.
> Science and Technology.

SAM taps on the door.

> C.J. (CONT'D)
>   (to SAM)
> Hey.
>   (to the AIDES)
> We're done.

The AIDES leave and SAM closes the door behind them. SAM
stands there, the two of them staring at each other for a
moment.

> SAM
> Hi.

> C.J.
> Hi.

There's another long beat before...

> SAM
> You wanted to see me.

> C.J.
> Yes.

> SAM
> I think I know why.

> C.J.
> Do you?

(CONTINUED)

13   CONTINUED:

                         SAM
           Yes, look--

                         C.J.
           You sussed it out, huh?

                         SAM
           C.J.--

                         C.J.
           Lemme tell you something, Sam, you're
           a smart guy, but if you could figure it
           out, and I could figure it out, what
           makes you think there's no one in my
           press room who could figure it out?

                         SAM
           There's nothing to figure out, C.J.

                         C.J.
           You can't spend time with a call girl,
           Sam, you're gonna get caught.

                         SAM
           Caught doing what?

                         C.J.
           Don't get cute with me.

                         SAM
           You are aware that I didn't know she was
           a call girl when I went home with her,
           right?

                         C.J.
           Yes, but you called her again and
           you went back to see her.

                         SAM
           I went back to see her, I didn't go back
           to solicit her.

                         C.J.
           It doesn't make a difference.

                         SAM
           It does make a difference.

                         C.J.
           You work in the White House, Sam,
           you work fifty feet from the Oval
           Office and you're consorting with
           a woman--

                                            (CONTINUED)

                    SAM
Consorting? I'm friendly with a woman.
I like this woman. This woman poses no
threat to the President. And it's very
likely that owing to my friendship, this
woman may start living her life inbounds,
insuring for herself a greater future,
and isn't that exactly what it is we're
supposed to be doing here.

                    C.J.
Ohhhhh...

                    SAM
C.J.--

                    C.J.
I seeee...

                    SAM
This is ridiculous.

                    C.J.
You're there to help her see the
error of her ways.

                    SAM
I am there because I like her. I'm there
because it's there that I'd be if this
were alcohol or drugs. I'm not sleeping
with her. This isn't tawdry.

                    C.J.
I don't care what it is, I care what
it looks like.

                    SAM
And I care what it is. And I think it's
high time we all spent a little less
time looking good--

                    SAM & C.J.
-- and a little more--

                    C.J.
--time being good?

                    SAM
Yes.

                    C.J.
Yeah, I've heard that one before. One
other thing--

                              (CONTINUED)

13   CONTINUED: (3)

                    SAM
Are we done?

                        C.J.
No, Sam, when I say "one other thing"
that means we're not done, that there's
one other thing.

                    SAM
Yeah. I'm resenting the hell out of this
conversation right now.

                        C.J.
It was tough to tell from your tone
of voice.

                    SAM
What do you want?

                        C.J.
I beg your pardon?

                    SAM
What's the one other thing?

                        C.J.
I'm your first phone call.

                    SAM
When?

                        C.J.
Before, now, in the future, anytime
you're into something and you don't
know what--and you can't <u>tell</u> me that
you thought there was nothing to it,
'cause you sat down with Josh and
you sat down with Toby -- <u>anytime</u> you're
into something and you don't know what,
you don't keep it from me. I'm your first
phone call. I'm the first line of
defense. You have to let me protect you,
and you have to let me protect the
President.

                    SAM
Is that what this is about?

                        C.J.
What this is about, Sam, is you're a high
profile, very visible, much noticed
member--

                                        (CONTINUED)

13   CONTINUED: (4)

> SAM
> You just said three things that all
> mean the same thing.

> C.J.
> You're not gonna let this outa your
> teeth.

> SAM
> Can I go now, C.J.? 'Cause what I
> think it's about is you, once again,
> letting the character cops win
> in a forfeit, because you don't have
> the guts or the strength or the courage
> to say "We know what's right from wrong
> and this is none of your damn business."

> C.J.
> Really.

> SAM
> Yes.

> C.J.
> Strength, guts or courage.

> SAM
> Yes.

> C.J.
> You just said three things that all
> mean the same thing.

> SAM
> C.J.--

> C.J.
> We're done talking now. You can go.

There's a terrible energy hanging in the air. SAM doesn't
want to leave on this note.

> SAM
> About the retaliatory strike, do you
> think we're gonna target--

> C.J.
> I really don't know what we're gonna
> target, Sam. The Commandant of the
> 2nd Division doesn't tend to include
> me in his thinking.

(CONTINUED)

13   CONTINUED: (5)   13

                         SAM
              I'll see you later.

                         C.J.
              Count on it.

SAM exits.

                                               CUT TO:

14   **INT. CORRIDOR - SAME TIME**   14

SAM has walked out. He slams the back of his fist against the
wall.

                                               CUT TO:

15   **INT. WHITE HOUSE SITUATION ROOM - DAY**   15

Several OFFICERS and CIVILIANS (Secretary of Defense,
National Security Advisor, etc.) sit around a conference
table, waiting for a meeting to get underway. Papers are laid
out over the table, charts are resting on easels. Four
digital LED read-outs show the time at "D.C.," "POTUS,"
"ZULU" and "ALPHA." ADMIRAL PERCY FITZWALLACE, the Chairman
of the Joint Chiefs of Staff, is drawing a cup of coffee from
a large urn on a side table. FITZWALLACE, anywhere from 55 to
65 and African-American, is a big bear of man with a calm,
powerful demeanor.

                         FITZWALLACE
              You know what I was just thinking?

                         OFFICER #1
              What's that, Admiral?

                         FITZWALLACE
              This is different coffee than we usually
              have.

The door opens and BARTLET and LEO come in. Everyone stands.

                         BARTLET
              Keep your seats.

                         FITZWALLACE
              Good morning, Mr. President.

                         BARTLET
              Whatta we got?

BARTLET and LEO take their seats.

                                               (CONTINUED)

15   CONTINUED:

> FITZWALLACE
> Three retaliatory strike scenarios.

> LEO
> When are they operational?

> FITZWALLACE
> At the President's command.

> LEO
> No prep time?

> OFFICER #2
> We're there.

> FITZWALLACE
> All three scenarios are comprehensive,
> meet the obligations of proportional
> response and pose minimum risk to
> American personnel and assets. Scenario
> One, or Paraclese-1 to use its code name,
> sir--

> BARTLET
> What is the virtue of a proportional
> response?

> FITZWALLACE
> I'm sorry?

> BARTLET
> What is the virtue of a proportional
> response? Why's it good?

There's an awkward silence in the room. They're not geared up
for these kinds of questions.

> BARTLET (CONT'D)
> They hit an airplane, so we hit a
> transmitter, right? That's a proportional
> response.

> FITZWALLACE
> Sir, in the case of Paraclese-1--

> BARTLET
> They hit a barracks, we hit two
> transmitters.

> FITZWALLACE
>   (pause)
> That's roughly it, yes sir.

(CONTINUED)

15   CONTINUED: (2)

> BARTLET
> And this is what we do, I mean...
> this is what we do.

> LEO
> Yes sir, it's what we do. It's what
> we've always done.

> BARTLET
> Well, if it's what we do, if it's what
> we've always done, don't they know
> we're gonna do it?

> LEO
> Sir, if you turn your attention
> to Paraclese-1--

> BARTLET
> I have <u>turned</u> my attention to
> Paraclese-1. It's two ammo dumps,
> an abandoned railroad bridge and a
> Syrian Intelligence Agency.

> FITZWALLACE
> Those are four highly rated
> targets, sir.

> BARTLET
> But they <u>know</u> we're gonna do that.
>   (beat)
> They <u>know</u> we're gonna do that. Those
> areas have been abandoned for three
> days now, we know that from the
> satellite, right? We have the
> intelligence.

> LEO
> Sir--

> BARTLET
> They did <u>that</u> so we do <u>this</u>, it's
> the cost of doing business, it's
> been factored in.
>   (beat)
> Right?

> LEO
> Mr. President--

> BARTLET
> Am I right or am I missing something
> here?

                                             (CONTINUED)

15   CONTINUED: (3)

>   FITZWALLACE
> No sir, you're right, sir.
>
>   BARTLET
> Then I ask again: What is the virtue
> of a proportional response?
>
>   FITZWALLACE
>   (pause)
> It isn't virtuous, Mr. President. It's
> all there is, sir.
>
>   BARTLET
> It's not all there is.
>
>   LEO
> Sir, Admiral Fitzwallace--
>
>   FITZWALLACE
> Excuse me, Leo. Pardon me, Mr.
> President, just what else is there?
>
>   BARTLET
> The disproportional response. Let the
> word ring forth, from this time and this
> place, gentlemen, you kill
> an American, any American, we don't come
> back with a proportional response, we
> come back with total disaster.
>
>   OFFICER #2
> Mr. President, are you suggesting we
> carpet-bomb Damascus?
>
>   BARTLET
> I am suggesting, General, that you and
> Admiral Fitzwallace and Secretary
> Hutchinson and the rest of the National
> Security team take the next 60 minutes
> and put together an American response
> scenario that doesn't make me think we
> are just docking somebody's *damn
> allowance*.

BARTLET gets up and walks out of the room. We HOLD on LEO for
a moment before we

                                                        CUT TO:

16   **INT. ROOSEVELT ROOM - DAY**   16

Waiting, standing in front of the table, is a very nervous
young man named CHARLES (CHARLIE) YOUNG.

                                                   (CONTINUED)

16   CONTINUED:

It's not like he's shaking or sweating or anything, but we
can tell from his posture and from the way he's trying hard
not to be noticed that he's out of his element and doing his
best to overcome fear. He's 20 years old, wearing his only
decent suit of clothes.

JOSH rounds the corner and enters--

                    JOSH
               (calling as walks)
          I haven't eaten lunch yet, so if
          anyone's going to the thing--

                    DONNA
          What do you want?

                    JOSH
          I would like salad, I would like
          a soup of some kind, and if you were
          to run across a sandwich, then
          hang the expense.

                    DONNA
          Right.

                    JOSH
          And I would like a bottle of water.

                    DONNA
          This is Charles Young.

CHARLIE stays standing until told otherwise.

                    JOSH
          I'm supposed to vet you.

                    CHARLIE
          I beg your pardon?

                    JOSH
          Vet you, I'm supposed to vet you.
          Investigate to discover if there
          are problems. Uh, I'm Josh Lyman, Deputy
          Chief of Staff.

                    CHARLIE
          How are you.

                    JOSH
          Is it Charles?

                    CHARLIE
          Charlie.

                                        (CONTINUED)

16   CONTINUED: (2)

> JOSH
> Charlie, you can have a seat if you like.

> CHARLIE
> I don't mind standing.

> JOSH
> (calling)
> Donna!

DONNA appears--

> JOSH (CONT'D)
> Never mind the salad, I'm not gonna
> eat it anyway.

> DONNA
> Fine.

> JOSH
> But, I would like a bottle of water as
> soon as humanly possible.

> DONNA
> Fine.

DONNA disappears.

> JOSH
> Let's have a seat.

CHARLIE sits.

> JOSH (CONT'D)
> I'm sure you understand why we have
> to go through this. It's a very sensitive
> job. It's also a very hard job. 20 hour
> days aren't uncommon, long trips at the
> last minute, a lot of wait and hurry-up.
> Moreover, there'll be times when you have
> to make yourself invisible in plain
> sight, as well as an undeniable force in
> front of those who want more time than we
> want to give. Sometimes the people I'm
> talking about will be Kings and Prime
> Ministers. Do you understand so far?

> CHARLIE
> Uh, sir, I'm sorry, but I think there's
> been some kind of mistake.

> JOSH
> Really?

(CONTINUED)

> CHARLIE
> See, I came here... I filled out an
> application for--

> JOSH
> I have your paperwork.

> CHARLIE
> Right. See, I came here... I was looking
> for a job as a messenger.

> JOSH
> Yes.

> CHARLIE
> And I had my interview with Miss
> DiLaguardia, and she told me to wait.

> JOSH
> Yes.

> CHARLIE
> And then she told me to come here.

> JOSH
> Yes, that's 'cause we asked Miss
> DiLaguardia to keep her eye out. She's
> recommending you for a different job.

> CHARLIE
> Sir, if you don't mind me asking--

> JOSH
> Personal Aide to the President, you don't
> have to call me sir.

> CHARLIE
>   (pause)
> I don't understand--

> JOSH
> Personal Aide to the President.
> Traditionally a young guy, 20 to
> 25 years old. Excels academically,
> strong on personal responsibility
> and discretion, presentable appearance--

> CHARLIE
> Sir--

> JOSH
> We obviously get quite a few candidates
> who meet those qualifications, so the
>   (MORE)

(CONTINUED)

16   CONTINUED: (4)

                         JOSH (cont'd)
         rest is just gut instinct.
              (beat)
         Or you could bribe me.

                         CHARLIE
         Sir, I--

                         JOSH
         Seriously, Charlie, we call the
         President "sir," everyone else is
         "Hey, when am I gonna get that thing
         I asked for."

                         CHARLIE
         See, that's not -- See, there's been a
         mistake.

                         JOSH
              (re: a paper in front of
              him)
         I'll say.
              (calling)
         Donna!

                         CHARLIE
         I should go.

DONNA appears in the doorway--

                         JOSH
         Insuccessful?

                         DONNA
         What's the problem?

                         JOSH
         I don't think we're allowed to make
         up our own words.

                         DONNA
         Oh and like there's no chance it's
         a typo.

                         JOSH
         Change it, would you? Serious people
         are gonna read that.

DONNA exits.

                         JOSH (CONT'D)
         Charlie, you're standing again.

                                        (CONTINUED)

> CHARLIE
> Well, I, see, I came here for a messenger
> job.

> JOSH
> Why aren't you in college?

> CHARLIE
> Well--

> JOSH
> These transcripts... your
> grades are better than <u>mine</u>.

> CHARLIE
> Mr. Lyman, I--

> JOSH
> Well not really, but they're close.

> CHARLIE
> It was an easy school. I--

> JOSH
> Nah, come on. I'm looking at
> recommendations from guidance counselors,
> I'm looking at A.C.T. scores, you didn't
> wanna go to college?

> CHARLIE
> Well, I, I have a little sister at home.

> JOSH
>   (beat)
> You take care of her?

> CHARLIE
> Yes sir.

> JOSH
> Your parents are gone?

> CHARLIE
> My mom, she's a police officer. She was
> shot and killed on duty a few months ago.
> Five months ago.

                                        FADE OUT.

<u>END OF ACT TWO</u>

ACT THREE

FADE IN:

18 **EXT. EST. THE WHITE HOUSE - LATE AFTERNOON**   18

It's raining now.

19 **INT. SITUATION ROOM - SAME TIME**   19

FITZWALLACE and the rest are seated and standing around the
table, whispering in groups of two and three as BARTLET walks
in. Everyone stands.

> BARTLET
> Keep your seats.

They all sit.

> BARTLET (CONT'D)
> There's a delegation of cardiologists
> having their pictures taken in the
> Blue Room. You wouldn't think you
> could find a group of people more
> arrogant than the 15 of us, but there
> they are, right upstairs in the Blue
> Room.
>   (beat)
> You called me.

> FITZWALLACE
> Yes, sir. Mr. President, we've put
> together a scenario by which we attack
> Hassan Airport; its three main terminals
> and two runways. In addition to the
> civilian casualties, which could register
> in the thousands, the strike would
> temporarily cripple the region's
> ability to receive medical supplies
> and bottled water. Now I think
> Mr. Cashman and Secretary Hutchinson
> would each tell you what I'm sure
> you already know, sir: That this strike
> would be seen both at home and abroad
> as a staggering over-reaction by a
> a first-time Commander in Chief. That
> without the support of our allies,
> without a Western coalition, without
> Great Britain and Japan and without
> Congress, you'll have doled out $5000
> worth of punishment for a fifty buck
> crime, sir.

> (MORE)

(CONTINUED)

19   CONTINUED: 19

                    FITZWALLACE
               (beat)
          Mr. President, a proportional response
          doesn't empty the options box for the
          future the way an all-out assault would--

                    BARTLET
          Thank you. Does, uh, anyone have a
          cigarette?

An OFFICER reaches into his pocket and slides a pack of
cigarettes and a lighter down the table to Bartlet. He takes
one out and lights it.

                    BARTLET (CONT'D)
          This other plan--

                    FITZWALLACE
          Paraclese-1.

                    BARTLET
          Paraclese-1, yes. No civilian casualties--

                    FITZWALLACE
          We can't promise that, sir.

                    BARTLET
          But you're as certain as you can be.

                    FITZWALLACE
          Yes sir.

                    BARTLET
          And what are the military implications?

                    OFFICER
          We'll cripple both their intelligence
          network and their surface-to-air
          strike capability.

                    BARTLET
               (pause)
          Very well. How does this work?

                    FITZWALLACE
          You give me the "go" order, sir.

A MILITARY AIDE punches some numbers into a secure phone and
holds the receiver ready for FITZWALLACE.

                    FITZWALLACE (CONT'D)
          Mr. President.

                                        (CONTINUED)

19   CONTINUED: (2)   19

BARTLET nods "yes." FITZWALLLACE takes the phone from the
AIDE.

                    FITZWALLACE (CONT'D)
          This is Fitzwallace, I have a go order
          from the President. Start the clock on
          Paraclese-1, stand by for confirmation
          code.

An OFFICER hangs up another phone.

                    OFFICER
          We're underway.

BARTLET gets up and heads to the door.

                    FITZWALLACE
          Well done, Mr. President.

                    BARTLET
          Fifty buck crime?
                    (beat)
          I honestly don't know what the hell
          we're doing here.

BARTLET leaves the room, as we:

                                                   CUT TO:

20   **INT. ROOSEVELT ROOM - LATE AFTERNOON**   20

A still confused CHARLIE is in the middle of his interview
with JOSH.

                    JOSH
          Charlie, I've got some questions
          here from the Counsel's office as well
          as the Department of Treasury and the
          Office of Internal Security. These
          questions are routine. There's no cause
          for concern. Ready?

                    CHARLIE
          Mr. Lyman--

                    JOSH
          Have you ever tried to overthrow the
          Government?

                    CHARLIE
          Is it because the messenger job is not
          available anymore, 'cause maybe if
          I came back at a different time--

                                                   (CONTINUED)

> JOSH
> Charlie, this job's actually better
> than the messenger job. It pays
> more, you don't have to ride around
> town on a bicycle, and instead of being
> a messenger, you get to be Personal Aide
> to the President.

> CHARLIE
> I see. So maybe if I come--

There's a KNOCK on the door and SAM steps in.

> JOSH
> Hey, Sam. This is Sam Seaborn,
> Deputy Communications Director. This
> is Charlie Young, he's here for Ted's
> job.

> SAM
> It's nice to meet you, don't get up.

> CHARLIE
> I was here for the messenger job.

> SAM
> Debbie's got an eye for personnel.

> CHARLIE
> I've got a driver's license and my own
> bike, so--

> JOSH
> I've gotta ask you some more questions
> here.

> SAM
> Have you ever tried to overthrow the
> Government?

> CHARLIE
> No, sir.

> SAM
> What the hell's been stopping you?

> JOSH
> Seriously, Charlie, I gotta ask you about
> your personal life.

> SAM
> No you don't.

(CONTINUED)

> JOSH
> Yes I do.

> SAM
> Why?

> JOSH
> Because I do.

> SAM
> Charlie, are you gonna come to work
> early, stay late, do your job efficiently
> and discreetly?

> CHARLIE
> Well, as I was saying to Mr. Lyman--

> SAM
> Thank you.
>   (to JOSH)
> What more do you need to know?

> JOSH
> Charlie, I wonder if you could tell me
> about your social life. Your friends,
> what you like to do.

> SAM
> Josh, I can not believe you.

> JOSH
> Sam--

> CHARLIE
> Well, there's my sister, Deanna, and...
> I'm sorry, I'm not sure what you're
> asking.

> SAM
> He's asking if you're gay, Charlie,
> and I wouldn't answer the damn question.

> JOSH
> Alright. That's it, Sam. Let's take a
> walk.

> SAM
> Feel free to sue our asses off. I'll
> represent you, if you like.

> JOSH
> Let's go.

(CONTINUED)

20   CONTINUED: (3)   20

JOSH and SAM head briskly out into:

21   **INT. CORRIDOR - CONTINUOUS**   21

We pick up JOSH and SAM at the end of the corridor as they
round the turn.

                    JOSH
          What the hell was <u>that</u> all about?

                    SAM
          This is ridiculous.

                    JOSH
          It's not all <u>that</u> ridiculous.

They walk into--

22   **INT. CORRIDOR - CONTINUOUS**   22

                    SAM
          I know the difference between right
          and wrong.

                    JOSH
          It's not like you didn't know you
          were gonna be held to a higher
          standard when you took this job.

                    SAM
          I don't mind being held to a
          higher standard, I mind being
          held to a <u>lower</u> one.

They bust through the doors to:

23   **INT. LOBBY - CONTINUOUS**   23

                    JOSH
          Sam, I gotta say digging
          your heels in--

                    SAM
          Look who's talking.

                    JOSH
          I understand--

                    SAM
          Digging my heels in?

                    JOSH
          I mean--

                                            (CONTINUED)

23   CONTINUED: 23

                        SAM
            Another word for that would be
            "principled," right?

                        JOSH
            I'm just saying--

They're intercepted by TOBY--

                        TOBY
            Leo's office.

                        JOSH
            What?

                        TOBY
            It's happening.

                                                        CUT TO:

24   **INT. LEO'S OFFICE - LATE AFTERNOON**   24

C.J. and a couple of STAFFERS are waiting. The STAFFERS are
on the phone. MARGARET enters from the side as JOSH, SAM and
TOBY enter through the front.

                        MARGARET
            He's right here.

                        SAM
            It's happening?

                        C.J.
            Yeah. That's what I hear.

LEO enters through the side. People begin writing as soon as
he begins talking.

                        LEO
            The order was given at 16:27, code
            name Paraclese-1. Four targets, all
            military. Two munitions dumps in
            Northern Rashan, Saffian Bridge and
            I.H.Q.

                        C.J.
            What's the estimated time?

                        LEO
            About 6:30 eastern. You can come
            to the sit room in twenty minutes
            for a weapons briefing. In the
            meantime, Toby, Sam, the President'll
                        (MORE)

                                                    (CONTINUED)

24   CONTINUED:

> LEO (cont'd)
> go on network at nine, so start
> zeroing in.

They start to leave--

> LEO (CONT'D)
> Hey guys? No phone calls in or out.

They go.

> LEO (CONT'D)
> And, C.J., nothing to the press until
> you get the high sign from me. No
> head starts.

> C.J.
> They're gonna wonder what all the
> fuss is about.

> LEO
> Then let's not have any fuss.

> C.J.
> I could use a few minutes with the
> President at some point.

> LEO
> You and me both.

> C.J.
> I'm not kidding, Leo, this is--

> LEO
> He'll be there.

> C.J.
> This is the first--

> LEO
> He'll be there, C.J.

> C.J.
> He'll talk to me?

> LEO
> Yes.

C.J. exits. JOSH is standing there.

> JOSH
> How are you doin'?

> LEO
> Fine.

(CONTINUED)

24   CONTINUED: (2)

                    JOSH
                (pause)
        Leo, Toby said he's snapping at the First
        Lady--

                    LEO
        Not now, Josh, okay? I mean, you're
        right, but not now.

                    JOSH
        Right.

                    LEO
                (calling)
        Margaret!

JOSH starts to leave, but turns around--

                    JOSH
        Hey, Leo, can I ask you a question?

                    LEO
        What?

                    JOSH
        I'm interviewing this kid for Ted
        Miller's job, and he's a real
        special kid. He's applied himself
        in school, I'm sure he'd be
        articulate if he weren't terrified.
        He's postponing college 'til his
        sister gets out of high school.

                    LEO
        Where are the parents?

                    JOSH
        His father's long gone, his
        mother was a uniformed cop
        here in D.C.

                    LEO
        Was?

                    JOSH
        She got shot and killed in the line
        five months ago.
                (beat)
        I really like him, Leo. I wanna hire
        him.

                    LEO
        What's the problem?

                                        (CONTINUED)

24   CONTINUED: (3)

                        JOSH
            He's black.

                        LEO
            So's the Attorney General and the
            Chairman of the Joint Chiefs.

                        JOSH
            They don't hold the door open
            for the President.

                        LEO
            What are you--

                        JOSH
            I'm not wild about the visual. A
            young black man holding his overnight
            bag--

                        LEO
            Josh, I hold the door open
            for the President. It's an honor.
            This is serious business, this isn't
            casting. We get the guy for the job
            and we take it from there.

                        JOSH
            Good.

                        LEO
            I'm fairly sure I'm right about this.

                        JOSH
            Yeah. Good.
                 (beat)
            Two hours?

                        LEO
            A little less.

    MARGARET enters--

                        MARGARET
            Leo?

                        LEO
            Yes.

                        MARGARET
            Chairman Fitzwallace.

                        LEO
            Send him in.

                                        (CONTINUED)

24   CONTINUED: (4)

> JOSH
> (to LEO)
> We'll be fine.

> LEO
> Yeah.

FITZWALLACE enters--

> FITZWALLACE
> Oh, things have moved since I was in this
> office last.

> JOSH
> How are you, Admiral, Josh Lyman.

> FITZWALLACE
> Josh, you don't have to introduce
> yourself. I'm fine thanks.

> JOSH
> Tough day.

> FITZWALLACE
> It'll be a lot tougher on them than on
> us.

> JOSH
> (pause)
> Good.

JOSH exits--

> FITZWALLACE
> You're gonna have to sit him down, Leo.

> LEO
> I know.

> FITZWALLACE
> He's gonna have to talk to the country
> a little bit. This is not the last one
> of these we're gonna have to do. But
> you're gonna have to sit him down.

> LEO
> Any advice?

> FITZWALLACE
> Oh, it's not my place.

> LEO
> Yeah it is.

(CONTINUED)

24   CONTINUED: (5)   24

                              FITZWALLACE
                    Tell him it's always like this the
                    first time. Tell him he's doing fine.

                              LEO
                    He's not doing fine.

                              FITZWALLACE
                    Yeah he is. Presidents don't make new
                    friends. That's why they gotta hang
                    on to their old ones. You'll know what
                    to say.

                              LEO
                    Yeah.

          FITZWALLACE starts to leave--

                              LEO (CONT'D)
                    Hey, Fitz?

                              FITZWALLACE
                    Yeah.

                              LEO
                    The President's personal aide. They're
                    looking at a kid--you have any problem
                    with a young Black man waiting on the
                    President?

                              FITZWALLACE
                    I'm an old Black man and I wait on
                    the President.

                              LEO
                    The kid's gotta carry his bags and all--

                              FITZWALLACE
                    You gonna pay him a decent wage?

                              LEO
                    Yeah.

                              FITZWALLACE
                    You gonna treat him with respect in the
                    workplace?

                              LEO
                    Yeah.

                              FITZWALLACE
                    Then why the hell should I care?

                                                    (CONTINUED)

24   CONTINUED: (6)   24

                              LEO
                That's what I thought.

                              FITZWALLACE
                I've got some real honest-to-God
                battles to fight, Leo. I don't have
                time for the cosmetic ones.

                              LEO
                Thanks Admiral. Good luck.

                              FITZWALLACE
                See ya later.

We follow FITZWALLACE out into

25   **INT. CORRIDOR - CONTINUOUS**   25

The entire communications area is alive with activity as
people come and go, delivering messages and information to
Toby and Sam's office and manning telephones. As FITZWALLACE
leaves the office, TOBY is passing from another direction and
in a hurry.

                              FITZWALLACE
                'Evening Toby.

                              TOBY
                     (without stopping)
                'Evening, sir. Sorry I can't stop--

                              FITZWALLACE
                Go.

We follow TOBY through the:

26   **INT. ROOSEVELT ROOM - CONTINUOUS**   26

JOSH is standing alone at one end of the room.

                              SHEILA
                Estimated BDA?

                              TOBY
                My first bombing. I don't know yet.

Josh calls to TOBY crossing through--

                              JOSH
                Toby, you need help?

                              TOBY
                No.

                                              (CONTINUED)

26   CONTINUED: 26

TOBY is gone out the other side...

> JOSH (CONT'D)
> Sheila, if you need me for anything, I'm
> standing here with absolutely nothing to
> do.

27   **INT. COMMUNICATIONS BULLPEN - CONTINUOUS**   27

As TOBY walks through and into his office. CATHY is answering
several phones at once.

> CATHY
> (into phone)
> White House Communications.
> (beat)
> I'm sorry, Toby's not available to
> speak on the phone at the moment. No,
> Sam's not available either.

C.J.'s walking through, CATHY puts her hand over the phone--

> CATHY (CONT'D)
> (to C.J.--seeking help)
> Why is no one available to speak on the
> phone?

> C.J.
> I don't know. They're planning my
> surprise party.

C.J. hasn't stopped walking. She goes into TOBY'S office--

28   **INT. TOBY'S OFFICE - CONTINUOUS**   28

TOBY and SAM are working--

> SAM
> "Unprovoked and cold-blooded--"

> TOBY
> It needs a third--

> C.J.
> Toby--

> TOBY
> (to C.J.)
> Quickly.

> C.J.
> The AGM-84E-SLAM.

(CONTINUED)

28   CONTINUED:

> TOBY
> Cathy, Sam cut the paragraph ten minutes
> ago.

> CATHY
> It's coming out on the red-line.

> C.J.
> The 84E-SLAM?

> TOBY
> "Stand-off Land Attack Missile."
> Distinguish it from the AGM-84D, or
> Harpoon, which is an anti-ship missile.

> C.J.
>   (out the door)
> Thank you.

> TOBY
>   (to SAM)
> A third thing--

> SAM
> "Unwarranted" unquote

> TOBY
> --yes, and cold-blooded. Unwarranted--

> SAM
> Unprovoked--

> TOBY
> --and cold-blooded. Great.

> SAM
> I just need--

> TOBY
> What are you--

> SAM
> Two seconds. Just two seconds.

SAM'S out the door and into

29   **INT. BULLPEN/CORRIDOR - CONTINUOUS**   29

> SAM
>   (calling out)
> C.J.!

SAM catches up to C.J.--

(CONTINUED)

                         SAM (CONT'D)
          Listen...

                         C.J.
          What.

                         SAM
          I'm sorry about before.

                         C.J.
          Yeah.

                         SAM
               (pause)
          I'm just really very fond of her is all.

                         C.J.
               (pause)
          Go back to work.

                         SAM
          Right.

C.J. continues on toward her office. She picks up a few
REPORTERS on her way. They ask questions as they walk.

                         REPORTER #1
          C.J., what's all the activity?

                         C.J.
          What activity?

                         REPORTER #1
          C.J., come on.

                         REPORTER #2
          Fitzwallace was in Leo's office.

                         C.J.
          Admiral Fitzwallace is Chairman of the
          Joint Chiefs. Leo McGarry is White House
          Chief of Staff. I'm your host C.J., let's
          play our game.

                         REPORTER #1
          Is it happening?

                         C.J.
          No.

                         REPORTER #1
          Would you know if it was?

                                              (CONTINUED)

29   CONTINUED: (2)   29

> **C.J.**
> Guys--

> **REPORTER #2**
> Why all the activity?

> **C.J.**
> Menudo's in the building. I gotta
> go.

C.J. turns the corner. DANNY's standing at her office door
waiting for her.

> **DANNY**
> C.J.--

> **C.J.**
> Oh man, I'd honestly think that you of
> all people--

> **DANNY**
> We need to talk.

> **C.J.**
> Danny, I haven't called a full lid,
> there'll obviously be a briefing if the
> President has engaged the use of military
> force.

> **DANNY**
> Thanks. Since I've only been a White
> House Reporter for seven years, I
> appreciate your clearing that up.

C.J. realizes that DANNY's talking about something else
entirely...

> **C.J.**
> What?

> **DANNY**
> Not for nothin', but I know Sam Seaborn's
> been going around with a $3,000 a night
> call girl and I thought you should know
> that I know.

C.J. looks at DANNY, looks down at the ground, looks
around... she can't believe she has to deal with this right
now.

> **DANNY (CONT'D)**
> Ask me inside, C.J.

(CONTINUED)

29   CONTINUED: (3)   29

                  C.J.
            (indicating her office)
      Inside.

They walk into C.J.'s office.

                           FADE OUT.

<u>**END OF ACT THREE**</u>

ACT FOUR

FADE IN:

30   **EXT. EST. WASHINGTON - NIGHT**   30

Now the rain's coming down pretty hard.

31   **INT. JOSH'S BULLPEN AREA - NIGHT**   31

JOSH walks in and strolls up to DONNA.

>   JOSH
>   Where's Charlie?

>   DONNA
>   He's filling out his employment stuff
>   at personnel.

>   JOSH
>   How's he doing?

>   DONNA
>   He looked pretty freaked.

>   JOSH
>   He's a gamer. I can pick 'em.

>   DONNA
>   If you say so.

>   JOSH
>   (pause)
>   I have nothing to do.

>   DONNA
>   I can see.

>   JOSH
>   (pause)
>   Whoa, excuse me. Everyone running around
>   like the future of the world depends on
>   it which, I suppose, it does. Everyone
>   running around working. Me, I got nothing
>   to do.

>   DONNA
>   Yes.

>   JOSH
>   Like a writer on a movie set.

>   DONNA
>   Have you ever been on a movie set?

                                          (CONTINUED)

31   CONTINUED:

> JOSH
> No, but I hear stories.

> DONNA
> You wanna do mail?

> JOSH
> At least there's some comfort in
> knowing that whatever's gonna
> happen today has already
> happened.

MANDY comes to the doorway of Josh's office--

> MANDY
> Josh, your office sucks.

JOSH hasn't even turned to look. He just keeps staring at
DONNA...

> JOSH
> I don't understand it. Why can't you
> tell me that there is a person in
> my office?

> DONNA
> Hey. The first time I didn't know.
> The second time I didn't care that
> much.

> MANDY
> I mean it, it's a hole.

JOSH goes into

32   **INT. JOSH'S OFFICE - CONTINUOUS**   32

> JOSH
> Why are you here?

> MANDY
> I start work next week. I came to
> get psyched.

> JOSH
> You picked a really bad time to
> get psyched.

> MANDY
> 'Cause the President gave the attack
> order and you're getting ready to go
> on the air?

(CONTINUED)

32   CONTINUED:

                    JOSH
          No, it's because--

                    MANDY
          Please, Josh, everyone's running around
          looking casual, Toby and Sam are locked
          in with the speech writers and you have
          nothing to do. What is it, I.H.Q.,
          a couple of armories?

                    JOSH
          You wanna say it a little louder,
          Mandy, I don't think Syrian Air Defense
          Command heard you.

                    MANDY
          I brought you a present.

                    JOSH
          Why are you being nice to me?

                    MANDY
          Because I'm really psyched to get started
          to work.

                    JOSH
          It's been pretty bad around here
          since it happened.

                    MANDY
          I had a hunch.

                    JOSH
          The combination of American lives
          and Morris, the idea of using
          any force at all...

                    MANDY
          We always said he'd be in his head.

                    JOSH
          He wasn't ready for it.

                    MANDY
          How do you get ready for it?

                    JOSH
          What'd you bring me?

                    MANDY
          What?

                                        (CONTINUED)

> JOSH
> I want my present.

> MANDY
> Yeah. It's a picture I found.

MANDY hands JOSH a framed picture with a bow tied around it.

> JOSH
> A picture of you and me. And
> someone's drawn all over my face
> with a magic marker.

> MANDY
> That was me.

> JOSH
> Ah.

> MANDY
> During my period of hating you.

> JOSH
>   (pause)
> Well, that could've been pretty much
> anytime, couldn't it?

> MANDY
> Sure. This was taken the night we
> met at that seafood place by the
> Democratic Leadership Conference.

> JOSH
> Look at that.

> MANDY
> You couldn't stop staring at me.

> JOSH
> Well you were wearing quite the
> ensemble that night, Madeline.

> MANDY
> I don't think it was the wardrobe
> you were lookin' at there, Lucky.

JOSH smiles.

> MANDY (CONT'D)
> You guys are doin' okay, Josh.

His phone RINGS...

(CONTINUED)

32   CONTINUED: (3)   32

JOSH picks up the phone--

> JOSH
> (into phone)
> Yeah.
> (beat)
> Yeah.

JOSH hangs up.

> JOSH (CONT'D)
> They found a job for me.

> MANDY
> Then I'll see you next week.

> JOSH
> Listen, you're not gonna be this
> nice to me when we're working
> together, right?

> MANDY
> Not a chance.

> JOSH
> That's what I thought.

MANDY exits as DONNA enters.

> JOSH (CONT'D)
> Hey, what's up.

JOSH and DONNA exit as we:

                                              CUT TO:

33   **INT. C.J.'S OFFICE - NIGHT**   33

DANNY's sitting across from C.J.'s desk.

> DANNY
> I mean I obviously don't have enough
> for a story, but as a courtesy to you,
> C.J., I just want to let you know
> I'm gonna be asking around.

> C.J.
> Danny, it's gonna be much ado about
> nothing.

> DANNY
> It doesn't look that way.

                                             (CONTINUED)

33   CONTINUED: 33

                              C.J.
                    But it <u>is</u> that way and I just
                    got through <u>telling</u> you it's
                    that way.

                         DANNY
                    C.J.--

                              C.J.
                    Sam knows the difference between
                    right and wrong and so do you. Would
                    it make my life easier if he wasn't
                    friends with this woman? Absolutely.
                    But Sam's a grown-up and I don't
                    get to choose his friends and your
                    readers don't get to judge them. And I'll
                    tell you what else: There's something
                    commendable about Sam's behavior here.
                    Don't ask me what, but there is, and
                    I'm gonna stick by him 'till the
                    President orders me otherwise, and
                    I'm gonna look very unfavorably on
                    those who seek only to make us look
                    like fools.

                         DANNY
                    Whoa, down girl.

                              C.J.
                    Danny--

                         DANNY
                    I'll drop it.

                              C.J.
                    Good.

                         DANNY
                    I'll drop it.

                              C.J.
                    Thank you.

                         DANNY
                    But, C.J., you better get dee'd-up
                    here, 'cause not everybody's a good
                    guy. And you're gonna start
                    to get traction on something that
                    maybe someone else isn't such a fan
                    of, and they're gonna put a tail on
                    Seaborn if they haven't already--'member
                    I found out about this somehow and I
                    wasn't there--

                                                    (CONTINUED)

33   CONTINUED: (2)

> C.J.
> I don't suppose you'd tell me how--

> DANNY
> No way. My point is they'll keep it in
> their pocket 'til the eve of
> something big: Bill signing, State of the
> Union, maybe the convention.

> C.J.
> I'm on it.

The phone RINGS.

> C.J. (CONT'D)
> (into phone)
> Yeah. I'll wait for him.
> (to DANNY)
> Hang on a second, I'm gonna
> give you a ten minute head-start
> on something.

> DANNY
> What for?

> C.J.
> Bein' a good guy.

> DANNY
> What's the tip?

> C.J.
> (into phone)
> Yeah. Thank you.
> (hanging up)
> We're out of Syrian air space.

DANNY immediately gets out a note pad as we

                                        CUT TO:

34   **INT. WEST CORRIDORS - NIGHT**   34

JOSH is taking CHARLIE through the West Wing.

> JOSH
> These used be White House Counsel's
> offices until Toby and the Communications
> staff conquered and pillaged.
> (pointing)
> Map Room, Roosevelt Room, Oval Office,
> Chief of Staff...I guess the only thing
> left for you to do is say hello to
> (MORE)

                                        (CONTINUED)

34   CONTINUED: 34

> JOSH (cont'd)
> the President.
> (JOSH starts walking)
> We're going on the air in a few minutes
> with a national address, so I don't know
> how much--

CHARLIE is standing frozen back at the spot where Josh said
"President."

> JOSH (CONT'D)
> Where the hell did he go? Charlie--

                                                        CUT TO:

35   **INT. OVAL OFFICE - NIGHT**   35

Television lights and a camera, along with all the cables,
sound equipment, monitors and CREW that go along with a live
address from the Oval Office are either in place or are being
put in place. LEO is standing off to the side. BARTLET is
working with TOBY and SAM as AIDES walk in and out. C.J. will
walk in eventually.

> BARTLET
> What happened to paragraph nine?

> SAM
> In the red-line?

> BARTLET
> I'm sorry, paragraph _eight_.

> SAM
> We cut that a half an hour ago.

> TOBY
> France'll read between the lines.

> BARTLET
> Well I want to see it again, please.

> TOBY
> If you look at the new paragraph--

> BARTLET
> I can't look at anything, fellas--
> (calling)
> Mrs. Landingham, I need my glasses!

> NANCY
> Sir, she's talking to the porters right
> now.

JOSH enters with CHARLIE--

                                                  (CONTINUED)

35   CONTINUED: 35

                  TOBY
Mr. President--

                  BARTLET
When do I get the BDA?

                  SAM
Uh, well, there's a problem with that,
sir.

                  BARTLET
Why?

                  TOBY
Ordinarily we'd get help with early
information from sources inside the
Syrian intelligence network.

                  BARTLET
So what's the problem?

                  TOBY
We just blew up the Syrian intelligence
network.

                  BARTLET
Oh, for crying out loud, will somebody
get on the phone to CNN and find out if
we hit anything.

A STAFFER comes in with some papers--

                  STAFFER
Mr. President, it's the BDA, sir.

                  BARTLET
Thank you, now if I only had my glasses--

MRS. LANDINGHAM has come in--

                  MRS. LANDINGHAM
The porters have searched your bedroom
from top to bottom--

                  BARTLET
This has been since this morning. We
should've brought in an optometrist
by now.

                  MRS. LANDINGHAM
An optometrist can't fold his equipment
in a briefcase--

                      (CONTINUED)

35   CONTINUED: (2)   35

                              NANCY
          They've got those machines with the
          lenses--

                              BARTLET
          I don't need an optometrist now. Thank
          you, Nancy. I just need the glasses he
          prescribed.

                              C.J.
          Mr. President, if you'll take a
          minute or two to familiarize yourself
          with the Phoenix, the press'll--

                              BARTLET
          I got the briefing on the Phoenix.

                              C.J.
          You understand I'm not talking about
          the Sidewinder.

                              BARTLET
          The Phoenix. I got the briefing on the
          Phoenix last night. I studied the report.
          Hutchinson was there. In my private
          study. The Phoenix. The A-61. The Sparrow
          and the Sidewinder. Are we covered?

      CHARLIE has leaned in and whispered something to JOSH while
      the action and the noise continue. JOSH smiles--

                              C.J.
          Yes sir.

                              BARTLET
          Very well.

                              FLOOR MANAGER
          Ten minutes to air, Mr. President.

                              JOSH
              (indicating BARTLET)
          Tell him.

                              BARTLET
          For want of a pair of eyeglasses--

                              C.J. (O.S.)
          Try mine, sir.

                              JOSH
          Tell him.

                                                        (CONTINUED)

35   CONTINUED: (3)

                    MRS. LANDINGHAM
          We're looking.

                    NANCY
          She's looking.

                    BARTLET
          Thank you.

                    TOBY
          While they're looking, sir. In the
          meantime, can you take a look at the new
          pact.

                    BARTLET
          Oh crap. I can't see anything with these.

                    JOSH
               (louder)
          Charlie, <u>tell</u> him.

                    CHARLIE
          Mr. President.

CHARLIE's voice quiets the room and now everyone is looking
at Josh and Charlie.

                    CHARLIE (CONT'D)
               (beat)
          You said you read the Phoenix report in--

                    BARTLET
          What?

                    CHARLIE
          You said you read the Phoenix report in
          your private study last night, sir.

                    BARTLET
          What of it? Who is this?

There's a bit of a stunned silence as everyone looks at
CHARLIE. After a moment, MRS. LANDINGHAM turns to NANCY--

                    MRS. LANDINGHAM
          Have a steward go to the President's
          study. Have him look under the papers
          on the coffee table.

NANCY goes. The room is still quiet.

                    JOSH
          Mr. President, this is Charles Young...

                                        (CONTINUED)

35   CONTINUED: (4)   35

This is the best Bartlet can do...

                    BARTLET
          I don't have any time for new people now.

The noise and activity resumes. CHARLIE half backs out of the
room, trying to make himself invisible. The activity goes on
a moment longer before--

                    LEO
          All right, that's it. Excuse me, Mr.
          President.
               (calling out)
          A minute please.

No one really knows what's going on--

                    TOBY
          Leo...

The Oval Office clears out except for BARTLET and LEO.
BARTLET leans against his desk. LEO stands on the other side
of the room.

36   **INT. LEO'S OFFICE - NIGHT**   36

                    BARTLET
          What do you need, Leo?

                    LEO
          Well you've gone through everyone
          who works for you and everyone who's
          married to you. I didn't know who
          else you could get mad at, so I
          was afraid the American people might
          be next. Oh, by the way, when we're done
          here, you're sending Abbey some flowers.

                    BARTLET
          Did you know that two-thousand years
          ago, a Roman citizen could walk across
          the face of the known world, free of
          the fear of molestation? He could walk
          across the Earth unharmed, cloaked only
          in the protection of the words: Civis
          Romanus. I am a Roman citizen. So great
          was the retribution of Rome universally
          understood as <u>certain</u> should any
          harm befall even one of its citizens.
               (beat)
          Where was Morris's protection? Or anybody
          else on that airplane. Where was the
          retribution for their families?
               (MORE)

                                              (CONTINUED)

> BARTLET (cont'd)
> And where was the warning to the rest of
> the world that Americans shall walk this
> Earth unharmed lest the clenched fist of
> the most mighty military force in the
> history of mankind *comes crashing down on*
> *your house*. In other words, Leo, what the
> hell are we *doing*, here?

> LEO
> We are behaving the way a superpower
> oughta behave.

> BARTLET
> Well our behavior has produced some
> crappy results. In fact, I'm not a
> hundred percent sure it hasn't induced
> it.

> LEO
> What are you talkin' about?

> BARTLET
> I'm talkin' about 286 American Marines
> in Beirut, I'm talkin' about Somalia, I'm
> talking about Nairobi--

> LEO
> And you think ratcheting up the body
> count's gonna act as a deterrent?

> BARTLET
> You're damn right I do.

> LEO
> Oh, then you're just as stupid as these
> guys who think capital punishment's
> gonna be a deterrent for drug
> kingpins, as if drug kingpins didn't
> live their day-to-day _lives_ under
> the possibility of execution. And
> their executions are a lot less dainty
> than ours, and tend to take place
> without the bother and expense of
> due process. So, my friend, if you
> wanna start using American military
> strength as the arm of the Lord,
> you can do that. We're the only
> superpower left, you can conquer the
> world like Charlemagne, but you
> better be prepared to kill _everyone_,
> and you better start with me,
> 'cause I will raise-up an army
> against you and I will beat you.

(CONTINUED)

> BARTLET
> He had a ten day-old baby at home.

> LEO
> I know.

> BARTLET
> We are doing nothing.

> LEO
> We are not doing nothing.

> BARTLET
> Destroy--

> LEO
> Four high-rated military targets--

The decibel level of the argument is starting to rise quickly--

> BARTLET
> And this is good?

> LEO
> Of course it's not good. There is no
> good! It's what there is! It's how
> you behave if you're the most powerful
> nation in the world! It's proportional.
> It's reasonable. It's responsible.
> It's merciful. It's not nothing. Four
> high-rated military targets--

> BARTLET
>   (shouting)
> Which they'll rebuild again in six
> months!

> LEO
>   (shouting)
> *Then we'll blow 'em up again in six*
> *months! We're getting really good at*
> *it!!!!*

The two men stand staring at each other. It's the feeling you
have when you've shouted as loud as you know and just
discovered the futility.

They catch their breath for a moment...

> LEO (CONT'D)
>   (easily)
> It's what our fathers taught us.

                                        (CONTINUED)

BARTLET looks at LEO for a long moment...

> BARTLET
> Why didn't you say so?

They smile...

> BARTLET (CONT'D)
> (with a sigh)
> Ah, man, Leo. I think of all the
> work you put into getting me to run,
> and when I think of all the work you
> did to get me elected...I could
> pummel your ass with a baseball bat.

This cracks them both up...

> LEO
> Oh, here's one you'll like: Bertram
> Coles--

> BARTLET
> Oh, I like anything that starts with
> Bertram Coles. Let's have it.

> LEO
> Coles goes on the radio yesterday
> and he says people in his district
> love America, and you better not come
> down there 'cause you might not get out
> alive.

They LAUGH--

> BARTLET
> Bert's callin' me out?

> LEO
> (laughing all the way)
> Apparently the people in Bert's
> district are so patriotic, that
> if the President of the United
> States himself were to show up,
> they'd kill him.

The two men LAUGH.

> BARTLET
> Ziegler must be ballistic.

> LEO
> Toby is on it.

(CONTINUED)

36   CONTINUED: (4)   36

                              BARTLET
             Oh, by the way, who was that kid before?
             The one who figured out where my glasses
             were?

                              LEO
             Well, if you want him, that's your
             new body man.

                              BARTLET
             What's his story?

                                                         CUT TO:

37   **INT. OVAL OFFICE/OUTER OFFICE - NIGHT**   37

Everyone is standing around quietly and nervously.   After a
moment...

                              SAM
             What do you think is going on in there?

                              TOBY
                 (beat)
             I don't know.

                              C.J.
             Hey, do you know anything about a story
             going around that has the Secret Service
             investigating Bertram Coles for
             threatening the life of the President?

                              TOBY
             No.

                              C.J.
             Maggie Greenwald is quoting you as
             saying, "the Secret Service investigates
             all threats made against the President,
             and it's White House policy not to
             comment."

                              TOBY
             Yeah.

                              C.J.
             Did you say that?

                              TOBY
             Yeah.
                 (beat)
             Hey, you don't suppose that's how the
             story got started, do you?

                                                      (CONTINUED)

37   CONTINUED:

> TOBY (CONT'D)
> You know what, C.J. You tell Bert Coles
> that Toby Ziegler said there's a new
> sheriff in town.

JOSH is in the outer office standing confidentially with
CHARLIE.

> JOSH
> (quietly)
> This was just, I think, a bad day. I
> have to tell you he's ordinarily
> an extremely kind man, placing a very
> high premium on civility. Today--

> CHARLIE
> Sure.

> JOSH
> It's just been a very difficult few days
> for him--

> CHARLIE
> I think I should probably go.

BARTLET's voice comes BOOMING from the Oval Office.

> BARTLET (O.S.)
> Excuse me, Charlie!

CHARLIE freezes and looks at the door just as BARTLET pops
his head out--

> BARTLET (CONT'D)
> Can I see you inside, please?

Everyone from the outer office has begun filing back into the
Oval Office where they'll move for places around monitors.

> BARTLET (CONT'D)
> (to CHARLIE)
> Come on, it's okay.

CHARLIE does as he's told. JOSH comes after and we follow
them back into

38   **INT. OVAL OFFICE - CONTINUOUS**   38

The monitors are displaying network anchors doing their lead-
ins to the President's address.

BARTLET takes CHARLIE aside, away from the bustle--

(CONTINUED)

38   CONTINUED:

                         BARTLET
          I'm Jed Bartlet.

                         CHARLIE
          I'm Charles Young.

                         BARTLET
          But you prefer Charlie, right?

CHARLIE nods "yes."

                         BARTLET (CONT'D)
          Listen, Leo McGarry filled me in on the
          situation with your mother. I'm so very
          sorry. I hope you don't mind, but I took
          the liberty of calling Tom Connolly, the
          FBI Director, and we had the computer
          spit out some quick information. Your
          mother was killed by a Westing 38
          revolver firing KTWs, or what are known
          as "cop killer" bullets. Now, we have
          not had a whole lot of success yet in
          banning that weapon and those bullets off
          the streets, but we're planning on
          taking a big whack at it when Congress
          comes back from recess.
               (beat)
          So, what do you say, you wanna come help
          us out?

                         CHARLIE
               (pause)
          Yes sir, I do.

                         BARTLET
          Thanks, Charlie.

                         FLOOR MANAGER
          30 seconds, please.

BARTLET pats CHARLIE on the arm and takes his place behind
his desk. A HAIR AND MAKE-UP WOMAN helps him with his jacket
and brushes him off.

                         LEO
          All set?

                         BARTLET
          You tell me.

                         LEO
          It's a pretty ugly tie.

                                        (CONTINUED)

38   CONTINUED: (2)

> BARTLET
> My granddaughter gave me this tie.

> LEO
> My nephew gave me an ashtray he made at
> summer camp--

> BARTLET
> Get away from me. Somebody
> throw this guy outa the building.

By the monitors, SAM stands next to C.J., TOBY next to JOSH
and CHARLIE.

> FLOOR MANAGER (O.S.)
> Stand by.

> BARTLET
> Thank you.

> CHARLIE
> (to JOSH; whispering)
> I've never felt like this before.

JOSH smiles...

> JOSH
> It doesn't go away.

> ANCHOR (ON TV)
> ...here now, the President.

> BARTLET (ON TV)
> My fellow Americans. Good evening. A
> short while ago I ordered our Armed
> Forces to attack and destroy four
> military targets in Northern Syria.

                                      DISSOLVE TO:

END TITLES

> BARTLET (ON TV)
> This in response to the unwarranted,
> unprovoked and cold-blooded downing three
> days ago of an unarmed Air Force jet
> carrying 58 passengers and the flag of
> the United States...

                                      FADE TO BLACK

                    END OF SHOW

THE
WEST WING
SEASON TWO

IN THE SHADOW OF
TWO GUNMEN

Parts I and II

Directed by Thomas Schlamme

Most TV shows have what are called Bibles. The staff gets together before the season starts and maps out an arc to the year. They break stories and they outline and they put some organization to the writing process.

I put no organization to the writing process. The writing is done on the fly. When I finish one script I have no idea what's going to happen in the next. The two-part second season premiere is the only time in the life of the series I knew something of what the story was going to be in advance. Sometime in the middle of the first season I had decided I wanted to do an episode with flashbacks showing the early days of the campaign. I had thought of the early scene with Josh and Leo and how Sam leaves his law firm and how C.J. leaves her P.R. firm. That was it but for me that's a lot. I wasn't sure how I was going to get into the flashbacks, but sometime later I thought of the shooting attempt and one of the characters' lives hanging in the balance.

Tommy directed it and Michael O'Neill gave a beautifully understated performance as the head of Bartlet's Secret Service detail.

In the Shadow of Two Gunmen

Part I

<u>TEASER</u>

From the DARKNESS we HEAR:

Police sirens. And the sound of a 7000 pound limousine racing across the Potomac on the Lincoln Bridge at 80 miles an hour.

FADE IN:

1   **EXT. LINCOLN BRIDGE - NIGHT**   1

TITLE:
                        Monday, 9:37 p.m.

                        BUTTERFIELD (V.O.)
            Zoey's secure.

                        BARTLET (V.O.)
            Get her again.

                        BUTTERFIELD (V.O.)
            She wasn't hit, sir.

                        BARTLET (V.O.)
            Get her on the radio please.

                        BUTTERFIELD (V.O.)
            Sir, she can't talk right now.

                                                        CUT TO:

2   **INT. BARTLET'S LIMO - NIGHT**   2

The blue/red lights of the motorcycle escort are flashing into the car as BARTLET and BUTTERFIELD sit in the back, stunned and expressionless but breathing hard.

                        BARTLET
            Why can't she talk?

                        BUTTERFIELD
            She's vomiting in the car.

                        BARTLET
            Oh, my God.

                        BUTTERFIELD
            She--it happens, sir.

                                                    (CONTINUED)

                              BARTLET
          Why's she vomiting?

                              BUTTERFIELD
          It happens. It could be shock.

                              BARTLET
          Ron--

                              BUTTERFIELD
          She might've got an elbow in the stomach.

                              BARTLET
          Gina with her?

                              BUTTERFIELD
          Gina put her in the car.

                              BARTLET
          She's not with her?

                              BUTTERFIELD
          She's got two other agents in the car,
          she's got Mike and Fred, sir, they're
          gonna have her back in the White House--

                              BARTLET
          Why isn't Gina in the <u>car</u>?

                              BUTTERFIELD
          Gina put Zoey in the car then stayed
          behind for the I.D. Agent. Mr. President,
          <u>please</u>.

BARTLET winces slightly and is still having a little trouble
catching his breath.

                              BARTLET
                    (pause)
          Is anybody dead back there?

                              BUTTERFIELD
          We don't know, we don't think so.

                              BARTLET
          What happened to your hand?

BARTLET's just noticed that BUTTERFIELD's got a bloodsoaked
handkerchief wrapped around his hand.

                              BUTTERFIELD
          I got hit.

                                                        (CONTINUED)

2   CONTINUED: (2)   2

> BARTLET
> Oh God--
> (to the DRIVER)
> Coop, turn around! We gotta go to the
> hospital.

> BUTTERFIELD
> We've gotta get you to the White--

> BARTLET
> We're going to the hospital, let's go!

> BUTTERFIELD
> I have to put you inside the White House,
> Mr. President, this isn't something we
> discuss.

> BARTLET
> This is--my daughter is throwing up on
> the floor in the car behind us, you're
> losing blood by the liter, not to
> mention, God knows how many broken bones
> you've got in your hand, but let's make
> sure that _I'm_ tucked in bed before we--

> BUTTERFIELD
> Mr. President...?

BUTTERFIELD's noticed something that's definitely got his
attention...

...a stream of blood is running down the corner of BARTLET's
mouth. BARTLET begins to look disoriented.

BUTTERFIELD runs his hands through the back of BARTLET's hair,
then puts his hand inside BARTLET's coat and reaches around
back. He pulls his hand back out and it's covered with blood.
He whips around to the DRIVER--

> BUTTERFIELD
> (to the DRIVER)
> *G.W.! BLUE! BLUE! BLUE!*

And the 7000 pound limousine screeches into a 180 degree turn
as we

                                               CUT TO:

3   **EXT. THE NEWSEUM - NIGHT**   3

We're only a few minutes removed from the shooting, and if the
chaos has died down a bit, it's only a bit. Additional police
and paramedics are starting to arrive on the scene.

                                               (CONTINUED)

Witnesses, in clumps, are giving statements, and we'll see a
few people pointing up to a blown-out window where the shots
came from.

We move over and find C.J. sitting on the curb with a bandage
pressed to the side of her forehead.

                    PARAMEDIC #1
          She's stable.

                    C.J.
          I'm really fine.

                    PARAMEDIC #2
          It's a scalp laceration, secondary to
          fall.

                    C.J.
          I hit my head on the ground.

                    PARAMEDIC #3
          No LOC.

                    C.J.
          Somebody pushed me down.

                    PARAMEDIC #3
          Are you C.J. Cregg?

                    C.J.
          Yeah.

                    PARAMEDIC #3
          Can you tell me what day it is?

                    C.J.
              (beat)
          It's still Monday.

                    PARAMEDIC #3
          Okay, C.J.? You're more shaken up than
          anything else. I don't think you're gonna
          need stitches, but you should find a
          place to lie down.

                    C.J.
          Is the President dead?

                    PARAMEDIC #3
              (beat)
          I wouldn't know anything about that.

                    PARAMEDIC (O.S.)
          You alright, ma'am?

                                              (CONTINUED)

3   CONTINUED: (2)   3

The PARAMEDICS move along, leaving C.J. alone at the curb. She gets up and takes a few steps over to the police car she was pushed down behind. She sees the exploded window.

SAM comes over.

                    SAM
          You alright?

                    C.J.
          What?

                    SAM
          Are you alright?

                    C.J.
          Where's the President?

                    SAM
          He's on his way back to the White House.
          So's Zoey. They just put Leo in the
          car. Are you alright?

                    C.J.
          Somebody put me down.

GINA's passing by--

                    SAM
               (calling out)
          Gina!

                    GINA
          I can't talk right now.

GINA heads to a cluster of SECRET SERVICE AGENTS, a little short of breath and speaks to an Asian-American man (TOMMY CHO).

                    GINA
          Gina Toscano.

                    TOMMY CHO
          Tommy Cho.

                    GINA
          You're the I.D. Agent?

                    TOMMY CHO
          Yeah.

                                        (CONTINUED)

3   CONTINUED: (3)   3

                              GINA
                    Two shooters in that window. We got
                    'em both from the roof. But there was
                    a signal.

                              TOMMY CHO
                    There was somebody on the ground?

                              GINA
                    White male. 20-25. Maybe 5-10.

                              TOMMY CHO
                    What else?

                              GINA
                    He was wearing a baseball cap.

                              TOMMY CHO
                    What kind of cap?

                              GINA
                         (beat)
                    Maybe it got knocked off in the crowd.

                              TOMMY CHO
                    What kind of cap?!

                              GINA
                         (beat--boy is <u>this</u> the
                          wrong answer)
                    I don't know.

TOMMY CHO keeps his gaze on GINA a moment before turning to an
AGENT--

                              TOMMY CHO
                    Fix a perimeter.
                         (SHOUTING across to an agent)
                    Close the airports, shut 'em down.
                         (as he walks away)
                    I want the Harbor Patrol and the Coast
                    Guard.
                         (calling)
                    Stevie. Paul.

The AGENTS disperse, nearly knocking down GINA as they ignore
her.

                              TOBY
                         (calling)
                    Josh. Josh.

TOBY passes CHARLIE--

                                                          (CONTINUED)

3   CONTINUED: (4)   3

                              TOBY
                    Hey, Charlie--

                              CHARLIE
                    Are you okay?

                              TOBY
                    Yeah. Have you seen Josh?

                              CHARLIE
                    He got in the car with Leo.

                              TOBY
                    No he didn't. Shanahan got in with Leo,
                    Josh didn't get in the car.

                              WOMAN (O.S.)
                         (calling)
                    Can we get some help?

                              CHARLIE
                         (calling O.S.)
                    Yeah, stay right there.

CHARLIE heads off and TOBY looks around. He walks up to a wall
where finally he sees JOSH, who is sitting on the ground with
his back resting against the wall.

                              TOBY
                    Josh. Didn't you hear me shouting for
                    you? I didn't know where the hell you--

And as TOBY stands in front of JOSH, he sees why JOSH hasn't
answered. TOBY's frozen for a moment in horror as JOSH, his
chest covered with blood, slumps down to the sidewalk.

                              TOBY
                         (shouting)
                    I need a... I need a doctor! I need help!

                                                  SMASH CUT TO:

MAIN TITLES

                              END OF TEASER

ACT ONE

FADE IN:

3A   **INT. GEORGE WASHINGTON HOSPITAL/EMERGENCY ROOM - NIGHT**   3A

It's a fairly light night in the E.R., which means about a
half-dozen patients in the waiting area. Maybe someone's got a
thermometer in their mouth, maybe two roommates are helping a
friend who got too high at a party.

> PA (V.O.)
> Dr. Partridge. Dr. Partridge.

A DOCTOR emerges and approaches the DUTY NURSE, who hands the
doctor a clipboard with some information--

> DUTY NURSE
> Hi

> DUTY NURSE
> Hey, your best friend's back.

> DOCTOR
> Thank you for that. Cynthia. Hi. You can
> follow me.

The PATIENT (CYNTHIA) follows the DOCTOR into the examining
area as another NURSE joins the DUTY NURSE at the desk.

> DUTY NURSE
> She's been in twice a week for the last
> three weeks 'cause she can't feel the
> baby kick. I should just tell her,
> "Ma'am, wait'll eight months, the kid'll
> be doing the Macarena, in the meantime,
> this is an emergency room."

> NURSE
> Did you really say that?

> DUTY NURSE
> No I'm sayin' I shoulda said that.

The PHONE RINGS--

> DUTY NURSE
> (answering the phone)
> Emergency Room.

But there's no one on the other end. The DUTY NURSE sees that
it's not the E.R. phone that's ringing, but a special red
phone with a single line.

(CONTINUED)

3A   CONTINUED: 3A

She picks it up--

                              DUTY NURSE
                        (into phone)
                  Station 1.

                                              INTERCUT WITH:

4   **INT. BARTLET'S LIMO - SAME TIME**   4

BARTLET's pressing a towel inside his jacket as BUTTERFIELD
talks on the phone--

                              BUTTERFIELD
                  We're coming in.

                              DUTY NURSE
                        (beat)
                  I copy that. Is this a drill?

                              BUTTERFIELD
                  No.

                              DUTY NURSE
                  The thing is, I have a few patients,
                  not many, but I do have a couple of kids
                  with alcohol poisoning and we're
                  expecting more in a bit, so if this is a
                  drill, I'd just as soon--

And now the DUTY NURSE hears the roar of the motorcycles and
the wail of the sirens with the blue/red flashes.

She hangs up the phone, grabs another and hits the PA button--

                              DUTY NURSE
                  Trauma One, Trauma One, Blue, Blue!
                  Trauma One. Blue!

And now the entire direction of the world changes. The first
group of SECRET SERVICE AGENTS flies in, mixing with the
DOCTORS and NURSES and SUPPORT STAFF and equipment that begin
to fill the room.

                              AGENT #1
                        (calling to the DUTY NURSE)
                  Is that priority?

                              DUTY NURSE
                  No priorities.

                                              (CONTINUED)

4   CONTINUED: 4

                         AGENT #1
              Put 'em in a van, they're going to
              Memorial.

                         DUTY NURSE
                    (to the patients)
              Okay, people--
                    (pointing to AGENT #2)
              I need you to follow this gentleman
              to the van that's waiting.

                         AGENT #1
                    (calling out)
              Get the South side cleared. There're two
              back doors and a loading dock. Put two
              units on the scaffolding and get some
              light out there.

                         KELLER (SURGEON)
              Gimme ultrasound and a crash cart.

                         AGENT #1
              Eagle's two minutes away.

                                                            CUT TO:

5   **INT. WEST WING LOBBY - NIGHT**   5

HOYNES is lined up in a photo-op with the members of the USC
Women's Volleyball Team and their coach, who are uniformly
dressed in blazers with patches.

                         PHOTOGRAPHER (V.O.)
              Mr. Vice President, could you hold the
              shirt up a little bit.

HOYNES raises the volleyball jersey he's been given with
"HOYNES" and the number "21" emblazoned on the back as the
flashbulbs pop.

                         HOYNES
              Now one of my roommates at SMU was Drew
              Harper. Anybody know that name?

                         VOLLEYBALL PLAYER
              '72?

                         HOYNES
              '72 Olympics in Munich. Well, I played
              against him in a pick-up game on the
              quad. And I thought I'd stuff him with an
              overhead slam, he sent that ball back at
              my face like I'd talked about his sister.

                                                         (CONTINUED)

5   CONTINUED: 5

Everyone laughs...

                          HOYNES
                Coach, I want to congratulate you and
                your team and the NCAA on a great season
                last year. I know you've got four
                starters returning, so I'm confident--

HOYNES stops talking as he sees a vision from his nightmares:
Eight SECRET SERVICE AGENTS hustling right toward him.

                          AGENT #3
                Excuse me, everyone stay where you are.
                Mr. Vice President, would you come with
                us, please.

It only takes HOYNES a beat to digest it. He exits without a
word and we

                                                    CUT TO:

6   **INT. WEST WING CORRIDOR - NIGHT**   6

As ABBEY flies down the hallway, she's joined by SECRET
SERVICE who seem to appear from every direction.

                          MADSEN (AGENT)
                Mrs. Bartlet--

                          ABBEY
                Is he conscious?

                          DIXON (AGENT)
                He's conscious and they're moving him
                to pre-op. He was hit in the side. Entry
                and exit.

They walk through the doors and out onto--

7   **EXT. CAR PORT - CONTINUOUS**   7

--as a black sedan screeches up in front and the passenger
door flies open.

                          ABBEY
                    (getting into the car)
                What about Zoey?

                          MADSEN
                They got her in the car, she's cool,
                she's on her way to GW.
                    (banging on the roof)
                Let's go, let's go, let's go!

                                              (CONTINUED)

7   CONTINUED: 7

The car screeches off and we

                                                                    CUT TO:

8   **INT. EMERGENCY ROOM - NIGHT**   8

The doors burst open and BARTLET's wheeled in on a gurney by
two PARAMEDICS and a few AGENTS, including BUTTERFIELD.

                         DUTY NURSE
               He's been shot in the abdomen. Visible
               entry and exit wound.

                         NURSE
               BP 134 over 78, pulse 108.

                         DOCTOR
               What's his pulse o.x.?

                         DOCTOR #1
               98.

                         KELLER
               Mr. President, I'm Dr. Keller, I'm
               the trauma surgeon on duty. The exit
               wound is a good indication, we like
               your vital signs.

                         BARTLET
               I swear to God, if I don't speak to my
               daughter in the next five minutes I'm
               gonna attack someone.

He's been wheeled into--

9   **INT. TRAUMA ROOM - CONTINUOUS**   9

                         BUTTERFIELD
               She's on her way.

                         BARTLET
                    (calling out)
               This guy's got about 7 broken bones
               in his hand, by the way, if somebody
               wants to get him an aspirin or something.

                         DOCTOR #1
               Okay, sir, we're just gonna get you
               stabilized.

                                                              (CONTINUED)

9   CONTINUED: 9

> BARTLET
> Listen...I want you to wait as long as
> you can before you give me the
> anesthesia. I need to speak to Leo
> McGarry before you give me the
> anesthesia.
>
> BUTTERFIELD
> He's on his way as well.
>
> DUTY NURSE
> I need to ask you some questions, sir.
> Do you have any medical conditions?
>
> BARTLET
> Well...I've been shot.

                                                        CUT TO:

10   **INT. MRS. LANDINGHAM'S OFFICE - NIGHT**   10

MRS. LANDINGHAM is walking as MARGARET falls in step with her--

> MARGARET
> Good evening, Mrs. Landingham
>
> MRS. LANDINGHAM
> (without looking up)
> Good evening, Margaret.
>
> MARGARET
> The President's not back yet?
>
> MRS. LANDINGHAM
> (still typing)
> I imagine he's schmoozing the rope line.
> You know he says he's coming straight
> back, but he can't resist a rope line.
> Never has. Oh he'll complain, but he just
> can't resist it. I remember a time in the
> Governor's mansion--it was about ten
> years ago--
>
> MARGARET
> Mrs. Landingham--
>
> MRS. LANDINGHAM
> More, maybe twelve--
>
> MARGARET
> Mrs. Landingham.

                                              (CONTINUED)

10   CONTINUED:

And MRS. LANDINGHAM looks up to see MARGARET staring in blank
terror at the words on a television screen:

SPECIAL REPORT

Then--

> ANCHOR (ON TV)
> Good evening. We are getting reports that
> multiple gunshots were fired at President
> Bartlet as he was leaving a public event
> in Rosslyn, Virginia. The shots were
> fired approximately seven minutes ago
> from an office building...

But MRS. LANDINGHAM is gone. An empty desk chair where she
used to be as we

CUT TO:

11   **INT. TRAUMA ROOM - CONTINUOUS**   11

ZOEY enters--

> ZOEY
> Dad--

> BARTLET
> I'm okay.

> ZOEY
> Daddy--

> BARTLET
> They didn't hit anything, they're just
> gonna look around and make sure.

> ZOEY
> You in a lot, a lot of pain?

> BARTLET
> No.

> ZOEY
> Are you lying?

> BARTLET
> Yeah, 'cause I want these guys to tell
> reporters that I was brave and joking
> around.

> ZOEY
> You are brave. You were so good tonight.

(CONTINUED)

11   CONTINUED:

> BARTLET
> Honey, I'm fine. I'm just so happy to see
> you.

> ZOEY
> Mom's on her way.

> BARTLET
> Mom's gonna be pretty pissed.

> ZOEY
> Yeah.

LEO comes in. He's still breathing kind of hard.

He and BARTLET look at each other for a long moment...

> LEO
>   (to ZOEY)
> How you doin', kid?

> ZOEY
> I'm fine.

> BARTLET
> She hooted all over the back of her
> car. You __know__ they're gonna bill me
> for that.

> LEO
> Yeah.

> BARTLET
> Honey, do me a favor, will you?

> ZOEY
> Yeah, I'll step outside, I'll go wait
> for Mom.

> BARTLET
> Tell her not to frighten the doctors.
> I'll see you in a couple of hours.

> ZOEY
> I love you.

> BARTLET
> I love you, too, hon.

ZOEY exits.

> BARTLET
> Anybody killed back there?

(CONTINUED)

11   CONTINUED: (2)

                         LEO
             The two shooters. They got 'em through
             the window.

                         BARTLET
             Anybody in the crowd?

                         LEO
             There were some injuries, they're
             coming right now.

                         BARTLET
             What about our people?

                         LEO
             C.J. hit her head on the ground but
             other than that--

                         BARTLET
             Get the Cabinet together.

                         LEO
             Yes, sir.

                         BARTLET
             And the Security Council. Tell Jerome
             to suspend trading on the stock exchange.

                         LEO
             Yeah.

                         BARTLET
             Do we know who the shooters were?

                         LEO
             No.

                         BARTLET
                 (pause)
             I'm gonna be under anesthesia for a
             couple hours.

                         LEO
             It'll be fine.

                         BARTLET
             You know what I'm talkin' about, right?

                         LEO
             I'll talk to Abbey.

        KELLER steps in with TWO ORDERLIES--

                                                    (CONTINUED)

11   CONTINUED: (3)   11

                    KELLER
              Sir, it's time.

                    BARTLET
              (to LEO)
              Hey, come here.

LEO leans down. BARTLET kisses him on the cheek...

                    BARTLET
              It's okay.

                    LEO
              I'll see you in a few hours, Mr.
              President.

LEO exits the trauma room as we

                                            CUT TO:

12   **INT. EMERGENCY ROOM - NIGHT**   12

ABBEY enters with a few AGENTS and ZOEY goes right to her.

                    ABBEY
              Oh, you alright?

                    ZOEY
              Yeah. And Dad's making jokes.

                    ABBEY
              Good ones--

                    ZOEY
              No.

                    ABBEY
              Okay.

LEO brings KELLER over to speak to ABBEY.

                    LEO
              Abbey.

                    ABBEY
              Hi.

                    LEO
              This is Dr. Keller.

                    ABBEY
              Oh yes. We spoke in the car.

                                            (CONTINUED)

12   CONTINUED: 12

KELLER
Hello.

ABBEY
What's his PAO2?

KELLER
It's good. It's a hundred.

ABBEY
You're gonna do a laparoscopy?

KELLER
Yeah, we want to make sure the
peritoneum's intact.

ABBEY
Who's the anesthesiologist?

KELLER
Dr. Lee.

ABBEY
(to ZOEY)
Right. You'll be okay for a minute?

ZOEY
Yeah.

ABBEY exits as we

CUT TO:

13   **INT. SCRUB ROOM - NIGHT**   13

The room looks through a glass partition onto the trauma room
where BARTLET's being prepped. LEE is scrubbing up as ABBEY
opens the door and steps in.

ABBEY
Dr. Lee?

LEE turns around.

LEE
Dr. Bartlet. I hope they told you that
it's looking very good.

ABBEY
There are 14 people in the world who
know this, including the Vice President,
the Chief of Staff and the Chairman of
the Joint Chiefs. You're gonna be the
(MORE)

(CONTINUED)

13   CONTINUED: 13

>   ABBEY (cont'd)
>   15th. Seven years ago my husband was
>   diagnosed with a relapsing/remitting
>   course of MS.
>   (beat)
>   When all this is over, tell the press,
>   don't tell the press. It's entirely
>   up to you.

ABBEY looks at him a moment longer, then exits into the trauma
room to join her husband as we

>   CUT TO:

14   **INT. EMERGENCY ROOM - NIGHT**   14

GINA's standing by herself. LEO goes over to her.

>   LEO
>   You alright?

>   GINA
>   Yeah.

>   LEO
>   Was there someone on the ground?

>   GINA
>   There was a signal. I couldn't give
>   a description.

>   LEO
>   Did they close the airports?

>   GINA
>   And Union Station. We've got Troopers
>   on the bridges and 300 field agents
>   working Rosslyn but I can't tell 'em
>   what they're looking for.

>   LEO
>   You got the girl in the car, Gina.

>   GINA
>   It's right in front of my face.

>   LEO
>   (pause)
>   Look--I'll--

But LEO's interrupted by a gurney bursting through the doors--

>   PARAMEDIC #5
>   (shouting)
>   Gunshot wound!

>   (CONTINUED)

> PARAMEDIC #6
> Decreased breath sound on the
> left, pulse o.x. is 92 on 15 liters.

> C.J. (O.S.)
> It's Josh--

> NURSE (DEBBIE)
> I've got hema--

> DOCTOR (HOLBROOK)
> Trauma panel, serial crits, cross him
> for 8 units.

> DEBBIE
> Get me a central line kit and an
> x-ray technician!

TOBY, SAM, C.J. and CHARLIE race in the door--

> LEO
> What happened?

> TOBY
> I don't know, he was behind us.

> HOLBROOK
> Single gun shot wound, entry left
> fifth intercostal space.

> SAM
> Josh, I'm here.

> JOSH
> I shouldn't be at this meeting.

> DEBBIE
> Trauma 1's ready.

> HOLBROOK
> --32, press.

> JOSH
> Senator...

> LEO
> (to the HOLBROOK)
> Tell me what's happening.

> HOLBROOK
> I don't have time.

They start to roll JOSH toward pre-op.

                                              (CONTINUED)

14   CONTINUED: (2)   14

                    JOSH
I shouldn't be at this meeting.

                    DEBBIE
Pulse o.x. 88.

                    JOSH
I need to get to New Hampshire.

                    SAM
We went to New Hampshire. We
both did. You came and got me.

                    HOLBROOK
On my count, one... two... three...

The gurney leaves SAM, TOBY, LEO, C.J. and CHARLIE and busts
through into--

15   **INT. TRAUMA ROOM - SAME TIME**   15

                    HOLBROOK
Josh a bullet collapsed your lung.
I'm putting in a tube to expand it

And now, as if we're hearing through JOSH's ears, the voices
and actions of the medical team begin to blur out of focus...

                    DEBBIE
He's got blood in the thoraseal.

                    DOCTOR (WHITAKER)
Over a liter out.

                    DEBBIE
Ready and done.

                    HOLBROOK
Okay, tube him. Now.

                    WHITAKER
8.0 tube.

The screen has DISSOLVED TO a blue/grey blur...

...and the voices have melted into an indecipherable sound.
And we hear this:

                    HOYNES (V.O.)
Social Security--

                    JOSH (V.O.)
Senator--

                                        (CONTINUED)

15   CONTINUED:

> HOYNES (V.O.)
> Social Security is the black hole--

> JOSH (V.O.)
> Senator--

> HOYNES (V.O.)
> Social Security--

> JOSH (V.O.)
> Senator--

> HOYNES (V.O.)
> Social Security--

> JOSH (V.O.)
> Yes--

> HOYNES (V.O.)
> Social Security is the black hole of
> national politics.

And we FADE UP on:

16   **INT. SENATE CONFERENCE ROOM - DAY**   16

HOYNES is conducting a meeting with about 18 staffers, one of whom is JOSH. People get up, get coffee, come, go...

> JOSH
> Yes.

> HOYNES
> Josh was cutting me off because he knew
> I was gonna say that. He knew I was
> gonna say that 'cause I've said it, what--

> JOSH
> A few hundred times, Senator.

> HOYNES
> It is the black hole of national politics
> and I would just as soon not get lost in
> it 13 weeks before the New Hampshire
> primary.

TITLE:

> **Capitol Hill Offices**
> **Senator John Hoynes**
> **(D) - Texas**

(CONTINUED)

> HOYNES
> It is the third rail. You step on it and
> you die.

> JOSH
> Of the 537 federal elected
> officials, there are 30 who've put
> their names on Social Security reform
> legislation and you're one of them,
> why not say so?

> AIDE #1
> He will say so, just not now.

> JOSH
> Mark, at 400 billion dollars, Social
> Security represents one-fourth of the
> Federal budget and it's gonna be bankrupt
> in exactly 17 years, right around the
> time you're going to check your mailbox.
> Half of the elderly population will be
> living in poverty. This now qualifies
> as a priority. And running for President
> of the United States not putting
> Social Security front and center is like
> running for president of the Walt Disney
> Corporation by saying you're gonna fix
> the rides at Epcot.

An AIDE has come in and whispered something to HOYNES.

> AIDE #1
> We're gonna get to Social Security,
> Josh, it's a long campaign, for now
> we focus on the tax cuts.

> AIDE #2
> It's what magicians call misdirection.

> JOSH
> Really, 'cause it's what the rest of us
> call bull--

> HOYNES
> Knock it off. I have a vote. The rest of
> you should stay here and work on the
> ethanol tax credit. Josh, come with me,
> would you?

JOSH follows HOYNES out into--

17   **INT. CORRIDOR - DAY**   17

                    HOYNES
       You don't seem to be having a very
       good time lately.

                    JOSH
        (beat)
       I don't think the point of this is for
       me to have--

                    HOYNES
       I'm saying you've been pissed off at
       every meeting for a month.

                    JOSH
       Senator, you're the prohibitive favorite
       to be the Democratic Party's nominee for
       President. You have 58 million dollars
       in a war chest with no end in sight, and
       I don't know what we're <u>for</u>.

                    HOYNES
       Josh--

                    JOSH
       I don't know what we're for, I don't know
       what we're against. Except we seem to be
       for <u>winning</u> and against somebody else
       winning.

                    HOYNES
       It's a start.

                    JOSH
       Senator--

                    HOYNES
       Josh, we're gonna run a good campaign.
       You're gonna be very proud of it. And
       when we get to the White House, you're
       gonna play a big role. In the meantime,
       cheer up. And get off my ass about Social
       Security. I've got a vote.

HOYNES heads down the corridor and disappears around the
corner. JOSH stands there a moment, then walks across the hall
and into--

18   **INT. STAFF OFFICES - CONTINUOUS**   18

JOSH walks into a bullpen ringed with small offices. STAFFERS are milling about and talking on the phone. We HEAR an unseen voice...

> MAN (O.S.)
> Josh?

JOSH turns around to see LEO, who's been waiting for him. This is clearly an unusual event as they haven't seen each other for a few years and it wasn't like they were beer buddies or anything.

> JOSH
> Mr. Secretary?

> LEO
> I hope you don't mind, I didn't make an appointment. I'm trying to fly under the radar a little.

> JOSH
> No, of course I don't mind, but the Senator just went down to the floor for a vote.

> LEO
> It's probably the annual vote to override the veto on the resolution to ship nuclear waste to Nevada.

> JOSH
> Yeah.

> LEO
> It won't pass.

> JOSH
> No kidding.

> LEO
> Actually I came to see you.

> JOSH
> Really?

> LEO
> Yeah.

> JOSH
> What can I do for you?

(CONTINUED)

18   CONTINUED:

                              LEO
                    You mind if we take a walk?

                              JOSH
                    Sure.

                                                         CUT TO:

19   **EXT. THE CAPITOL BUILDING - DAY**   19

LEO and JOSH walk along the exterior....

                              LEO
                    I heard your dad was in the hospital
                    again.

                              JOSH
                    Yeah, they think they got it all this
                    time.

                              LEO
                    Is he taking it easy?

                              JOSH
                    No, he does the opposite. Seven every
                    morning, comes home at eight every night.
                    On the weekends he cleans the gutters and
                    yells at the squirrels.

                              LEO
                    Why does he yell at the squirrels?

                              JOSH
                    'Cause they eat the seeds out of the
                    birdfeeder.

                              LEO
                    You know they make a thing now.

                              JOSH
                    He knows, but he prefers to admonish
                    them. Listen, I need to get back to
                    this meeting--

                              LEO
                    Josh, I'd like you to come to Nashua,
                    New Hampshire Thursday night and hear Jed
                    Bartlet speak.

                              JOSH
                         (pause)
                    I work for Senator Hoynes.

                                                    (CONTINUED)

> LEO
> Yeah.

> JOSH
> (pause)
> Mr. Secretary--

> LEO
> I'm not in the Cabinet anymore, Josh,
> call me Leo.

> JOSH
> Look, Hoynes has the nomination sewn up--

> LEO
> Yeah.

> JOSH
> --and if Bartlet's looking to be Treasury
> Secretary or a slot at the convention,
> this really isn't the--

> LEO
> Come to Nashua Thursday night.

> JOSH
> Why?

> LEO
> 'Cause that's what sons do for old
> friends of their fathers'.
>   (beat)
> I'll see you then.

LEO starts to leave...

> JOSH
> Mr. Secretary--

> LEO
> Leo.

> JOSH
> Leo, the Democrats aren't gonna nominate
> another liberal academic former governor
> from New England. I mean we're dumb, but
> we're not that dumb.

> LEO
> (he smiles)
> Nah. I think we're exactly that dumb.

(CONTINUED)

19   CONTINUED: (2)   19

LEO walks on and disappears. JOSH stands there a moment. This
is the last thing he needed right now. He opens his cell phone
and hits a speed dial button...

                    JOSH
                 (into phone)
            Yeah Janet, I need you to set up some
            train tickets for me... late tomorrow.

                                              FADE TO BLACK

                    <u>END OF ACT ONE</u>

ACT TWO

FADE IN:

20   **EXT./EST. NEW YORK CITY - DAY**   20

                         GAGE (V.O.)
             All in, showroom floor to your garage, 18
             million dollars.

                         LOCH (V.O.)
             18 million is a cheap price, isn't it?

                         GAGE (V.O.)
             Yes it is, but what you're happy about
             isn't the price, it's the structure of
             the deal.

21   **INT. GLASS CONFERENCE ROOM - CONTINUOUS**   21

A half-dozen LAWYERS are passing papers back and forth with a
half-dozen EXECUTIVES. A few SECRETARIES are taking notes and
bringing in coffee.

                         LOCH
             Well, how do you figure that?

                         GAGE
             Sam's gonna tell you about it. Sam?

                         SAM
             Hm?

                         GAGE
             Structure vs. cost.

                         SAM
             Yeah, what Jack means is that if you were
             getting these tankers for a buck eighty-
             five in trading stamps, it would still be
             a bad deal if we didn't limit your
             liability.

                         CAMERON
             And did you do that?

TITLE:

                         Gage Whitney Pace
                         Midtown Manhattan

                         SAM
             We did.

                                            (CONTINUED)

21   CONTINUED: 21

                         LOCH
          How?

                         SAM
          The same way we do with any other
          asset acquisition. Create a separate
          corporation for each one of them,
          then mortgage the boats top to bottom.

                         CAMERON
          Ships.

                         SAM
          I'm sorry?

                         CAMERON
          Oil tankers aren't boats, they're ships.

                         SAM
          Mr. Cameron, you want me to buy the
          boats, you're not asking me to be the
          First Mate, right?

                         CAMERON
          No.

                         SAM
          You wanna finance the tankers a hundred
          percent so if litigation does penetrate
          the liability shield we've set up for
          you, there are no real assets at the end
          of the line, just debt. You're judgement
          proof. Lemme run back to my office and
          get the tax figures while David and Rita
          talk to you about IMO regulations.

     SAM gets up and exits into--

22   **INT. CORRIDOR - CONTINUOUS**   22

     --where his SECRETARY meets him.

                         SECRETARY
          Sam, there's a guy waiting in your office
          who said he's a friend of yours.

                         SAM
          What's his name?

                         SECRETARY
          Josh Lyman.

                                                            (CONTINUED)

22 CONTINUED: 22

                        SAM
            Seriously?

                        SECRETARY
            Yeah.

It's Christmas morning for SAM as he hustles into--

23 **INT. SAM'S (NEW YORK) OFFICE - CONTINUOUS**   23

--where JOSH is waiting for him.

                        SAM
            Hey! How you doin'?

They hug.

                        SAM
            Hey, you look fit.

                        JOSH
            You made partner?

                        SAM
            Next month. Listen, I'm hungry, you
            want to go get a hot dog or something?

                        JOSH
            It's nine-thirty in the morning.

                        SAM
            Yeah, they'll be fresh. Come on.

                        JOSH
            Okay.

                                                      CUT TO:

24 **EXT. ROCKEFELLER PLAZA - DAY**   24

SAM and JOSH are buying hot dogs at a stand.

                        JOSH
            You know, I was gonna call before I came
            here, but the strangest thing happened.

                        SAM
            What?

                        JOSH
            I forgot the name of your firm.

                                                      (CONTINUED)

                    SAM
Gage Whitney?

                    JOSH
Yeah.

                    SAM
You couldn't remember Gage Whitney?

                    JOSH
I know.

                    SAM
The second biggest law firm in New York.

                    JOSH
I know.

                    SAM
The Shearson deal.

                    JOSH
Yeah.

                    SAM
Transcom.

                    JOSH
I really do know Gage Whitney, I'm
saying...I'm just... having a brain
problem.

                    SAM
What are you doing in town?

                    JOSH
I'm on my way to Nashua.

                    SAM
What's in Nashua?

                    JOSH
A waste of time. Listen, you know why I'm
here?

                    SAM
You want me to quit my job and come work
for Hoynes.

                    JOSH
He's gonna win, Sam.

                                        (CONTINUED)

                    SAM
          So what does he need me for?

                    JOSH
          A better campaign. Come do some speech
          writing.

                    SAM
          Lisa and I are getting married in
          September.

                    JOSH
               (pause)
          Ah.

                    SAM
          Yeah.

                    JOSH
               (pause)
          Okay.
               (pause)
          Listen, I gotta go. I should let you--

                    SAM
          I gotta get back to this thing.

                    JOSH
          It's good seeing you again.

                    SAM
          It's good seeing you, too. I miss you.

They start to walk their separate ways.

                    JOSH
          Hey, congratulations on the partnership.

 SAM turns back--

                    SAM
          Josh.

JOSH turns around.

                    SAM
          Hoynes. He's not the real thing, is he?

                    JOSH
               (pause)
          See, the thing you gotta know about
          Hoynes is--

                                                    (CONTINUED)

24   CONTINUED: (3)

                        SAM
            It's okay.

                        JOSH
            No, I'm saying--

                        SAM
            Josh, what are you doin'?

                        JOSH
                (beat)
            I don't know.
                (beat)
            What're you doing?

                        SAM
            Protecting oil companies from litigation.
            They're our client. They don't lose legal
            protection 'cause they make a lot of
            money.

                        JOSH
            I can't believe no one ever wrote a folk
            song about that.

    SAM and JOSH look at each other for a moment...

                        JOSH
            If I see the real thing in Nashua, should
            I tell you about it?

                        SAM
            You won't have to.

                        JOSH
            Why?

                        SAM
            You've got a pretty bad poker face.

                        JOSH
                (beat)
            Okay. Take it easy.

                        SAM
            Okay.

                                                CUT TO:

25   **INT. VIP ROOM - NIGHT**   25

    --as the DUTY NURSE has to reach around SAM for a ringing
    phone on the wall.

                                        (CONTINUED)

25   CONTINUED:

                    DUTY NURSE
          Ugh.

                    SAM
          I'm sorry.

                    DUTY NURSE
          That's okay.

                    SAM
          I'm sorry. I was just--

                    DUTY NURSE
               (into phone)
          George Washington emergency. We're not
          giving any information.

SAM steps away as a Hospital Administrator (LEWIS) comes in.

                    LEWIS
          Dr. Bartlet.

                    ABBEY
          Yes.

ABBEY goes over to him. The two of them speak quietly and out
of earshot of the rest.

                    LEWIS
          The President's gonna be fine.

                    ABBEY
          Oh.

                    LEWIS
          You can see him in the recovery room in
          about two hours.

                    ABBEY
          Thank you. No organ damage?

                    LEWIS
          No ma'am. And the blood loss was minimal.
          Dr. Keller was able to visualize the
          entire abdomen and he's secure with the
          diagnostic sensitivity of the
          laparoscopy.

                    ABBEY
          What about Josh?

                                                        (CONTINUED)

25   CONTINUED: (2)   25

                              LEWIS
                    The bullet lacerated his pulmonary
                    artery.

ABBEY's face barely betrays how ominous that news is.

                              ABBEY
                    Can they try a Gortex graft?

                              LEWIS
                    No. They're gonna have to stay in and
                    try to repair the artery primarily.

                              ABBEY
                         (beat)
                    Thank you.

ABBEY turns to the group as LEWIS stands away at a respectful
distance.

                              ABBEY
                    The President's gonna be fine. The bullet
                    seems to have gone out of its way not to
                    hit anything.

Everyone breathes a sigh of relief, though they're nowhere
near out of the woods.

                              ABBEY
                    Now, here's what's happening with Josh:

                                                         CUT TO:

26   **INT. WHITE HOUSE BASEMENT CORRIDOR - NIGHT**   26

We see on a security tv monitor that LEO's just getting off a cell
phone call as Air Force General SHANNON punches a code into a
security panel next to an outer door.

                              LEO (ON TV MONITOR)
                         (into phone)
                    Thank you.

                              SHANNON (ON TV MONITOR)
                    What do you know?

They walk into--

26A   **INT. VESTIBULE - CONTINUOUS**   26A

                              LEO
                    He'll be out of surgery in about two
                    hours. Fitzwallace is on a plane?

                                                         (CONTINUED)

26A   CONTINUED: 26A

> SHANNON
> He was on his way to Manila. They turned
> around and he'll be back in about four
> hours.

> LEO
> You got him by phone?

> SHANNON
> Yeah.

They walk into--

CUT TO:

27   **INT. SITUATION ROOM - NIGHT**   27

It's become a command center. MILITARY, CIVILIAN, SECRET
SERVICE...they're talking on phones, getting faxes, checking
pictures, talking among themselves.

> LEO
> Good evening.

> AIDE #3
> Good evening, Mr. McGarry.

> LEO
> Where's the National Security Advisor?

> AIDE #3
> She's on her way, sir.

> SHANNON
> So is the Vice President.

And NANCY MCNALLY, the National Security Advisor, strides into the
room from another door. She's a strikingly handsome African-
American woman who, at the moment, is wearing a formal evening
gown and a string of pearls.

> NANCY
> Good evening, everybody. Mike, could
> you have somebody send over some clothes
> from my office, please, I look like an
> idiot.

> MIKE
> Yes, ma'am.

> LEO
> Nancy, you've seen the KH-10 pictures?

(CONTINUED)

27   CONTINUED: 27

                              NANCY
                    Yeah.

                              LEO
                    And you know what they mean?

                              NANCY
                    Well I wouldn't go that far.

HOYNES enters.

                              NANCY
                    Good evening, Mr. Vice President.

                              HOYNES
                    Good evening, Nancy.
                         (to LEO)
                    Leo.

Some of the OFFICERS at the far end of the room have either
not seen HOYNES come in or simply aren't used to standing for
the Vice President.

                              LEO
                         (quietly prompting SHANNON)
                    Jack.

SHANNON sees what LEO's talking about.

                              SHANNON
                    Ten-hut.

                              HOYNES
                    No, as you were. It's okay. Bobby,
                    you report on domestic activity.

(*Note: HOYNES does not sit in the President's chair. It
remains vacant.)

                              BOBBY (CIVILIAN)
                    Yes sir, there's not much. Air traffic
                    control was down for 22 minutes at Logan.
                    CitiBank computers were off line for a
                    little more than an hour and the lights
                    went out for seven minutes at the Delta
                    Center.

                              HOYNES
                    Now somebody tell me. These shooters.
                    They didn't have a wallet on 'em, they
                    didn't have a drivers license?

                                                        (CONTINUED)

27   CONTINUED: (2)   27

> SHANNON
> They didn't have anything on 'em, Mr.
> Vice President, they knew we were gonna
> get 'em through the window.

> HOYNES
> If this signal guy isn't in custody in
> one hour, I'm gonna Federalize the
> Virginia and Maryland National Guard.

> NANCY
> It's worth mentioning that at this moment
> we do not know the whereabouts of about a
> half-dozen cell leaders including bin
> Laden, but that's not my concern right
> now.

> HOYNES
> What is your concern?

> NANCY
> Can we look at the KH-10s?

> LEO
> I've seen 'em, not worried about it.

LEO passes some satellite photos to HOYNES.

> NANCY
> Leo, these images show a sudden build-up
> of frontline Republican Guard units along
> the Tigris and Euphrates rivers.

> LEO
> The build-up isn't sudden, they do it
> every couple of months.

> NANCY
> And they're moving South. Not 13 hours
> ago they shot down an F-117 in the no-
> fly, the rescue mission invaded their
> airspace with armed M-50 Pave Hawks, and
> my recommendation would be that the
> President order Fitzwallace to put the
> 32nd Tactical on Ready-Alert and take us
> to DefCon-4.

> LEO
> The President is under general anesthesia
> right now. If he weren't, I'm sure he'd
> be comforted by knowing that RDF can put
> marines on the ground in 36 hours.

(CONTINUED)

27   CONTINUED: (3)   27

                          NANCY
          We may not have 36 hours.

                          LEO
          The Iraqi Republican Guard can't find
          their car keys in 36 hours.

                          NANCY
          Look at the pictures, Mr. Vice President,
          I think they found 'em.

There's silence as everyone looks to HOYNES...

                          HOYNES
               (beat)
          Nancy, we're gonna follow Leo for the
          moment.

                          LEO
               (pause)
          Jack, what's the best way to get a
          message to Iraq?

                          SHANNON
          King of Jordan.

                          LEO
          Okay.

                          HENRY
          Leo, what do you want the message to be?

                          LEO
          Don't mess with us tonight.

                                                    CUT TO:

28   **INT. VIP ROOM - NIGHT**   28

TOBY, SAM, C.J....

                          LEWIS
          Uh...excuse me. We can't make you very
          comfortable here and Josh's procedure is
          likely to take 12 to 14 hours, so--

Everyone suddenly turns their attention to the door, where
DONNA's just walked in.

There's an uncomfortable moment.

                                              (CONTINUED)

                            DONNA
I'm sorry. They told me I should come
back here.
        (pause)
I'm sorry.
        (pause)
Is there word on the President?

                            C.J.
        (beat)
The President's gonna be fine.

                            DONNA
        (not knowing whether to
         laugh or cry)
Oh thank God.
        (beat)
Oh thank God. That's the best news I ever
heard.
        (beat)
I got here as fast as I could. I had a
hard time getting in, I, I had to find an
agent who knew me. I was shaking. It was
just, I didn't know anything--

                            TOBY
Donna.

DONNA, who's sensed that something was wrong when she came in,
looks at TOBY.

                            TOBY
Josh was hit.

                            DONNA
        (pause)
Hit with what?

                            TOBY
He was shot in the chest.

                            C.J.
He's in surgery right now.

                            DONNA
I don't understand.
        (pause)
I don't understand. Is, is it serious?

                            TOBY
Yes. It's critical. The bullet collapsed
his lung and damaged a major artery.

                            (CONTINUED)

28   CONTINUED: (2)

The horror is silently taking hold of DONNA. After a moment...

                    LEWIS
                 (to the GROUP)
         I was just saying we can't make you very
         comfortable here and the procedure's
         likely to take 12 to 14 hours. We won't
         know anything until morning. I'm sure
         there are things you're supposed to be
         attending to right now. So, if you'd
         like, we can stay in touch with you at
         your homes and offices throughout the
         night.

After a long moment, they start to get themselves together...

                    C.J.
         Leo's gonna meet with the leadership in
         ten minutes. When he's done I'll talk to
         the press.

                    CHARLIE
         Well, I'm gonna go back to the residence
         and pick up some things for the
         President.

The room starts to clear out. DONNA sits down slowly, not
really looking at anything or anyone, and puts her hands
together in her lap.

                                 FADE TO BLACK

                END OF ACT TWO

ACT THREE

FADE IN:

29   **INT. PRESS BRIEFING ROOM - NIGHT**   29

There are a little over a thousand people with White House press
credentials, and it would appear that they're all in the briefing
room right now. There's a lack of orderliness--

              ALL
C.J.!

              KATIE
C.J., when can we talk to the medical
team?

              C.J.
Benjamin Keller, the Chief Surgeon and
Admiral Jarvis, the President's personal
physician will be made available for a
de-briefing in a few hours.

              ALL
C.J.!

              DANNY
Has there been any discussion of the
25th Amendment?

              C.J.
No.

              ALL
C.J.!

              DANNY
Why not?

              C.J.
I'm sorry?

              DANNY
Why hasn't there been a discussion of the
25th Amendment?

              C.J.
Danny, as I've said before, the
President's wounds are relatively
superficial, he'll be out of surgery
before morning and he's expected to make
a full and speedy recovery.

                       (CONTINUED)

                         ALL
          C.J.! C.J.!

                         LUCY
          C.J. Anything on the identity of the
          shooters?

                         C.J.
          I'm sorry?

                         LUCY
          Anything on the identity of the shooters?

                         C.J.
          Not yet.

                         LUCY
          Well you know, A.P.'s reporting that two
          bodies were brought out of the office
          building.

                         C.J.
          I don't have anything for you on that.

                         LUCY
          You know, they're also reporting that
          there is now a massive manhunt underway
          for a possible third accomplice on the
          ground.

                         C.J.
          I don't have anything for you on that
          either.

                         ALL
          C.J.!

                         KYLE
          Can you tell us why the A.P. knows more
          than you do?

                         C.J.
          I don't believe they do know more than I
          do, I just believe they're willing to
          tell you more than I am.

                         ALL
          C.J.!

                         C.J.
          One more question. Arthur.

                                                    (CONTINUED)

CONTINUED: (2)

> ARTHUR
> In previous administrations, the
> President entered and exited public
> buildings under a tent or canopy, the
> Secret Service wanting to limit his
> visibility in open air. Can you talk at
> all about why this precaution isn't taken
> for President Bartlet, or at least why it
> wasn't tonight?

> C.J.
> Arthur, it's policy not to comment on
> protection procedures.

> ARTHUR
> Well, C.J., if you won't answer the most
> straightforward questions--

> C.J.
> Arthur--

> ARTHUR
> Is there anything you <u>can</u> tell us?

Something about the question strikes C.J. as odd, but only she
knows why...

> C.J.
> I'm sorry.

> ARTHUR
> Is there anything you know, is there
> anything you can tell us?

> C.J.
> I'll be back for briefing in an hour and
> a half. Hopefully we'll know more then.

C.J. exits with CAROL into--

30   **INT. CORRIDOR - CONTINUOUS**   30

> CAROL
> There's a meeting in five minutes.

> C.J.
> What the hell was that supposed to mean?
> "Since you can't seem to give us
> answers."

> CAROL
> You scratched your neck.

(CONTINUED)

30   CONTINUED:

                         C.J.
          What?

                         CAROL
          The side of your neck.

C.J. feels her neck...

                         C.J.
          I lost my necklace.
               (beat)
          It must have come off when...

                         CAROL
               (pause)
          When what?

                         C.J.
          Somebody pushed me down. It must have
          come off when somebody pushed me down.

DANNY comes around the corner--

                         DANNY
          C.J.?

                         C.J.
          Yeah.

                         DANNY
          I'm sorry. I'd like to not be a reporter
          for a few minutes and just--but you gotta
          answer my question.

                         C.J.
          What was the question?

                         DANNY
          The President's been under anesthesia for
          more than an hour and he'll probably be
          on a morphine drip in post-op. Without
          the 25th, who's in charge?

                         C.J.
          The Vice President, the Secretary of
          State, the National Security Advisor, the
          Secretary of Defense, the Chairman of the
          Joint Chiefs, the White House Chief of
          Staff--

                         DANNY
          You just named six people. Who's in
          charge?

                                        (CONTINUED)

30   CONTINUED: (2)   30

                         C.J.
          The Canadians.

                         DANNY
          C.J.--

                         C.J.
          You understand what I'm talkin' about?
          The hockey team.

                         DANNY
          Look--

                         C.J.
          Just gimme a little time.

C.J. walks off as we

                                                       CUT TO:

31   **INT. LEO'S OFFICE - CONTINUOUS**   31

LEO, TOBY and NANCY MCNALLY are in mid-discussion with several
AIDES standing nearby.

                         LEO
          Fitzwallace agrees with me, Nancy. Any
          upgrade in our DefCon posture and the
          whole world's gonna wake up in the middle
          of the night.

C.J. slips in.

                         NANCY
          The world's awake, Leo. Look at the tv.
          Look out the window. Now there was more
          than one shooter. We think they had a guy
          on the ground. If we think they had one,
          we have no reason to believe they didn't
          have more than one. Somebody had to get
          them into that office. This wasn't a
          lonely guy who lived with his cats, there
          was a plan. And one of the things we have
          to assume is that we're under attack
          right now.

                         AIDE #4
          In which case the Vice President should
          order the 32nd tactical on Ready-Alert
          and take us to DefCon 4.

                         LEO
          Counsel's office isn't sure he can.

                                                  (CONTINUED)

31   CONTINUED:

> TOBY
> Why not?

> LEO
> He never signed a letter.

> TOBY
> What letter?

> NANCY
> Customarily, if the President's gonna be
> under a general anesthetic--

> TOBY
> He's gotta sign a letter giving the Vice
> President power?

> NANCY
> Absent the 25th, the Constitution doesn't
> give it to him unless the President's
> dead.

> TOBY
> He's hemorrhaging, and he's supposed to
> draft a memo?

> NANCY
> Yeah.

> C.J.
> I'm getting questions from Danny
> Concannon on it.

> NANCY
> It gets more complicated if you've read
> Section 202 of the National Security Act
> of 1947.

> C.J.
> Let's assume I haven't.

> NANCY
> It says that the Secretary of Defense
> will be the principle assistant to the
> President on all matters relating to
> the National security.

> C.J.
> What does principle assistant mean?

> NANCY
> It doesn't specify.

(CONTINUED)

31   CONTINUED: (2)   31

                              TOBY
              No, it wouldn't, 'cause this is an area
              of Federal law where you'd want as much
              ambiguity as possible.

                              NANCY
              Yeah.

                              TOBY
              Excuse me.

                              C.J.
              I'm gonna go back to the hospital.

                              LEO
              I'll be there in a little bit.

         C.J. and TOBY exit into--

32   **INT. CORRIDOR - CONTINUOUS**   32

                              TOBY
              Do you wanna hold Danny off for a few
              hours till the Counsel's office tells us
              where we are.

                              C.J.
              Yeah. Listen--

                              TOBY
              You scratched your neck.

                              C.J.
              What?

                              TOBY
              Your neck.

                              C.J.
              Yeah,that's where my necklace--Listen,
              Toby, they're asking me about the canopy
              the Secret Service used to use for
              outdoor entrances and exits.

                              TOBY
              Who asked you?

                              C.J.
              It was...Arthur Leeds and then a couple
              of others stopped me.

                                                      (CONTINUED)

32   CONTINUED: 32

                              TOBY
                         (beat)
                    Okay.

                              C.J.
                    We don't comment on protection procedure
                    so--

                              TOBY
                    Yeah.

                              C.J.
                    --I don't think we'll have to answer the
                    question.

                              TOBY
                    Yeah.

                              C.J.
                         (beat)
                    Okay.

                              TOBY
                    See you at the hospital.

                              C.J.
                    Yeah.

          C.J. peels off and TOBY continues into--

33   **INT. COMMUNICATIONS BULLPEN - CONTINUOUS**   33

          --where GINGER is standing in her coat.

                              TOBY
                         (calling out)
                    I need Section 202 of the National
                    Security Act of 1947. Hey, Ginger, I
                    didn't know you were here.

                              GINGER
                    I just got here.
                         (beat)
                    I just...I turned on the TV.

          TOBY looks at her face and is reminded of the enormity of the
          horror that's walked into their house.

                              TOBY
                    It's okay. Come here.

          He takes GINGER in his arms...

                                                            (CONTINUED)

33   CONTINUED:

                         TOBY
                      (quietly)
              It's alright. It's okay.

                         GINGER
                      (into his shoulder)
              I'm sorry.

He looks at her...

                         TOBY
              You alright?

                         GINGER
              Yeah.

                         TOBY
              You ready to go to work?

                         GINGER
              Yeah.

                         BARTENDER (V.O.)
              You want another one of those?

TOBY turns back--

                         TOBY
              What?

                         GINGER
                      (pause)
              I didn't say anything.

                                                    CUT TO:

34   **INT. MOTEL BAR - NIGHT**   34

                         BARTENDER
              You want another one of those?

                         TOBY
              Yeah.

TOBY's talking to a local bar-fly, the two of them among the only
ones in the vicinity to be drinking at three in the afternoon.

                         TRACY
              I gotta tell ya.

                         TOBY
              Yeah?

                                              (CONTINUED)

34   CONTINUED:

> TRACY
> I didn't even know Bartlet was running.

> TOBY
> Yeah, we keep that secret pretty good.

TITLE:

> **Hank's Tavern**
> **Nashua, N.H.**

> TOBY
> You know he's speaking at the VFW hall
> tonight, you should come.

> TRACY
> I'm not very political.

> TOBY
> There'll be free chicken.

> TRACY
> You've been, uh, uh--what'd you call it?

> TOBY
> Professional political operative.

> TRACY
> You've been one your whole life?

> TOBY
> Well there was a while there I was in
> elementary school--

> TRACY
> You any good at it?

> TOBY
> I'm very good at it.

> TRACY
> What's your record?

> TOBY
> My record?

> TRACY
> How many elections have you won?

> TOBY
> All together, including City Council, two
> Congressional races, Senate race,
> Gubernatorial campaign and a national
> campaign...none.

(CONTINUED)

34   CONTINUED: (2)

                          TRACY
                    (beat)
              None of 'em?

                          TOBY
              You gotta be impressed with my
              consistency.

                          TRACY
              So lemme ask you something.

                          TOBY
              Sure.

                          TRACY
              How come you're drinking so much so early
              in the day?

                          TOBY
              I'm about to get fired.

TOBY throws some money on the bar and gets up.

                          TOBY
              It was good meeting you.

TOBY grabs his coat and walks out.

                                        FADE TO BLACK

                    END OF ACT THREE

ACT FOUR

FADE IN:

35   **INT. VFW HALL - NIGHT**   35

The house is about three-quarters full. A few AIDES are standing
along the side of the wall. TOBY stands in the back of the room. A
microphone stands at the front of each aisle and BARTLET stands on
a platform at the front, hands in his pockets.

There's something about his manner that tells us he hasn't yet
fully committed to the idea of doing any of this.

There's something that seems smaller about him.

> BARTLET
> That has less to do with the overall
> consumer spending than it does with
> the consumer price index.

TITLE:

> **VFW Hall**
> **Nashua, N.H.**

> BARTLET
> The markets tend to be late in
> responding to those trends, and
> as a result, you get what doctors
> would call a false positive. The
> science of economics is a lot less
> of an exact science than we pretend.
> We build complex models with thousands
> of interdependent and independent
> variables to predict exactly how the
> economy will work.

As BARTLET continues, an aide (CAL EVANS) leaves his spot against
the side wall and walks up next to TOBY.

> CAL
> (quietly)
> What's he gonna say?

> TOBY
> (quietly)
> About what?

> CAL
> If he's asked the question.

> TOBY
> What question?

(CONTINUED)

> CAL
> The New England DFC.

> TOBY
> I don't know.

> CAL
> You talked to him, didn't you?

> TOBY
> Yeah.

> CAL
> Well, what's he gonna say?

> TOBY
> I don't know.

> CAL
> You talked to him about the New England
> DFC?

> TOBY
> Yes.

> CAL
> You wrote him a memo?

> TOBY
> Yes.

> CAL
> And I'm asking what's he gonna say.

> TOBY
> I have no new information since the last
> time you asked me that question.

They turn their attention back to BARTLET...

> BARTLET
> Let me put it another way. You and
> your husband are paying $600 <u>more</u>
> every year than you would if <u>you</u> were
> unmarried, living together and filing
> individually. Couples who live together
> outside the covenant of marriage do so
> for reasons that have nothing...

JOSH is sitting, doing a crossword puzzle--

                                          (CONTINUED)

35   CONTINUED: (2)   35

                         CAL
                    (to TOBY)
          You told him to go ahead and piss off the
          dairy farmers, didn't you. If he's asked
          about the New England DFC? You told him
          to piss off the dairy farmers.

                         TOBY
                    (pause)
          I asked him about his vote. He told me. I
          said that if asked about it tonight, he
          should--if only because it's the easiest
          thing to remember--tell the truth.

                         CAL
                    (beat)
          Do you enjoy losing?

                         TOBY
          Not that much, no. But then again I
          really don't have a lot to compare it to,
          so...

CAL walks away and rejoins the others on the side of the wall.

                         BARTLET
          ...the bulk of other previous losses--
          which in effect is a much larger tax on
          overstated "real" profits.

                         QUESTIONER
          Yes.

                         BARTLET
          You didn't really understand any of that,
          right?

                         QUESTIONER
          A little.

                         BARTLET
          Me too.
                    (calling on the next
                     QUESTIONER)
          Yeah.

                         QUESTIONER #2
          Governor Bartlet, when you were a member
          of Congress, you voted against the New
          England Dairy Farming Compact.

CAL looks over to TOBY...here it is...

                                                    (CONTINUED)

35   CONTINUED: (3)   35

                              QUESTIONER #2
                    That vote hurt me, sir. I'm a businessman
                    and that vote hurt me to the tune of
                    maybe 10 cents a gallon. And I voted for
                    you three times for Congressman. I voted
                    for you twice for Governor, and I'm here,
                    sir, and I'd like to ask you for an
                    explanation.

There's a tense moment as BARTLET looks down, then back up, then
back over to the QUESTIONER.

                              BARTLET
                    Yeah. I screwed you on that one.

JOSH looks up from his crossword puzzle. On the side of the room,
the AIDES want to kill themselves. In the back, TOBY's poker-
faced.

                              QUESTIONER #2
                         (pause)
                    I'm sorry?

                              BARTLET
                    I screwed you. You got hosed.

                              QUESTIONER #2
                    Sir, I--

                              BARTLET
                    Not just you. A lot of my constituents. I
                    put the hammer to farms in Concord,
                    Salem, Laconia, Pelham...Hampton,
                    Hudson...you guys got Rogered but <u>good</u>.
                         (pause)
                    Today...for the first time in
                    <u>history</u>...the largest group of
                    Americans living in poverty...are
                    <u>children</u>. One in five children live in
                    the most abject, dangerous, hopeless,
                    back-breaking gut wrenching poverty
                    anybody could imagine. One in five. And
                    they're children. If fidelity to freedom
                    and democracy is the code of our civic
                    religion, then surely the code of our
                    humanity is faithful service to that
                    unwritten Commandment that says "We shall
                    give our children better than we
                    ourselves received." Let me put it this
                    way...
                         (pause)
                              (MORE)

                                                          (CONTINUED)

35   CONTINUED: (4)   35

> BARTLET (cont'd)
> I voted against the bill 'cause I didn't
> want to make it harder for people to buy
> milk.
>   (beat)
> I stopped some money from flowing into
> your pocket. If that angers you, if you
> resent me, I completely respect that. But
> if you expect anything different from the
> President of the United States, you
> should vote for someone else.
>   (pause)
> Thanks very much, everybody, I hope you
> enjoyed the chicken.

The audience gives Bartlet a round of polite applause at best. It
wasn't his crowd, he didn't have his best stuff, but mostly that
last answer wasn't what they wanted to hear.

Except for one guy.

As the people are getting up and putting on their coats and
clearing out, we reveal...

...JOSH. An AMTRAK ticket sticking out of the breast pocket of his
overcoat which he never bothered taking off. Stunned. Floored.
Unable to stand up.

                                                          CUT TO:

36   **EXT. GEORGE WASHINGTON HOSPITAL - NIGHT**   36

TITLE:
                        Tuesday 1:45 a.m.

A black SUBURBAN with flashing lights and sirens arrives at
the hospital, where a large crowd of people are gathered.

                                                          CUT TO:

37   **INT. RECOVERY ROOM - NIGHT**   37

ABBEY, ZOEY and KELLER are at BARTLET's bedside. BARTLET's doing
his best to plead his case.

> ABBEY
> Jed, please. I want you to lie still for
> a few hours.

LEO comes in--

> LEO
> Mr. President--

                                                     (CONTINUED)

37   CONTINUED: 37

                          BARTLET
              I want to see him.

                          LEO
                    (to ABBEY)
              Is he okay?

                          ABBEY
              I told him about Josh.

                          BARTLET
              Please help me to the door.

                          LEO
              You should stay in bed.

                          BARTLET
              Charlie brought me clothes. Please.
                    (beat)
              Let me see him.

ABBEY looks at KELLER...KELLER nods slightly...

                          ABBEY
              Okay, just for a minute.

KELLER takes down the guard rail on the side of the bed as we
HEAR--

                          BARTLET (V.O.)
              What's next?

                                                          CUT TO:

38   **INT. VFW HALL - NIGHT**   38

Everyone has cleared out and BARTLET, LEO, CAL, TOBY and the other
AIDES are sitting around having a quick post-mortem on the event
that just ended.

BARTLET has little patience for this group. They're not much more
than a necessary evil, and LEO's the only one he relates to as a
peer, if he bothers to relate to anyone at all.

                          AIDE #2 (JERRY)
              The thing about saying the name--

                          BARTLET
              I understand.

                          JERRY
              If I could just re-frame the point that
              Cal was making--

                                                          (CONTINUED)

38   CONTINUED: 38

                    BARTLET
I understood the point that Cal was
making. I was sitting next to him when he
made it. My ears are connected to my
brain just like everybody else, and I'm
saying What's Next?

                    CAL
Sir, not to put my head in the lion's
mouth, but by repeating the name of your
opponent in public, you're essentially
giving him free advertising.

                    AIDE #4 (STEVEN)
Cal thinks you should start referring to
him as "my opponent" or "the other guy,"
"the other side." I don't know, maybe
there are other suggestions--

                    BARTLET
You want me to refer to Senator John
Hoynes of Texas, who at the moment has a
48 point lead for the Democratic
nomination, as "the other guy"?

                    STEVEN
Sir--

                    BARTLET
You're not afraid it's gonna make me look
like I can't remember his name?

                    STEVEN
No.

                    BARTLET
I am. I think it's gonna make me look
like I can't remember his name. I think
it's gonna make me look addled. I think
it's gonna make me look dotty. And even
if it didn't make me look like those
things, it would remain a stupid idea.
What's next? Nothing? Excellent.

BARTLET gets up and leaves...there's quite a bit of tension in the
room.

                    LEO
Okay, what's next?

                    CAL
Leo, we have to talk about what
happened tonight.

                                        (CONTINUED)

38   CONTINUED: (2)   38

                         LEO
          I thought he did well. I'd like to
          have seen more of those seats filled--

                         CAL
          That's not what I'm talking about.

                         LEO
          What are you talking about?

                         TOBY
          He's talking about the Governor's answer
          tonight.

They all look at TOBY...

                         TOBY
          I'm just guessing.
               (beat)
          I'm pretty drunk.

                         CAL
          I am talking about the Governor's answer
          tonight, but I'm also talking about--
          every day there's some--Look. Toby. We
          can talk about this with you in the room
          or if you're more comfortable--

                         LEO
          Cal, listen, I don't have time to make
          people comfortable. If a change has to be
          made, it has to be made. Jerry, Cal,
          Mack, Steve, you're fired.

                         CAL
          What?

                         TOBY
          What?

                         LEO
          No kidding, it's Moving Day. I want Toby,
          the rest of you thanks very much.

The AIDES still haven't gotten up. This must be some kind of gag.

                         LEO
          Fellas, look at my face. You're done.

The AIDES quietly gather their things. The room clears and TOBY is
looking at LEO.

LEO gets up and heads to the door...

                                               (CONTINUED)

38   CONTINUED: (3)

                        LEO
              Don't screw up.

LEO exits, leaving TOBY alone as we

                                                          CUT TO:

39   **EXT. STREET - NIGHT**   39

LEO exits the VFW hall and starts heading toward his suburban
which is parked on the all-but-deserted street. He sees
BARTLET waiting for him next to a State Trooper's car.

                        LEO
                   (calling)
              It's freezing cold in October. I don't
              know how you people live here.

                        BARTLET
              Did you just fire Cal Evans?

                        LEO
              Yeah.

                        BARTLET
              You fired him.

                        LEO
              Yeah. And, uh Jerry and Mack and Steve
              and the other guy.

                        BARTLET
              Is there anyone you kept?

                        LEO
              I kept Toby Ziegler.

                        BARTLET
              Oh, you kept Toby Ziegler and you fired
              everybody else.

                        LEO
              Yeah.

                        BARTLET
              Toby Ziegler's the only person working
              for us I don't know and he's the one you
              kept?

                        LEO
                   (to the STATE TROOPER)
              Take him home, would you.

                                                          (CONTINUED)

> BARTLET
> Those were the only people I knew.

> LEO
> Those people were worthless, it's time we
> bring in what we need.

> BARTLET
> So you made that decision on your own.

> LEO
> Yeah. You know why? 'Cause you're a
> crappy politician. I think you'll find
> that I'll be making a lot of decisions on
> my own, so start getting used to it.

> BARTLET
> You know I got elected to Congress by
> this state. This state sent me to
> Congress three times and then elected me
> Governor. All without your help.

And with this, LEO starts laughing...

> BARTLET
> Don't start.

> LEO
> No seriously, that's...that's a real
> political accomplishment considering
> your family <u>founded</u> this state.

> BARTLET
> Hey--

> LEO
> Were you even <u>opposed</u> in any
> of those elections?

> BARTLET
> You got rid of all the people I know.

> LEO
> Yeah. Have a good night.

LEO starts toward his car...

> BARTLET
> Why are you doing this?

LEO stops.

(CONTINUED)

> BARTLET
> You're a player.
>   (beat)
> You're bigger in the party than I am.
> Hoynes'd make you National Chairman.
>   (beat)
> Leo, tell me this isn't one of the twelve
> steps.

> LEO
>   (pause)
> That's what it is. Right after admitting
> that we're powerless over alcohol and
> that a higher power can restore us to
> sanity, that's where you come in.

> BARTLET
>   (wanting him to be serious)
> Leo--

> LEO
> Because I'm tired of it. Year after year
> after year after year, having to choose
> between the lesser of who cares. Of
> trying to get myself excited about the
> candidate who can speak in complete
> sentences. Of setting the bar so low I
> can hardly look at it. They say a good
> man can't get elected president, I don't
> believe that, do you?

> BARTLET
>   (pause)
> And you think I'm that man.

> LEO
> Yes.

> BARTLET
> Doesn't it matter that I'm not as sure?

> LEO
> No.
>   (beat)
> "Act as if ye have faith and faith
> shall be given to you". Put it another
> way, Fake It Till You Make It.

LEO starts toward his car and calls back--

> LEO
>   (calling)
> You did good tonight.

                                                        (CONTINUED)

39   CONTINUED: (3)   39

                              BARTLET
                   Yeah.

                              LEO
                         (pause)
                   This is the time of Jed Bartlet, old
                   friend. You're gonna open your mouth and
                   lift houses off the ground. Whole houses,
                   clear off the ground.

As the REPORTERS continue, we go through a series of QUICK
DISSOLVES:

40   **INT. HOSPITAL CORRIDOR - NIGHT**   40

BARTLET and LEO are walking.

                              MALE REPORTER #1 (V.O.)
                   And it's unknown at this time whether or
                   not the President before going under
                   anesthesia, signed a letter that would
                   give temporary...

41   **EXT. STREET - NIGHT**   41

A REPORTER is on the scene.

                              FEMALE REPORTER #1
                   ...shuttling back and forth between the
                   White House and George Washington
                   Hospital, where several thousand people
                   have begun to...

42   **EXT. GEORGE WASHINGTON HOSPITAL - NIGHT**   42

A CROWD has gathered.

                              MALE REPORTER #2 (V.O.)
                   ...begun to gather behind the police
                   barricades.

43   **INT. SAM'S OFFICE - NIGHT**   43

SAM sits while contemplating.

                              MALE REPORTER #2 (V.O.)
                              (CONT'D)
                   An impromptu vigil with prayers being
                   made...

                              FEMALE REPORTER #2 (V.O.)
                   ...understandably are rocked on their
                   heels at this hour to put it mildly.

44   **INT. TOBY'S OFFICE - NIGHT**   44

TOBY sits while contemplating, then lowers his face in his
hands.

>FEMALE REPORTER #2 (V.O.)
>(CONT'D)
>*Press Secretary C.J. Cregg has appeared*
>*at her briefing to be shaken and*
>*distraught.*

45   **INT. C.J.'S OFFICE - NIGHT**   45

C.J. sits, touching the area on her neck where her necklace
used to be.

>FEMALE REPORTER #2 (V.O.)
>(CONT'D)
>*She was unable...*

>MALE REPORTER #3 (V.O.)
>*Officials at George Washington University*
>*Hospital...*

>MALE REPORTER #4 (V.O.)
>*And in the fourth hour of a massive*
>*manhunt for a third suspect, airports up*
>*and down the Atlantic Coast are closed.*

46   **EXT. THE NEWSEUM - NIGHT**   46

FBI agents investigate the blown-out car window.

>MALE REPORTER #4 (V.O.)
>(CONT'D)
>*National Guard units in Baltimore,*
>*Virginia, Delaware...*

47   **EXT. STREET - NIGHT**   47

Police cars with lights flashing form a road-block check-
point.

>MALE REPORTER #5 (V.O.)
>*...reported massive delays, cancellations*
>*and closures at major airports, rail*
>*stations...*

>FEMALE REPORTER #3 (V.O.)
>*...rail stations, bus stations, and*
>*harbors. Travelers are strongly advised*
>*to either wait or...*

48   **INT. SITUATION ROOM - NIGHT**   48

A MAP of Iraq is projected on a wall in b.g. and a radar
display is in f.g.

> MALE REPORTER #6 (V.O.)
> ...*Navy carrier groups as well as the
> 32nd Marine Tactical Division have been
> put on a state of heightened alert.*

49   **INT. HOSPITAL WAITING ROOM - NIGHT**   49

GINA, DONNA and MRS. LANDINGHAM wait.

> FEMALE REPORTER #4 (V.O.)
> ...*Special Agent Ron Butterfield had to
> be cut from Secret Service detail. He was
> shot in the hand during the attack on the
> President.*

50   **INT. OPERATING ROOM - NIGHT**   50

The SURGICAL TEAM is working on JOSH.

And now we

                                                         CUT TO:

51   **INT. HOSPITAL CORRIDOR/OPERATING ROOM - NIGHT**   51

LEO is standing behind BARTLET, who is looking through the glass
partition at JOSH being operated on....

> BARTLET
> Look what happened.

                                                  FADE TO TITLE:

                    End of Part I

                                                  FADE TO BLACK

68.

In the Shadow of Two Gunmen

Part II

<u>TEASER</u>

FADE IN:

2-1   **EXT. THE DIXIE PIG BAR-B-Q - NIGHT**   2-1

TITLE:
                    Tuesday, 3:28 a.m.

                         TV ANCHOR (V.O.)
              ...emergency surgical team. The White
              House is telling us that there will be a
              press conference at 7:30 Eastern, in
              about... four hours from now. Deputy
              White House Chief of Staff--

2-2   **INT. THE DIXIE PIG BAR-B-Q - NIGHT**   2-2

The television plays somewhere near the cash register. The
news report has a quality we've become familiar with, which is
to say we're in the sixth hour of 24 hour coverage of a story
that hasn't changed since the first hour.

A YOUNG MAN is getting his change back after paying for a
couple of packs of cigarettes.

                         TV ANCHOR (ON TV)
              ...White House Chief of Staff Joshua
              Lyman is currently undergoing extensive
              surgery to repair a collapsed lung and to
              remove a bullet that remains lodged in
              his thoracic region. And for an update on
              his condition, let's go live now to Lynn
              Blakley who's standing by at George
              Washington Hospital... Wait, we're not
              going there just yet. Now, I'm being told
              that authorities are reporting another
              gunshot victim...

He's opening one of the packs as he walks out into--

2-3   **EXT. THE DIXIE PIG BAR-B-Q - NIGHT**   2-3

He's heading to his car as he puts a cigarette in his mouth.
He's about to light it with a Bic disposable when--

--a spotlight hits him from above. The light is shining from
above and before he can figure out that it is coming from a
helicopter hovering overhead--

                                                      (CONTINUED)

--the flashing lights of about 983 law enforcement vehicles
come screeching up and surround the YOUNG MAN. The doors fly
open and COPS, FBI, SECRET SERVICE, STATE TROOPERS,
brandishing everything from pistols to rifles to automatic
weapons, shout a chorus of "Federal agents"! "Get your hands
in the air"! "Federal Officers"! "Freeze"! "FBI"! "U.S. Secret
Service"! "Get your goddam hands in the air"!

                                                      SMASH CUT TO:

MAIN TITLES

                           <u>END OF TEASER</u>

ACT ONE

FADE IN:

2-4   **INT. PRESS BRIEFING ROOM - NIGHT**   2-4

The crowded room is taking its seats as C.J. walks up to the
podium.

> C.J.
> We're confirming now that a suspect has
> been taken into custody and is being
> questioned by Federal law enforcement.

That got things started in a hurry as notebooks flash open and
cameras whirr.

> C.J. (CONT'D)
> At this time, we can not, we are not,
> releasing any information whatsoever
> about the suspect.

> REPORTER (STEVE)
> C.J. can you tell us anything, his name,
> where he's from, ethnicity, if you guys
> suspect a motive...?

> C.J.
> (pause)
> Yes, Steve, I can tell you all those
> things. Because when I said we weren't
> releasing any information whatsoever, I
> meant except his name, his address, his
> ethnicity and what we think his motive
> was.

> ALL
> C.J.!

> C.J.
> (beat)
> I am releasing the name of Stephanie
> Abbott, A-B-B-O-T-T, of Silver Spring,
> Maryland, who was in the crowd and
> sustained an injury to the left femur,
> which is the thigh bone. The President
> remains in stable condition in the
> recovery room, and is expected to be
> released sometime Wednesday. Josh Lyman
> is now in his--

CUT TO:

2-5 **INT. VIP WAITING AREA - NIGHT**   2-5

SAM, DONNA, TOBY, ABBEY and a few others. C.J.'s briefing is
on TV.

       C.J. (FROM TV)
   --sixth hour of surgery to repair a
   collapsed lung and a ruptured pulmonary
   artery. We likely won't have an update
   on his condition until the procedure is
   complete, which they expect won't be for
   another six or eight hours. We'll keep
   you updated in the next hour. Thank you
   very much.

      REPORTERS (V.O.)
   C.J., what about the conference?

       SAM
   Ma'am, does the President know they've
   arrested a suspect?

       ABBEY
   Yes, I told him. He's pretty groggy after
   the anesthesia.

An AIDE steps in--

       AIDE
   Sam. Toby. You've got a phone call in the
   other room.

SAM and TOBY get up and exit.

       ABBEY
    (to DONNA)
   Donna, you wanna throw some water on your
   face?

       DONNA
   You know, I should ask, is there anything
   I'm supposed to be doing right now?

       TOBY
   No.

       DONNA
   I mean anything that Josh's office is
   supposed to be doing... should... should
   I be making sure it's farmed out?

             (CONTINUED)

2-5   CONTINUED: 2-5

                         ABBEY
              No. I'm sure it's covered.

                                               CUT TO:

2-6   **INT. C.J.'S OFFICE - NIGHT**   2-6

    As C.J. comes in--

                         C.J.
              You got 'em on the phone?

                         CAROL
              Yeah.

                         C.J.
                    (into speaker phone)
              Guys?

                                               CUT TO:

2-7   **INT. HOSPITAL COMMAND CENTER - NIGHT**   2-7

    Not at all what it sounds like. It's a small room where
    they've set up some phones.

                         SAM
              Yeah, we're here.

                                          INTERCUT WITH:

2-8   **INT. C.J.'S OFFICE - SAME**   2-8

    She's on speaker as she checks print releases that CAROL is
    handing her.

                         C.J.
              Sam, I need you to come over to the White
              House and speak to Nancy McNally about a
              letter the President was supposed to
              sign. She'll know what you're talking
              about.

                         SAM
              Yeah, alright.

                         C.J.
              And Toby?

                         TOBY
              Yeah.

                                               (CONTINUED)

                         C.J.
          They're still asking about the tent.

                         TOBY
          Yeah.

                         C.J.
          I'd be more comfortable with a no comment
          coming from the Secret Service, so--

                         SAM
                (to TOBY)
          What's this?

                         TOBY
          They want to know why the President
          exited the building in the open air.

                         SAM
                (pause)
          I'll talk to somebody at Treasury.

                         TOBY
          I'll do it.

                         SAM
          Let me.

                         TOBY
          No.

                         C.J.
          Someone.

                         SAM
          Toby, we were all in the meeting
          together.

                         TOBY
          Go back to the office.

                         SAM
          Okay.
                (beat)
          Okay.

SAM walks out as we HEAR--

                         LAWYER (V.O.)
          Can the ships pass inspection?

                                              (CONTINUED)

2-8   CONTINUED: (2)   2-8

                        LAWYER (ELLEN)(V.O.)
            The ships'll be registered in Libya and
            Panama--

                                                          CUT TO:

2-9   **INT. CONFERENCE ROOM - DAY**   2-9

The same oil tanker people from PART I. SAM, GAGE and a few
other LAWYERS, LOCH, CAMERON and a few oil tanker guys. The
rain beats against the window on one side while life in the
law firm can be seen through the glass on the other.

Once again, people are coming in and out and passing things
around...

        TITLE:

                        Gage Whitney Pace
                        Midtown Manhattan

                        LAWYER (ELLEN)
            --so they won't be subject to the OPA,
            which wouldn't allow an American company
            to keep a tanker like this in service
            very long.

                        LAWYER #2 (RICK)
            I think 2017.

                        ELLEN
            I think 20_15_, and we'll check that, but
            you get the idea.

                        GAGE
            I think all that's left is to dot the
            "T"s.

                        SAM
            Actually...

Everyone's listening.

                        SAM (CONT'D)
            I have a thing. I have a thing I was
            gonna mention. Just a proposal to throw
            out there. When I was a Congressional
            aide, we had an expression, "No idea was
            too stupid to say out loud." So here it
            is, and bear me out: Instead of buying
            these ships, _don't_ buy these ships. Buy
            other ships. Buy better ships.
                (pause)
            That's my idea.

                                                       (CONTINUED)

                       LOCH
What's he talking about?

                       GAGE
That's a perfectly fair question. Sam,
what the hell are you talking about?

                       SAM
And the good news is we have a no-penalty
clause we can exercise if we pull out
before the first of December.

                       CAMERON
But, Sam, we want these ships. This is as
little as we've ever paid for a fleet.

                       SAM
Well, there's a reason why they don't
cost a lot of money. They're 20 year-old
single-hull VLCCs that nobody else wants.
When they hit things, they will break.
And they will hit things, because they
don't have state of the art navigation
systems, they don't have G-3 tank
gauging, or EM-5000 engine monitoring,
the recommended staletronic or
electroneumatic ballast.

                       GAGE
And yesterday he didn't know the
difference between a ship and a boat.

                       CAMERON
Sam, I thought you said you covered our
liability.

                       SAM
       (pause)
I did.
       (beat)
Strictly speaking, I did. But there's a
broader liability to think about. People
drove past Exxon stations after Valdez.

                       CAMERON
We've got PR firms for PR problems.

                       SAM
There's a Suez tanker ready to launch in
the Koje Island Shipyard in Korea.
Chevron just dropped the option and it's
sitting in the cradle. Let's go get it.

                                 (CONTINUED)

2-9   CONTINUED: (2)   2-9

                              GAGE
              Sam, could I talk to you for a second.

                              SAM
              308,000 deadweight tons, carries 2.2
              million gallons. You can have it today
              for 46 million.

                              GAGE
              Sam?

SAM gets up to step outside the room with GAGE--

                              LOCH
              46 million dollars?

                              SAM
                   (calling back)
              That's a good price.

SAM and GAGE step out into--

2-10 **INT. CORRIDOR - CONTINUOUS**   2-10

The meeting can be seen through the glass, though nothing much
can happen until these two get back.

                              GAGE
              Sam, what are you doing?

                              SAM
                   (pause)
              I think I have an obligation--

                              GAGE
              What are you doing?

                              SAM
                   (pause)
              Maybe they <u>want</u> to buy safer boats, but
              we never gave 'em the option.

                              GAGE
              Are you trying to get fired?

                              SAM
              Maybe they're really gonna thank us for
              this suggestion.

                              GAGE
              Knock it off, Sam.

                                                          (CONTINUED)

2-10 CONTINUED: 2-10

                    SAM
               (pause)
          Look--

                    GAGE
          Knock it off.

GAGE goes back into the conference room, followed by SAM as
we--

                                                        CUT TO:

2-11 **EXT. GRAND CENTRAL STATION - MORNING**   2-11

JOSH is getting soaked at a payphone. He's got his overnight
bag.

                         JOSH
                    (into phone)
          I'm looking--uh... uh... operator--I'm
          looking for the number of a law firm in
          Manhattan. Here's the thing, I can't
          quite remember the <u>name</u> of the firm, no,
          wait, wait, wait--I just came back from
          New Hampshire where I saw this guy and
          now I have to -- listen, it's a very
          famous firm, that handled Shearson, you
          must know--

JOSH looks up at the buildings and decides to make a run for
it.

                         JOSH
          Okay, you know what, I'm just -- okay
          bye.

JOSH starts jogging off in the rain as we

                                                        CUT TO:

2-12 **INT. CONFERENCE ROOM - DAY**   2-12

The rain continues. The meeting continues.

                         CAMERON
               That's amortized over--

                         ELLEN
          15 years.

                         LOCH
          Pre-tax.

                                                    (CONTINUED)

2-12 CONTINUED:

                    GAGE
     Sam?

                    SAM
     Hm?

                    GAGE
     15 year pre-tax amortization?

                    SAM
          (beat)
     Eleven million extra dollars.

               LOCH
     We're back to this.

                    SAM
     Money is gonna be spent, Mr. Loch. You
     can spend it now or you can spend it
     later, but it's cheaper to spend it now.

                    CAMERON
     Sam--

                    SAM
     It's also the right thing to do. Spend
     eleven million extra dollars.

                    GAGE
     Sam--

                    SAM
     Spend it on a better boat.

                    GAGE
     Dammit--

                    SAM
     The Amoco Cadiz, 68 million gallons of
     crude oil off Brittany, France. Braer, a
     Liberian tanker, 26 million gallons off
     the Shetland Islands. I just pulled these
     off the internet last night. The Exxon
     Valdez, the Aegean Sea, the Argo Merchant
     -- look it up.

                    GAGE
     I'm sure they're aware--

                    SAM
     Spend eleven million extra dollars.

                                        (CONTINUED)

> GAGE
> Sam, that's enough.

> SAM
> You don't want to pay it? Pass the
> expense on to us.

> ELLEN
> Sam--

> SAM
> A half a penny at the tank. Here's five
> bucks, a thousand people are on me.

> GAGE
> Sam--

At the moment GAGE says "Sam," we hear a KNOCK on the glass.
SAM looks over to where the knock came from. JOSH is standing
outside the conference room glass. Soaking wet and still
breathing heavy from his run over here.

> ELLEN
> (pause)
> Sam, we are in the middle of a meeting.

> SAM
> Yeah.

SAM continues looking at JOSH, he can't imagine what this is
all about.

> LOCH
> Sam, we're not indifferent to the
> concerns for the environmentalist--excuse
> me, Sam?

> SAM
> Yeah.

SAM doesn't understand what JOSH wants. JOSH points to his
face. "Look at my face!"

> LOCH
> It doesn't quite feel like I have your
> attention.

> SAM
> Yeah.

JOSH nods his head "yes," meaning this means what you think it
means.

                                              (CONTINUED)

2-12 CONTINUED: (3)   2-12

                          SAM
            Yeah.

SAM stands up and starts to absently gather some things as if
the meeting's over. Then he puts all the papers back,
realizing--

                          SAM
            I'm not gonna need that.

                          GAGE
            Sam? Sam? Sam, please keep your seat.
            Sam, where are you going?

                          SAM
            New Hampshire.

SAM exits and disappears with JOSH as we

                                        FADE TO BLACK

                    END OF ACT ONE

ACT TWO

FADE IN:

2-13 **EXT./EST. WHITE HOUSE - NIGHT**   2-13

2-14 **INT. WHITE HOUSE CORRIDOR - NIGHT**   2-14

TITLE:

Tuesday, 3:55 a.m.

C.J.'s standing in the doorway--

                    C.J.
          Sam.

                    SAM
          Yeah.

                    C.J.
          I wanted to see if, uh--

                    SAM
          How's your head?

                    C.J.
          Uh, fine. I wanted to see if you talked
          to Nancy McNally.

                    SAM
          Yeah, and she talked to Counsel's Office,
          and they're gonna work on a few things to
          see what we'd like, but I can tell you,
          we're not gonna--

                    C.J.
               (beat)
          Sam, you didn't happen to notice... when
          the shooting started, you didn't happen
          to notice who pulled me to the ground,
          did you?

                    SAM
          No.

                    C.J.
          They pulled me down behind a police car.
               (beat)
          And my necklace came off.

                    SAM
          No.

                                    (CONTINUED)

2-14 CONTINUED:

> C.J.
> You talked to Nancy McNally?

> SAM
> Yeah.

> C.J.
> Okay.

She walks into--

2-15 **INT. COMMUNICATIONS BULLPEN - CONTINUOUS**   2-15

--where she hooks up with CAROL.

> CAROL
> Oh, C.J.?

> C.J.
> What?

> CAROL
> You need to call back Debbie at the Today
> Show.

> C.J.
> Why?

> CAROL
> You said you might be willing to do the
> morning shows when they go on the air at
> seven.

> C.J.
> No, that's not a good--

> CAROL
> They just wanted--

> C.J.
> No, I'm not gonna do any interviews just
> yet. I'm not doing it.

> CAROL
> I'll take care of it.

> C.J.
> Which one of our people said--

They've walked into--

2-16 **INT. PRESS BULLPEN - CONTINUOUS**   2-16

> CAROL
> It was a mistake, I'll take care of it.

DANNY comes in--

> DANNY
> C.J.--

> C.J.
> Yeah.

> DANNY
> I really don't want to be this guy--

They walk into--

2-17 **INT. C.J.'S OFFICE - CONTINUOUS**   2-17

> C.J.
> Somebody around here thought I should do
> the morning shows.

> DANNY
> I still don't have an answer.

> C.J.
> Who was in charge?

> DANNY
> For the three and a half hours the
> President was under anesthesia.

> C.J.
>   (beat)
> Danny, it's a little complicated.
> There's something called the National
> Security Act of 1947, there's the 25th,
> Nancy McNally, Bill Hutchinson, and the
> White House Counsel, they're all working
> on it right now.

> DANNY
> Yeah, but they're gonna tell me who was
> supposed to be in charge. I want to know
> who was in charge.

> C.J.
> And we are working on that information.
>   (beat)
> We're working on it.

(CONTINUED)

2-17 CONTINUED: 2-17

The phone on C.J.'s desk RINGS--

                                                        CUT TO:

2-18 **INT. C.J.'S BEDROOM - EARLY MORNING**   2-18

Her sleeping hand finds the phone receiver in the dark.

                        C.J.
                    (into phone)
                Hello?
                    (beat)
                Yeah?
                    (she holds--then)
                Isobel, it's six-thirty in the morning.
                    (beat)
                Yeah.

C.J. hangs up the phone and sits up as we

                                                        CUT TO:

2-19 **EXT./EST. LOS ANGELES - MORNING**   2-19

        TITLE:
                        Triton-Day Public Relations
                        Beverly Hills, California

                    ASSISTANT (V.O.)
                Excuse me.

2-20 **INT. ISOBEL'S OFFICE - CONTINUOUS**   2-20

                        ASSISTANT
                C.J.'s here.

                        ISOBEL
                Thank you.

ISOBEL is the owner and president of this high-end PR firm,
and with her is ROGER BECKER, who's very unhappy right now.

C.J. is shown into the office--

                        C.J.
                Good morning, Isobel. Hello, Roger.

                        ROGER
                I asked her to be here 45 minutes ago.

                        C.J.
                I'm sorry?

                                                    (CONTINUED)

                    ROGER
          I said I asked you to be--

                    ISOBEL
          Roger--

                    C.J.
          It was 6:30 in the morning, Roger, I
          wasn't quite ready for work. But I am
          now, how can I help you?

                    ROGER
          Are you aware the Golden Globe
          nominations were announced this morning?

                    C.J.
               (beat)
          I wasn't.
               (beat)
          Am I up for something?

                    ISOBEL
          C.J., Atlantis only got two nominations.

                    ROGER
          For the entire studio. Best Comedy Score
          and Supporting Actor for the kid. That's
          what twenty-thousand a month bought us.

                    C.J.
          Roger, I think we put together a very
          aggressive campaign--

                    ROGER
          Two nominations.

                    C.J.
          That's two nominations more than a lot of
          people got.

                    ROGER
          Are you aware that the new Premiere
          Magazine list is coming out Monday?

                    C.J.
          The hundred most powerful people in
          Hollywood?

                    ROGER
          Yeah.

                                        (CONTINUED)

2-20 CONTINUED: (2)

> C.J.
> Yes I am. And I can tell you that you're
> on it, and congratulations, and it must,
> you know, feel good being that powerful.

> ROGER
> I went from third to ninth. I dropped to
> ninth. Do you know how that looks? Do you
> know how many other people were ahead of
> me?

> C.J.
> (beat)
> Eight?

> ROGER
> Lady, you're--

> C.J.
> The movies were <u>bad</u> Roger. All of them.
> Even the little kid was bad. But he was a
> little kid, he had a couple of scenes,
> big eyeglasses, little lisp, he's going
> to the Golden Globes. You know why the
> New Coke marketing campaign failed?
> Because nobody liked New Coke. The movies
> were bad. If the movies were <u>unknown</u>, I
> could help you. But they weren't. They
> were just bad.

> ISOBEL
> (pause)
> Roger, would you excuse us for just a
> second, please?

ROGER nods. ISOBEL and C.J. step out into--

2-21 **INT. CORRIDOR - CONTINUOUS**   2-21

> C.J.
> Sorry I talked to him like that, but do
> you really think he had *The Maltese
> Falcon* out there?

> ISOBEL
> The thing is, C.J., he's big business for
> me.

> C.J.
> I'll apologize to him, Isobel. I'll find
> someone to make him man of the year. I'll
> ask around in Vegas.

(CONTINUED)

2-21 CONTINUED:

> ISOBEL
> He wants you fired. He thinks you're a
> smart mouth.

That got C.J.'s attention...

> C.J.
> He's gonna pull his business unless you
> fire me?

> ISOBEL
>   (beat)
> This is never what you wanted to be
> doing, C.J. You've always felt it was
> beneath you.

> C.J.
> It is beneath me.

> ISOBEL
> C.J.--

> C.J.
> So take me off film and television, I
> don't know anything about it anyway. We
> have plenty of accounts--

> ISOBEL
> I need to keep his business. I'm sorry.

> C.J.
>   (pause)
> You're firing me?

> ISOBEL
> I'm sorry.

> C.J.
> Out here in the hallway?

> ISOBEL
> C.J.--

> C.J.
> I need someone to call me a cab.

> ISOBEL
> I'm sorry?

(CONTINUED)

2-21 CONTINUED: (2)   2-21

                         C.J.
          I couldn't get my contacts in this
          morning and I broke my glasses getting
          out of the car. I can't drive myself
          home, I need someone to call me a cab.

                         ISOBEL
                    (to the ASSISTANT)
          Could you call a taxi for C.J. please?

The ASSISTANT begins dialing...

                         ISOBEL
          I have to go back in.

ISOBEL starts back into her office...

                         C.J.
          It was a bad movie, Isobel.

                         ASSISTANT
          Yes, I need a taxi for Beverly Hills,
          please.

                                                    CUT TO:

2-22 **EXT. C.J.'S HOUSE - MORNING**   2-22

A cab pulls up and C.J. gets out with a carton of stuff from
her office and pays the driver.

She notices that there's a rental car in her driveway. She
looks around--

                         C.J.
                    (calling out)
          Hello?

C.J. walks down the drive-way to the back of the house and
opens the gate into--

2-23 **EXT. C.J.'S BACKYARD - CONTINUOUS**   2-23

C.J. has a pool.

                         TOBY (O.S.)
          Hey, C.J.!

TOBY's sitting in a patio chair...

                         C.J.
                    (pause)
          Who is that?

                                              (CONTINUED)

> TOBY
> It's me.

> C.J.
> (squinting)
> Toby?

> TOBY
> Yeah.

> C.J.
> What the hell are you--

C.J. can't finish her sentence 'cause she turned the corner
too early and just walked into her pool.

TOBY's fairly unconcerned. He knows C.J. pretty well.

> TOBY
> C.J. you fell into the pool, there.

> C.J.
> I can't see!

> TOBY
> Yeah. Well maybe, kinda try and feel your
> way to dry land. You want a hand?

> C.J.
> Shut up.

C.J.'s made it to the side and is about to climb out when...

> C.J.
> Avert your eyes.

> TOBY
> What?

> C.J.
> I'm climbing out of the pool, my clothes
> will be clingy, avert your eyes.

> TOBY
> C.J., I really didn't come here--

> C.J.
> *Avert your eyes.*

C.J. climbs out of the pool and stands there, water draining
off her body.

(CONTINUED)

2-23 CONTINUED: (2)

                    C.J.
          Oh turn around.

                    TOBY
          I tried calling you at your office. They
          said you were fired. Were you stealing
          things?

                    C.J.
          Roger Becker dropped from third most
          powerful person in Hollywood to ninth
          most powerful person in Hollywood.

                    TOBY
             (beat)
          Does he still make the playoffs, or is
          the cutoff line--

                    C.J.
          They take it seriously.

                    TOBY
          C.J., Jed Bartlet's very impressed with
          you. He likes the work you did with that
          girls' group with the stupid name.

                    C.J.
             (pause)
          Emily's List?

                    TOBY
          Yes.

                    C.J.
          That girls' group with the stupid name?

                    TOBY
          Yes.

                    C.J.
          Emily's List. Early Money is Like Yeast.

                    TOBY
          Yeah.

                    C.J.
          It helps raise the dough.

                    TOBY
          I get it.

(CONTINUED)

> C.J.
> They raise money for women candidates.
> Early Money is Like Yeast. It helps raise
> the dough.
> (beat)
> For the candidates.

> TOBY
> I really do get it.

> C.J.
> Bartlet's impressed with me?

> TOBY
> Very impressed. And one of the big keys
> to his game plan is bringing you on as
> press secretary.

> C.J.
> He's never heard of me, has he.

> TOBY
> No.

> C.J.
> Toby--

> TOBY
> I'm here on instructions from Leo
> McGarry.

> C.J.
> (beat)
> McGarry wants me?

> TOBY
> (beat)
> Yes.
> (beat)
> Come join the campaign.

This is a very serious offer for C.J. She tries not to look
too ridiculous as she stands there dripping wet.

> C.J.
> How much does it pay?

> TOBY
> How much were you making before?

> C.J.
> 550,000 a year.

(CONTINUED)

                    TOBY
        This pays six-hundred dollars a week.

                    C.J.
        So this is less.

                    TOBY
        Yes.

                    C.J.
              (pause)
        Toby, does he know I've only ever worked
        statewide. Does he know I've never worked
        on a national campaign?

                    TOBY
        Yes, it's graduation day.

                    C.J.
              (beat)
        You really think I can do this?

                    TOBY
        Yeah.

                    C.J.
        Is Jed Bartlet a good man?

                    TOBY
        Yeah.

                    C.J.
        Toby?

                    TOBY
        Yes.

                    C.J.
              (pause)
        Then let's go into the house so I can
        change my clothes and we'll talk about
        it.

        C.J. starts to walk off...

                    TOBY
        C.J.?

                    C.J.
        Yeah.

                    TOBY
        The house is over there.

                                    (CONTINUED)

> C.J.
> Okay.

> BUTTERFIELD (V.O.)
> One of them was using a 9mm Beretta, the
> other had a 357 Desert Eagle.

CUT TO:

2-24 **INT. BARTLET'S HOSPITAL ROOM - EARLY MORNING**   2-24

BARTLET's sitting up in bed and ABBEY, ZOEY, and BUTTERFIELD
are all in the room.

> ABBEY
> Ron's saying that these were absolutely
> the wrong weapons to use for a shooting
> of this kind and that's why the injury
> count was as low as it was.

> BARTLET
> We don't <u>know</u> what the injury count
> is yet.

> ABBEY
> Yeah, but his point is--

The door opens and CHARLIE enters. He senses that something's
up...

> CHARLIE
> Excuse me, sir, I was told you wanted to
> see me.

> BARTLET
> Yeah.
>   (beat)
> Charlie, the guy the Secret Service have
> in custody is named Carl LeRoy. He gives
> a statement in which he says that he and
> the two shooters were members of an
> organization called West Virginia White
> Pride.

BARTLET and everyone else in the room is gonna let CHARLIE
take a moment to absorb this. After a moment...

> CHARLIE
> They tried to kill the President because
> Zoey and I are together?

> ABBEY
> No.

(CONTINUED)

2-24 CONTINUED: 2-24

                         CHARLIE
                    (pause)
               Why did--

                         BUTTERFIELD
               Charlie, the President wasn't the target.
                    (beat)
               According to the statement, the President
               wasn't the target.

                         CHARLIE
                    (pause)
               Oh.
                    (pause)
               Okay.
                    (pause)
               Okay, well....
                    (pause)
               Okay.
                    (pause)
               Thank you, Mr. President.

CHARLIE exits.

                         ZOEY
                    (indicating that she wants to)
                    be with CHARLIE)
               Dad, I'm gonna--

                         BARTLET
               Go.

ZOEY exits....

                         BARTLET
               We don't know what the injury count is
               yet.

                                        FADE TO BLACK

                    END OF ACT TWO

ACT THREE

FADE IN:

TITLE:
Tuesday, 6:15 a.m.

2-25 **INT. LEO'S OFFICE - EARLY MORNING**   2-25

> MARGARET
> He was supposed to sign a letter?

> LEO
> The President is going under general
> anesthesia, usually signs a letter
> handing over executive powers to the Vice
> President.

> MARGARET
> And the President didn't sign a letter?

> LEO
> Nope, we blew that play.

> MARGARET
> Is there gonna be trouble?

> LEO
> We'll see. To be honest with you, I don't
> really care right now.

> MARGARET
> Can I just say something? You know, for
> the future?

> LEO
> Yeah.

> MARGARET
> I can sign the President's name. I have
> his signature down pretty good.

> LEO
> You can sign the President's name?

> MARGARET
> Yeah.

> LEO
> On a document removing him from power and
> handing it to someone else?

(CONTINUED)

>   MARGARET
> Yeah.
>   (beat)
> Or do you think the White House Counsel
> would say that was a bad idea?

>   LEO
> I think the White House Counsel would
> say that's a coup d'etat.

>   MARGARET
>   (pause)
> I'd probably end up doing some time for
> that.

>   LEO
> I would think.

C.J. enters--

>   LEO
>   (calling to MARGARET as she
>   leaves)
> And what the hell are you doing
> practicing the President's signature?

>   MARGARET (O.S.)
> It's just for fun.

>   LEO
>   (to C.J.)
> We've got separation of powers, checks
> and balances, and Margaret, vetoing
> things and sending them back to the Hill.

>   C.J.
> Leo, who thought it was a good idea for
> me to do the morning shows?

>   LEO
> I did.

>   C.J.
> Why?

>   LEO
> The President's not ready for cameras, if
> it's the Vice President it's gonna look
> like we don't have a President, and I'd
> like the White House to start climbing
> out from behind the bushes.

(CONTINUED)

> C.J.
> I think it's a bad idea.

> LEO
> Why?

> C.J.
> I just--First of all, I think it's
> inappropriate while Josh--you know,
> until--

> LEO
> What's wrong?

> C.J.
> Nothing.

> LEO
> C.J.

> C.J.
> Nothing.
>   (beat)
> I'd rather not do it, but obviously--

> LEO
>   (pause)
> Have Sam do it.

> C.J.
> Okay. Listen, the letter--

> LEO
> Yeah.

> C.J.
> The three and a half hours.

> LEO
> Yeah.

> C.J.
> I don't know how much longer I can dance
> around Danny and it's gonna be Danny
> times a hundred by lunchtime.

> LEO
> Have him come see me.

> C.J.
> Yeah?

(CONTINUED)

2-25 CONTINUED: (3)   2-25

                         LEO
               Yeah.

                         C.J.
               Okay.

          LEO exits...

2-26 **INT. WHITE HOUSE CORRIDOR - CONTINUOUS**   2-26

          TOBY joins LEO and they walk in step.

                         LEO
               She doesn't want to do the morning shows.

                         TOBY
               She said she's been getting a couple
               questions about why the President exited
               in the open air. They remember that the
               Secret Service used to construct a tent
               or a canopy.
                    (beat)
               I'm gonna talk to Ron Butterfield.

                         LEO
                    (beat)
               He's gonna say the Secret Service doesn't
               comment on procedure.

                         TOBY
               I know, but... maybe I can talk him out
               of it. I should try anyway.

                         LEO
               You don't have to, Toby.

                         TOBY
               Yeah I should, though.

                         LEO
                    (beat)
               Okay.

          TOBY exits...

                                                            CUT TO:

2-27 **INT. BARTLET HEADQUARTERS - DAY**   2-27

          An empty storefront, but the place is taking on steam. *BARTLET
          FOR AMERICA* posters can be seen and new phone lines are being
          installed. YOUNG VOLUNTEERS are working the phones and
          stuffing envelopes and bringing in coffee and sandwiches.

                                                      (CONTINUED)

BARTLET, LEO, TOBY, SAM, C.J., JOSH and about a half-dozen
STAFFERS are looking at the TV.

> TV ANCHOR #2
> *--won the non-binding straw poll, pulling
> in 48% of the vote. Senator William Wiley
> of Washington State drew a poorer than
> expected 22% of the vote, but the story
> this morning is the 19% of the vote
> picked up--*

TITLE:

> ### Bartlet Campaign Headquarters
> ### Manchester, New Hampshire

> TV ANCHOR #2
> *--by former New Hampshire Governor Jed
> Bartlet, who leap-frogged several
> Democratic candidates to finish a
> surprising third. And we're gonna go now
> to Governor Bartlet who's standing by
> live... Okay, I'm told we don't have the
> Governor at this moment, so while we try--*

And C.J. clicks off the tape they've been watching.

> C.J.
> Okay, who can tell me what we did wrong
> there?

> BARTLET
> I blew it, what's next.

> C.J.
> We didn't have the candidate, that's
> right. Anybody who answered "We didn't
> have the candidate--"

> BARTLET
> What's next.

> JOSH
> Toby wants to say something.

> BARTLET
> Which one is Toby?

> TOBY
> I am.

> BARTLET
>   (to JOSH)
> And which one are you?

(CONTINUED)

                    JOSH
          I'm Josh.

                    LEO
               (to TOBY)
          What was it you wanted to say?

                    TOBY
          Let's get out of New Hampshire.

                    LEO
          Why?

                    TOBY
          Nothing to win here.

                    SAM
          He's right.

                    BARTLET
               (quietly to LEO)
          The New Hampshire primary isn't held
          in New Hampshire anymore?

                    TOBY
          You can't win the New Hampshire primary.

                    BARTLET
          I'm gonna win the New Hampshire primary.

                    TOBY
          Which is why you can't win it.

                    JOSH
          You're incredibly popular in this state.

                    SAM
          You're a Democrat who was elected with
          69% of the vote, that's unheard of.

                    TOBY
          There's no way you can exceed
          expectations, all you can hope for is an
          "as expected" and there's the possibility
          you can embarrass yourself.

                    BARTLET
          I appreciate that, thanks.

                    JOSH
          Toby meant in the polls.

                                        (CONTINUED)

> BARTLET
> I know what he meant.

> TOBY
> So Hoynes will be in a fight with Wiley
> for a strong second place finish in New
> Hampshire, meantime we're gonna be in
> South Carolina and we're gonna be the
> only ones there.

> BARTLET
> We're not gonna beat Hoynes in South
> Carolina.

> TOBY
> We don't have to beat Hoynes in
> South Carolina.

> C.J.
> We just have to beat Wiley.

> BARTLET
>   (beat--then to LEO)
> Wiley's gonna drop out after South
> Carolina?

> LEO
> If he doesn't finish higher than third.

> BARTLET
> Are we gonna get his endorsement?

> LEO
> We're gonna get his money, that's for
> sure.

> BARTLET
> It's for sure?

> LEO
> Josh thinks it is.

> BARTLET
> Which one is Josh?

> JOSH
> I am.

> BARTLET
> Okay.

(CONTINUED)

2-27 CONTINUED: (4)

                    TOBY
So we finish second in South Carolina, we
pick up some steam, some endorsements,
mostly some money going into South
Dakota, Vermont and Maine--

                    SAM
--where we'll come away with a split,
maybe better, and now the prohibitive
nominee for the Democratic nomination
has lost three of the first seven
contests--

                    C.J.
--half the actual primaries--

                    SAM
--leading into Super Tuesday.

                    JOSH
Hoynes'll win the South, we'll take the
North and the Pacific Northwest.

                    TOBY
This race will be decided a week later in
Illinois.

                    C.J.
Illinois is gonna be High Noon.

                    LEO
Sam, if we win in Illinois, do we have a
shot at California and New York?

                    SAM
If we win in Illinois we're gonna run the
table.

                    BARTLET
Well that's it then. And we've saved
people the trouble of voting. What's
next?

                    JOSH
Our, our point is that it's--

                    BARTLET
I understood the point. We're going to
South Carolina to set up Illinois. When I
ask "What's next," it means I'm ready to
move on to other things. So. What's next?

                                        (CONTINUED)

> LEO
> We're done.

> BARTLET
> Fantastic.

BARTLET gets up and leaves...

> JOSH
> Well, I feel bathed in the warm embrace
> of the candidate, Leo.

> LEO
> He's really very easy to like once you
> get to know him.

> JOSH
> How many people get that far?

> LEO
> Not that many.

> JOSH
> Okay.

JOSH walks through the bullpen to his tiny office on the
perimeter. Inside the office, DONNA is standing at a desk and
answering the phone.

> DONNA
> (into phone)
> Josh Lyman.
> (listens)
> Uh, no, he's not available right now.
> (listens)
> Uh, this afternoon he's got a media
> session and then four o'clock with
> finance. If you leave your name, I can
> give Josh the message when he gets back.

JOSH is standing in front of DONNA watching all this with
curiosity.

> DONNA
> (into phone)
> Thank you very much.

DONNA hangs up the phone.

> JOSH
> Hi.

(CONTINUED)

2-27 CONTINUED: (6)

> DONNA
> Hi.

> JOSH
> Who are you?

> DONNA
> I'm Donna Moss, who are you?

> JOSH
> I'm Josh Lyman.

> DONNA
> Ahhhhh.

> JOSH
> Yesssss.

> DONNA
> I'm your new assistant.

> JOSH
> Did I have an old assistant?

> DONNA
> Maybe not.

> JOSH
> Who are you?

> DONNA
> I'm Donna Moss. I came in to volunteer
> and the woman assigned me to you?

> JOSH
> Which woman?

> DONNA
> Betsy.

> JOSH
> You mean Margaret?

> DONNA
> Yes.

> JOSH
> Who are you?

> DONNA
> I'm Donna Moss, I'll be working as
> your assistant.

(CONTINUED)

> JOSH
> I'm gonna talk to Margaret.

> DONNA
> Actually, Josh?

> JOSH
> Yeah?

> DONNA
> When I said I was assigned to you?

> JOSH
> Yeah?

> DONNA
> I may have been over-stating it a little.

> JOSH
>   (beat)
> Who are you?

DONNA falls in step with JOSH as he walks away.

> DONNA
> I'm Donna Moss. I drove here from
> Madison, Wisconsin.

> JOSH
> When did your boyfriend break up with
> you?

> DONNA
>   (pause)
> What makes you think my boyfriend broke
> up with me?

> JOSH
> Well, you're too old for your parents to
> have kicked you out of the house.

> DONNA
> I'm here because I want to work for
> Bartlet. I'm a college graduate with a
> degree in political science and
> government.

> JOSH
> Where did you graduate?

> DONNA
> Hm?

(CONTINUED)

2-27 CONTINUED: (8)

                    JOSH
Where did you graduate?

                    DONNA
Okay, when I said I graduated?

                    JOSH
Yeah?

                    DONNA
I may have been over-stating a little.

                    JOSH
Look--

                    DONNA
I... I was a couple of credits short.

                    JOSH
         (pause)
From where?

                    DONNA
University of Wisconsin.

                    JOSH
And you majored in Political Science and
Government.

                    DONNA
And, uh, Sociology and Psychology.

                    JOSH
Uh huh--

                    DONNA
And Biology for a while. With a minor in
French.

                    JOSH
Okay--

                    DONNA
And, uh, drama.

                    JOSH
You had five majors and two minors in
four years?

                    DONNA
Two years.

They step into--

2-28 **INT. JOSH'S (CAMPAIGN) OFFICE - CONTINUOUS**   2-28

    --where JOSH stands behind his desk and DONNA stands in front
of it.

> JOSH
> Uh, listen--

> DONNA
> I had to drop out.
>   (pause)
> I had to drop out.

> JOSH
> Your boyfriend was older than you?

> DONNA
> I think that question's of a personal
> nature.

> JOSH
> Donna, you were just at my desk, reading
> my calendar, answering my phone and
> hoping I wouldn't notice that I never
> hired you. Your boyfriend was older?

> DONNA
> Yes.

> JOSH
> Law student.

> DONNA
> Medical student.

JOSH sits.

> JOSH
> And the idea was you drop out and pay the
> bills till he's done with his residency.

> DONNA
> Yes.

> JOSH
> And did you?

> DONNA
> Yes.

> JOSH
> And why did Dr. Freeride break up with
> you?

(CONTINUED)

2-28 CONTINUED:

                       DONNA
       What makes you think he broke up with me?

DONNA sits. JOSH just looks at DONNA...

                       JOSH
       Donna, this is a campaign for the
       presidency and there's nothing I take
       more seriously than that. This can't be a
       place for people to come to find their
       confidence and start over.

                       DONNA
         (pause)
       Why not?

                       JOSH
       I'm sorry?

                       DONNA
       Why can't it be those things?

                       JOSH
         (pause)
       Because--

                       DONNA
       Is it gonna interfere with my typing?

                       JOSH
         (pause)
       Donna, we're picking up today and going
       to South Carolina. If you want to stay in
       the Manchester office--

                       DONNA
       I want to come to Charleston.

                       JOSH
       I can't carry you, Donna. I got a lot of
       guys out there not making the trip.

                       DONNA
       I'll pay my own way.

                       JOSH
       With what?

                       DONNA
       I'll sleep on the floor, I'll sell my
       car. Eventually you're gonna put me on
       salary.

                               (CONTINUED)

JOSH is looking at DONNA...

                    JOSH
          Donna--

                    DONNA
               (pause)
          Look, I think I can be good at this. I
          think you might find me valuable.

The PHONE RINGS...JOSH is looking at DONNA...it RINGS again...

                    JOSH
               (re: the phone)
          Go ahead.

DONNA picks up the phone--

                    DONNA
               (into phone)
          Bartlet for America, Josh Lyman's office.
               (listens)
          Yes.
               (listens)
          I think I'm gonna have somebody from the
          press office get back to you if it
          relates to--
               (listens)
          Yes.

JOSH takes off his laminated ID tag on a chain that hangs
around his neck and hands it to DONNA.

                    DONNA
               (into phone)
          Uh, yes... yes... yes.

DONNA holds the tag in her hand, trying not to show that it's
the first piece of jewelry anyone's ever given her.

                                        CUT TO:

2-29 **INT. CORRIDOR OUTSIDE O.R. - EARLY MORNING**   2-29

DONNA is watching the operation through the glass, her hand
absently holding the White House ID tag around her neck.

                    SURGEON (V.O.)
          Suction.

                                        (CONTINUED)

2-29 CONTINUED:

                    NURSE (V.O.)
          Pressure is holding 131-65.

                                        FADE TO BLACK

                <u>END OF ACT THREE</u>

ACT FOUR

FADE IN:

2-30 **EXT./EST. WHITE HOUSE - DAY**   2-30

TITLE:
          Tuesday, 8:46 a.m.

2-31 **INT. SAM'S OFFICE - MORNING**   2-31

SAM's at his desk when C.J. sticks her head in, knocks on the
door once, and says--

                    C.J.
          Hey, Spanky.

SAM looks up...

                    SAM
               (beat)
          Oh God, what'd I do?

                    C.J.
          Take a walk with me, would you?

SAM gets up and follows C.J. out into--

2-32 **INT. COMMUNICATIONS BULLPEN/CORRIDOR - CONTINUOUS**   2-32

--where they start heading toward the Press Briefing Room.

                    C.J.
          They're taking him off bypass now.

                    SAM
          Yeah, I just heard, I'm gonna head to the
          hospital.

                    C.J.
          You did well on the morning shows.

                    SAM
          Thanks.

                    C.J.
          I told Leo the reason I didn't want to do
          it was it didn't feel right with Josh
          still in surgery.

                    SAM
          Yeah.

                                        (CONTINUED)

2-32 CONTINUED:

They go through the doors and into--

2-33 **INT. ANOTHER CORRIDOR - CONTINUOUS**   2-33

                         C.J.
          You know what the real reason was?

                         SAM
          The real reason?

                         C.J.
          Yeah.

                         SAM
          No.

                         C.J.
          I think you do.

                         SAM
               (pause)
          Listen, C.J.....

                         C.J.
               (calling out)
          Suzanne?

                         SUZANNE
          Right.

                         C.J.
          The real reason I couldn't go on the
          morning shows and give a first-hand
          account of what happened is that I
          couldn't <u>remember</u> what happened.

SUZANNE gets on the PA--

                         SUZANNE
               (into PA)
          Take your seats.

                         C.J.
          I remember walking out of the building. I
          remember somebody knocking me down. I
          know my necklace came off and I know a
          police car window exploded over my head.
          All night long I've been doing my press
          briefings using notes from other people's
          accounts.
               (beat)
                    (MORE)

(CONTINUED)

2-33 CONTINUED:

      C.J. (cont'd)
But it's morning now and I listened to
you on the morning shows and I know what
happened.

     SAM
C.J.--

      C.J.
Sam, I think you have my necklace.

     SAM
  (pause)
I didn't want you to feel beholden to me.
I didn't want it to be like an episode of
I Dream of Jeannie where now you get to
save <u>my</u> life and the time/space
continuum--

      C.J.
Sam--

     SAM
--or following me around with coconut
oil and hot towels--

      C.J.
Sam. I don't--coconut oil?

     SAM
I'm just saying--

      C.J.
Sam, I don't feel beholden to you.

     SAM
  (pause)
Why not? I saved your life.

      C.J.
Can I have my necklace back.

SAM reaches in his pocket and hands C.J. her necklace.

      C.J.
Thank you.

     SAM
I'll be in my office.

SAM starts to head back...

      C.J.
Sam.

          (CONTINUED)

2-33 CONTINUED: (2)   2-33

                        SAM
        Yeah.

                        C.J.
        Were you scared?

                        SAM
        Yeah.

                        C.J.
        Me too.
                (pause)
        Thanks.

SAM turns and goes...C.J. watches him, smiles, and heads into--

2-34 **INT. PRESS BRIEFING ROOM - CONTINUOUS**   2-34

--where the PRESS is coming to order.

                        C.J. (O.S.)
        Good morning. We have an update and I can
        give you a ballistics report so let's get
        started.

                                                   CUT TO:

2-35 **EXT. GEORGE WASHINGTON HOSPITAL - MORNING**   2-35

The CROWD, the PRESS, the POLICE, none of it has died down
any. BUTTERFIELD is standing out there as TOBY comes along...

                        TOBY
        Ron?

                        BUTTERFIELD
        Hey Toby. I heard they're about to take
        him off bypass.

                        TOBY
        Pretty soon, yeah. Listen, can I talk to
        you for a second?

                        BUTTERFIELD
        Yeah. Sergeant, I want those people on
        that corner backed up another 200 feet.

                        SERGEANT
        Yes sir.

                        BUTTERFIELD
        And if they move in again, handcuff 'em
        to a parking meter.

                                              (CONTINUED)

> TOBY
> How's your hand?

> BUTTERFIELD
> It's fine.

> TOBY
> You should be home.

> BUTTERFIELD
> What's on your mind?

> TOBY
> C.J.'s starting to get some questions
> about why the President's exit wasn't
> covered in Rosslyn.

> BUTTERFIELD
> The Secret Service doesn't comment on
> procedure.

> TOBY
> Yeah.
> (beat)
> Ron, a few weeks after the President was
> sworn in, you got a memo about his
> protection.

> BUTTERFIELD
> Yeah.

> TOBY
> It said he wanted to enter and exit in
> the open air. He didn't like the feeling
> of traveling around in an armored tank.

> BUTTERFIELD
> Yeah.

> TOBY
> Specifically it said he wouldn't use the
> tent or the canopy anymore.

> BUTTERFIELD
> Yeah.

> TOBY
> I wrote that memo. And the President
> signed it at my urging.

> BUTTERFIELD
> I know.

(CONTINUED)

2-35 CONTINUED: (2)

                    TOBY
          Ron, I don't think it's right that the
          Secret Service be blamed for what
          happened last night. I want the Treasury
          Department to hand over my memo to the
          press.

                    BUTTERFIELD
          No, we can't do that.

                    TOBY
          There are gonna be a lot of questions.

                    BUTTERFIELD
          There are always a lot of questions.

                    TOBY
          Ron--

                    BUTTERFIELD
          Don't worry about it, Toby.

                    TOBY
          It's not right. You're the guys- Look at
          your hand.

                    BUTTERFIELD
          My hand is fine.

                    TOBY
          Your hand is not fine.

                    BUTTERFIELD
          Toby--

                    TOBY
          Lemme go over there and tell 'em it was
          my fault.

                    BUTTERFIELD
          It wasn't your fault.

                    TOBY
          Ron--

                    BUTTERFIELD
          It wasn't your fault, it wasn't Gina's
          fault, it wasn't Charlie's fault, it
          wasn't anybody's fault, Toby, it was an
          act of madmen, you think a tent was gonna
          stop 'em?
                    (beat)
          We got the President in the car, we got
                    (MORE)

                                        (CONTINUED)

2-35 CONTINUED: (3)

> BUTTERFIELD (cont'd)
> Zoey in the car, and at 150 yards and
> five stories up, the shooters were down
> 9.2 seconds after the first shot was
> fired.
> (beat)
> I would never let you not let me
> protect the President. You tell us you
> don't like something, we figure out
> something else. It was an act of madmen.
> (beat)
> Anyway, the Secret Service doesn't
> comment on procedure.

> TOBY
> (pause)
> Okay.
> (pause)
> Good job last night.

> BUTTERFIELD
> Thank you.

CUT TO:

2-36 **INT. PRESS BRIEFING ROOM - MORNING**   2-36

C.J.'s in the middle of her briefing.

> C.J.
> Secret Service agents carry a weapon
> called a 357 Sig Sauer. The agents on the
> roof shot the two gunmen with .726
> caliber rifles that are referred to as
> JAR, which believe it or not stands for
> Just Another Rifle, they're made
> specifically and exclusively for the
> Secret Service.

LEO's been watching from the back of the room. As C.J.
continues, he nods to MARGARET, who steps down and taps DANNY
on the shoulder and whispers something to him. DANNY gets up
and follows MARGARET back to LEO.

C.J. stops for a moment...

> C.J.
> I wanted to mention something:

> DANNY
> Leo--

LEO stops DANNY mid-sentence so he can listen to C.J.'s
editorial. DANNY also turns his attention to C.J.

(CONTINUED)

2-36 CONTINUED:

> C.J.
> This is our fifth press briefing since
> midnight, and obviously there's one story
> that's going to be dominating the news
> around the world for the next few days
> and it would be easy to think that
> President Bartlet, Joshua Lyman and
> Stephanie Abbott were the only people who
> were victims of a gun crime last night.
> They weren't. Mark Davis and Sheila Evans
> of Philadelphia were killed by a gun last
> night. He was a biology teacher and she
> was a nursing student. Tina Bishop and
> Belinda Larkin were killed with a gun
> last night. They were twelve. There were
> 36 homicides last night. 480 sexual
> assaults, 3411 robberies, 3685 aggravated
> assaults. All at gunpoint. And if anyone
> thinks those crimes could've been
> prevented if the victims themselves had
> been carrying guns, I'd only remind you
> that the President of the United States
> was shot last night while surrounded by
> the best trained armed guards in the
> history of the world
> (beat)
> Back to the briefing.

> DANNY
> She's good.

> LEO
> Yes she is.

> C.J.
> The bullet that hit the President was a
> 9mm flat point. The FMJ or Full Metal
> Jacket--

> DANNY
> Leo--

> LEO
> I'm going to the hospital, why don't you
> ride with me.

DANNY follows LEO out.

> SAM (V.O.)
> We're starting to get some exit polling
> in Stark County and Rock Island.

CUT TO:

2-37 **INT. HOTEL SUITE - NIGHT**   2-37

The suite is large and overpopulated with people, TV monitors, room service carts and fax machines. The people, who are gathered in different clumps around the suite, include SAM, TOBY, C.J., LEO, JOSH, ABBEY and BARTLET. The TV monitors are all showing network newscasts.

                    LEO
          How good?

TITLE:

                    Sheraton Centre Hotel
                    Chicago, Illinois

                    SAM
          We're running at 53 to 58 with the
          undecideds from 72 hours ago in the 12th,
          14th and 15th--

                    LEO
          That's the money.

                    SAM
          --DeWitt County, Cumberland...

JOSH is to the side on his cell phone.

                    LEO
          Josh.

                    JOSH
          Yeah.

                    LEO
          Who you talking to?

                    JOSH
          I'm talking to nobody, there's no one at
          my house.

                    LEO
          What's going on?

                    JOSH
          Nothing. My dad had his chemo today,
          these exit polls are gonna cheer him up.

JOSH hangs up his cell phone.

                    LEO
          Sam says we got the 72 hour undecideds
          in the 14th and 15th.

                                        (CONTINUED)

2-37 CONTINUED:

ABBEY comes up to them--

>   ABBEY
> Leo, is there any food in this room
> that isn't fried?

>   LEO
> Well if there is, let's get rid of it.

>   ABBEY
> I'm not kidding.

>   LEO
> There's good exits from Stark County and
> Rock Island.

>   ABBEY
> How good?

>   LEO
> Good.

BARTLET comes out of a bedroom with several sheets of paper.

>   BARTLET
> Leo, what the hell is this?

>   JOSH
> That's Sam's draft of your victory
> remarks, Governor.

>   BARTLET
>   (to LEO)
> "I congratulate my opponent on a
> well-fought campaign in Illinois"?

>   LEO
> You don't want to congratulate him?

>   BARTLET
> Yes, I want to congratulate him, but I'd
> like to call him by his name. Are we back
> to this crap again?

>   JOSH
> Governor, we can--

>   BARTLET
> Leo, I want to go over this whole thing
> with you.

BARTLET walks away...

(CONTINUED)

                    LEO
Excuse me.

LEO follows after BARTLET. JOSH and ABBEY stand alone.

                 BARTLET (O.S.)
It's the exact same crap all over again.
It's amateur hour. Damn student--

                 ABBEY
You can say it, you know. It's not like I
haven't heard it before.

                 JOSH
Your husband's a real sonofabitch, Mrs.
Bartlet.

                 ABBEY
He doesn't like being handled.

                 JOSH
Well, I think if he looked around, he'd
see that nobody has handled him.

                 ABBEY
He's not ready yet, Josh. He's terrified.

                 JOSH
Is he gonna <u>be</u> ready?

                 ABBEY
You bet your ass he will.
    (beat)
In the meantime, you wanna kick
something, kick me.

All of a sudden SAM shouts across the room to TOBY--

                 SAM
Toby!

                 TOBY
Got it.

                 C.J.
Here it comes.

The volume is bumped up on the monitor--

(CONTINUED)

> TV ANCHOR #3
> *...with 17% of the precincts reporting,*
> *we are now ready to call the Illinois*
> *Primary for former New Hampshire Governor*
> *Jed Bartlet...*

--but everything after "Governor" was drowned out by the
cheering. C.J. comes over to JOSH and gives him a hug.

> JOSH
> Hit the music.

> TV ANCHOR #3
> *...putting him at the top in what can*
> *only be described as a remarkable*
> *victory.*

JOSH POINTS to SAM, who silently MOUTHS the words "Thank you."
LEO comes back over to JOSH and gives him a hug.

> LEO
> Hey, way to go. Now let's get to
> California.

> JOSH
> Nice job.

Somebody's turned up "Celebration" on a tape deck. It only
takes a few moments before everyone starts singing and dancing
to the music.

DONNA has walked over to JOSH--

> JOSH
> Leo.

> DONNA
> Josh.

> JOSH
> Leo, we gotta replace this music.
> (calling out)
> We gotta replace it with some Doobie
> Brothers.

> DONNA
> Josh.

> JOSH
> We gotta get happy, Donna. You just won
> the Illinois primary.

(CONTINUED)

2-37 CONTINUED: (4)

>   DONNA
> No. Josh.

>   JOSH
> Come dance with me.

>   DONNA
> No. Josh, your father died.

>   TV ANCHOR #3
> *...there's a lot of very happy Bartlet*
> *supporters. We are told the candidate is*
> *in his suite refining his remarks. He's*
> *due to make an appearance here any*
> *moment. Just a little under an hour ago*
> *now, this...*

And as the celebration continues in the background, DONNA
stares at JOSH, unable to speak. They stand there a long
moment before we

                                        CUT TO:

2-38 **INT. AIRPORT LOUNGE - NIGHT**   2-38

JOSH is sitting by himself. No suitcase. No newspaper.

>   PA (V.O.)
> Welcome to O'Hare International Airport.
> We'd like to remind you this is a smoke-
> free airport.

A figure walks by him that catches his attention as peculiar.
He looks and sees that it was a man in a dark suit who's now
planted himself by a pillar about 20 feet away. Then he sees
ANOTHER MAN in a dark suit stake out a position near-by. And
JOSH notices the wire coming out of his collar and sticking in
his ear.

>   BARTLET
> Josh?

And now JOSH turns back in the other direction to see BARTLET
standing right next to him.

>   JOSH
>   (pause)
> Governor....

>   BARTLET
>   (pause)
> Your father died, Josh, I can't believe
> it.

                                        (CONTINUED)

2-38 CONTINUED:

                         JOSH
          Yeah. Governor you, you shouldn't be
          here.

                         BARTLET
          What happened?

                         PA (V.O.)
          Flight leaving for St. Louis.

                         JOSH
          He went in for his chemotherapy and he
          unexpectedly developed what's called a
          pulmonary embolism, it's a--

                         BARTLET
          It's a blood clot.

                         JOSH
          Yeah. It went to his heart and there was
          cardiac arrest.

                         BARTLET
          Yeah.
               (pause)
          Yeah.

                         JOSH
          Governor, you should, you should really
          get back to the ballroom so you can get
          on a plane and get to California.

                         BARTLET
          He was a lawyer?

                         JOSH
          Yeah. A litigator.

                         BARTLET
          Did he like that you were in politics?

                         JOSH
               (pause)
          I think he would've liked grandchildren
          more.

                         BARTLET
               (smiles)
          He would've.

                         JOSH
               (pause)
          He liked that I was working for you.
                         (MORE)

                                        (CONTINUED)

2-38 CONTINUED: (2)

                    JOSH (cont'd)
He liked that we were starting to do
well. He would've liked tonight.
        (beat)
At least his friends and neighbors'll be
spared all the, you know--

            BARTLET
He'd been doing some bragging right now?

            JOSH
Yeah. And your name wouldn't have come
up, by the way. "My son won the Illinois
primary tonight."
        (beat)
Three more hours and he would have been
able to say that. He'd have been proud.

            BARTLET
He was already. Trust me, Josh, I'm a
father. He was already.

            JOSH
        (pause)
I appreciate that Governor. You should
really get back to the hotel.

            BARTLET
No.

            JOSH
        (beat)
Sir, not that I don't appreciate your
having come down here, but there's a
ballroom full of people waiting for a
victory speech.

            BARTLET
They'll wait.

            JOSH
Yeah they will, but the people watching
television won't.

            BARTLET
I've been a real jackass to you, Josh.

            JOSH
        (pause)
Well...

            BARTLET
To everybody. Toby Ziegler, C.J. Cregg,
Sam Seaborn...

                                    (CONTINUED)

                              JOSH
          Yeah.

                              BARTLET
          Don't think I don't know what you gave up
          to work for this campaign. And don't
          think I don't know your value. And I'll
          never make you think I don't again.
                    (beat)
          And you gotta be a little impressed I got
          those names right just now.

BARTLET smiles...then JOSH does...

                              PA (V.O.)
          Delta Airlines Flight 175 for Kennedy
          International now boarding at Gate 56.

                              JOSH
          They're calling my flight.

                              BARTLET
          You want me to go with you?

                              JOSH
          Go with me?

                              BARTLET
          Maybe you want some company on the plane.
          I'll get a ticket and go with you.

JOSH looks around the airport terminal in exasperation, not
knowing whether to kiss this man or beat him with a two-by-
four.

                              JOSH
                    (finally)
          Governor, California! You have to go to
          the ballroom and give a victory speech in
          primetime, and go to California.

                              BARTLET
          I guess you're right.

                              JOSH
          You _guess_ I'm right? Listen to me,
          Governor, if you don't lose this election
          it isn't gonna be because you didn't try
          hard enough.
                    (pause)
          But it was nice of you to ask, thank you,
          I appreciate it.

                                              (CONTINUED)

2-38 CONTINUED: (4)

> PA (V.O.)
> Final boarding for Delta Airlines, Flight
> 175 to Kennedy International, now
> boarding at Gate 56.

> BARTLET
> They're calling your flight.

JOSH nods and heads off. He turns around to see BARTLET
watching him go. LEO, who's been there the whole time, joins
BARTLET.

> LEO
> Is he gonna be alright?

> BARTLET
> He is gonna be fine.

> LEO
> Good.

> BARTLET
> Leo?

> LEO
> Yeah.

> BARTLET
> I'm ready.

We stay on their backs as they walk up the center terminal
corridor and into the distance...

...the sound of 20,000 people cheering fades up.

> BARTLET
> *"Tonight, what began at the Commons in*
> *Concord, Massachusetts as an alliance of*
> *farmers and workers, of cobblers and*
> *tinsmiths, of statesmen and students,*
> *of mothers and wives, of men and boys,*
> *lives two centuries later as America.*
> *My name is Josiah Bartlet, and I accept*
> *your nomination for the Presidency of the*
> *United States."*

The cheering becomes deafening before it's pierced by--

> HOLBROOK (V.O.)
> Josh.
> (beat)
> Josh.

(CONTINUED)

2-38 CONTINUED: (5)   2-38

The sound of the name isn't pleading, just firm, as we

                                                    CUT TO:

2-39 **INT. RECOVERY ROOM - DAY**   2-39

BARTLET and LEO stand at JOSH's bed with a couple of doctors
and nurses..

                        DOCTOR
            Josh. Wake up. It's okay, I want you
            to wake up.

JOSH opens his eyes. His expression is oddly undistressed,
almost blank. It's hard to say if he knows where he is or
what's happened or what was a dream and what wasn't.

It's silent for a long moment, but in no way tense.

JOSH tries to say something, but it's barely audible.

                        BARTLET
            I couldn't hear you, Josh.

BARTLET leans closer to him and JOSH tries again...

                        LEO
            What'd he say?

                        BARTLET
                (pause)
            He said "What's next."

                                                FADE TO BLACK

                        END OF SHOW

17 PEOPLE

Directed by Alex Graves

NBC gives us a lot of money to do the show. The problem is it costs us <u>quite</u> a lot of money to do the show, so Warner Bros. comes up with the rest in deficit financing. They lose a significant amount of money every time we make an episode in the hope that we'll make enough episodes (about 100) to sell the show into syndication at which point they hope the episodes will be worth more than what they spent and that's how they make a living. But until (and if) that happens, they lose a lot of money per episode.

When we stay on budget.

Which we've never done.

The West Wing is an expensive show to make. Our set is bigger than any two other sets combined, we take four trips a year to D.C. to shoot locations, we hire sought after guest cast, Air Force One has to look like Air Force One, but mostly it takes us a little longer to shoot and that means overtime and that's the real money.

So the word came down from Warner Bros. that some budget overruns had to be made up and that for the next episode I write we should use no guest cast, no locations, no new sets, no extras and no film.

In other words, I got to write a play. It was time for Bartlet to start coming clean about his MS. Alex Graves directed (ironically, giving us the most visual opening we've ever had on the show) and Richard Schiff tore up even the highest expectations.

17 People

<u>TEASER</u>

We end "Previously on *The West Wing*" with the shot from "The Stackhouse Filibuster" of Toby alone in his office, bouncing the ball against the wall.

We FADE TO BLACK for the title card, and

From the BLACK we HEAR--

--the ball bouncing against the wall.

And again.

FADE IN:

1   **INT. TOBY'S OFFICE - NIGHT**   1

TITLE:
The Same Night

TOBY's working on something in his head as he methodically bounces the ball against the wall.

Two bounces.

Three.

Then he catches the ball and holds it for a long moment...

Then he bounces it again and we

FADE OUT.

TITLE:
Two Nights Later

FADE IN:

2   **INT. TOBY'S OFFICE - NIGHT**   2

A crumpled piece of paper banks into a small trash can. Then another one.

FADE OUT.

TITLE:
Two Nights After That

(CONTINUED)

2   CONTINUED: 2

FADE IN:

3   **INT. TOBY'S OFFICE - NIGHT**   3

TOBY's typing away at his computer, working off some reference
material on his desk. But then a nagging thought distracts him
and he stops. He looks out his window, across the darkened and
unpopulated bullpen and Roosevelt Room and sees that a light
is on in Leo's office. What the hell. He gets up and we--

                                                            CUT TO:

4   **INT. LEO'S OFFICE - NIGHT**   4

LEO's working at his desk as TOBY appears in the doorway.

                         TOBY
            Leo?

                         LEO
            Hey, I didn't know you were still here.

                         TOBY
            Yeah.

                         LEO
            What's goin' on?

                         TOBY
            I've been thinking about why Hoynes
            volunteered to slap down big oil.

                         LEO
            It was his polling information.

                         TOBY
            Yeah, but why did he put the poll in the
            field at all is what I'm saying.

                         LEO
            John Hoynes is an egomaniac who needs to
            be told what people think of him.

                         TOBY
            Well that's pretty unusual for
            Washington.

                         LEO
            Yeah.

                                                        (CONTINUED)

4   CONTINUED: 4

> TOBY
> Leo, has there been a discussion in some
> room, someplace, anywhere on any level,
> about Hoynes being dropped from the
> ticket in 2002?

> LEO
> No.

> TOBY
> You sure?

> LEO
> Yeah.

> TOBY
> 'Cause I thought maybe it was an
> Eisenhower/Nixon--

> LEO
> No. Toby, I wouldn't give it a lot of
> thought.

> TOBY
> Okay.

                                                        FADE OUT.

TITLE:
                       The Next Night

And we HEAR the bouncing ball.

FADE IN:

5   **INT. TOBY'S OFFICE - NIGHT**   5

The wheels are still turning...

                                                        FADE OUT.

TITLE:
                       The Next Morning

FADE IN:

6   **INT. LEO'S OFFICE/MARGARET'S OFFICE - EARLY MORNING**   6

As LEO flicks a light switch, revealing TOBY sitting there and
waiting.

> TOBY
> Hey.

                                                        (CONTINUED)

6   CONTINUED: 6

                    LEO
          Scared the hell outa me.

                    TOBY
          The poll that Hoynes put in the field--

                    LEO
          Hoynes is gonna run for President one
          day, why shouldn't he do his own polling?

                    TOBY
          He's gonna run for President six years
          from now, what good does last week's do?

                    LEO
          I really don't know.

                    TOBY
          Okay.

                                              FADE OUT.

TITLE:

                    That Night

From the BLACK we HEAR

                    TOBY
          It's never happened before, right?

FADE IN:

7   **INT. LEO'S OFFICE - NIGHT**   7

TOBY stands in his overcoat, ready to go home.

                    LEO
          No.

                    TOBY
          A Vice President would never challenge a
          sitting President for the nomination.

                    LEO
          Of course not.

                    TOBY
          You see his itinerary for the weekend?

                    LEO
          Who?

                                              (CONTINUED)

7   CONTINUED: 7

> ### TOBY
> The Vice President.
>
> ### LEO
> I don't keep tabs on John--
>
> ### TOBY
> He's giving a speech at a semi-conductor
> plant. The title of the speech is "Clean
> Air Industry in the High Tech Corridor of
> the Industrial Northeast."
>
> ### LEO
> Where?
>
> ### TOBY
> Nashua, New Hampshire.

And TOBY's got LEO's attention...

> ### LEO
> (pause)
> Toby, nobody, and particularly not
> Hoynes, would be naive enough...What I
> mean to say is if he's going to New
> Hampshire for the reason you're thinking,
> he would mask it with something, it
> wouldn't be an official trip, he'd make
> up a benign excuse to be up there.
>
> ### TOBY
> I know.
>
> ### LEO
> So why are you concerned about the
> speech?
>
> ### TOBY
> Because it comes in the middle of a three
> day camping trip to Killington.

TOBY's staring straight at LEO...

> ### TOBY
> (pause)
> Why does Hoynes think the President isn't
> gonna run again?

And we HEAR the bouncing ball.

TOBY has him in check...

                                              (CONTINUED)

7   CONTINUED: (2)   7

                         TOBY
                       (pause)
                What's going on, Leo?

The two of them keep staring at each other...

and staring...

and staring...

...and we

                                              SMASH CUT TO:

MAIN TITLES

                        <u>END OF TEASER</u>

ACT ONE

FADE IN:

8   **EXT./EST. THE WHITE HOUSE - NIGHT**   8

TITLE:

The West Wing
11:35 PM

CUT TO:

9   **INT. THE OVAL OFFICE - NIGHT**   9

BARTLET's at his desk reading a briefing book. LEO comes in from his office.

>   LEO
> Excuse me, Mr. President.

>   BARTLET
> I closed the embassies in Tanzania and
> Brussels.

>   LEO
> What about domestic?

>   BARTLET
> I don't have to make that call yet.

>   LEO
> How much time do you have?

>   BARTLET
> About an hour.

>   LEO
> Mr. President, I've got Toby waiting in
> his office right now.

>   BARTLET
> Why?

>   LEO
> We've gotta tell him.

>   BARTLET
> Tell him what?

LEO doesn't say anything, and now, for the first time, BARTLET lifts his head up from his briefing book...

(CONTINUED)

9   CONTINUED:

                              LEO
               We've gotta tell him.

                            BARTLET
               What happened?

                              LEO
               He got curious when Hoynes volunteered to
               step in for Bill Trotter, and then more
               curious when he found out it was 'cause
               Hoynes put a poll in the field.

                            BARTLET
               Yeah.

                              LEO
               Now he's camping in Killington, Vermont
               with a quick stop--

                            BARTLET
               Come on--

                              LEO
               --in New Hampshire and Toby's not an
               idiot.

                            BARTLET
               He--

                              LEO
               None of them are.

        BARTLET and LEO are looking at each other...

                            BARTLET
                 (pause)
               He scheduled a trip to New Hampshire?

                              LEO
               High Tech corridor of the Northeast.

                            BARTLET
               Yeah, thanks to who?

                              LEO
               What does that matter right now?

        BARTLET closes the briefing book...thinks...then picks up the
        briefing book and *slams* it down on his desk...

                              LEO
               I think you gotta see this as an
               opportunity.

                                                        (CONTINUED)

9   CONTINUED: (2)

> BARTLET
> To do what?

> LEO
> To gauge reaction.

> BARTLET
> You think Toby's reaction is gonna be the
> same as the public's?

> LEO
> I meant the staff.

> BARTLET
> Which will be?

> LEO
> I'm sorry, sir?

> BARTLET
> The staff's reaction will be what?

> LEO
> I don't know. Shock. Betrayal, confusion,
> concern about our future. I don't know.

> BARTLET
> What do I tell him?

> LEO
> Everything.

> BARTLET
> (pause)
> Go get him.

> LEO
> Yes sir.

LEO exits.

BARTLET's left alone...

> BARTLET
> Now it starts.

                CUT TO:

10   **INT. SAM'S OFFICE - NIGHT**   10

SAM and JOSH are both sitting and reading copies of a brief
speech.

             (CONTINUED)

10   CONTINUED:

                          SAM
              Hm.

                          JOSH
              Yes.

SAM finishes first and puts the speech down.

                          SAM
              Well.

Then JOSH finishes...

                          JOSH
              You know what the problem with this is?

                          SAM
              Yes.

                          JOSH
              It's supposed to be funny.

                          SAM
              And yet?

                          JOSH
              It's not.

                          SAM
              No.

                          JOSH
              Who worked on this?

                          SAM
              Jay Breech, Janet Lippman, Andy Kyle
              worked on it a little.

                          JOSH
              You know what they did?

                          SAM
              Yeah.

                          JOSH
              They forgot to bring the funny.

                          SAM
              Yeah.

                          JOSH
              How much time do we have?

                                        (CONTINUED)

10   CONTINUED: (2)

                         SAM
          I want to show it to him within the hour.

JOSH gets up, opens the door and walks out into--

11   **INT. COMMUNICATIONS BULLPEN - CONTINUOUS**   11

--where he stands in TOBY's open doorway. TOBY's sitting at
his desk.

                         JOSH
          Toby.

                         TOBY
          Yeah.

                         JOSH
          Sam and I are gonna stay and punch up
          some of the jokes for the Correspondents'
          Dinner.

                         TOBY
          Yeah, I read it.

                         JOSH
          They forgot the funny.

                         TOBY
          Yeah.

                         JOSH
          You want to stay?

                         TOBY
          Where are you gonna be?

                         JOSH
          We'll find a place.

                         TOBY
          I'll hook up with you in a little bit.

                         JOSH
          What's goin' on?

LEO comes by--

                         LEO
          Nothing.

TOBY gets up from his desk and follows LEO out of the bullpen.
JOSH watches them go as DONNA comes through.

                                            (CONTINUED)

11   CONTINUED:
                                                                                    11

                              DONNA
                    Hello.

JOSH falls in step with her.

                              JOSH
                    How you doin'?

They walk out into--

12   **INT. CORRIDOR - CONTINUOUS**   12

                              DONNA
                    I'm doing fine.

                              JOSH
                    Did you get the flowers?

                              DONNA
                    Yes I did.

                              JOSH
                    Did you like them?

                              DONNA
                    They were very pretty.

                              JOSH
                    Do you know why I sent them?

                              DONNA
                    I know why you <u>think</u> you sent them.

                              JOSH
                    It's our anniversary.

They walk into--

13   **INT. LOBBY - CONTINUOUS**   13

The place is empty except for the SECURITY GUARD at the desk
and maybe one at the door.

                              DONNA
                    No it's not.

                              JOSH
                    I'm the sorta guy who remembers those
                    things.

                              DONNA
                    No, you're the sorta guy who sends a
                    woman flowers to be mean.
                              (MORE)

                                                              (CONTINUED)

13   CONTINUED: 13

                         DONNA (cont'd)
              You're really the only person I've ever
              met who can do that.

                         JOSH
              I'm quite something.

                         DONNA
              Yes.

                         JOSH
              I sent them to mark an occasion.

                         DONNA
              Are we really gonna do this every year?

They walk into--

14   **INT. JOSH'S BULLPEN - CONTINUOUS**   14

Also fairly deserted. Maybe one or two people working late
with desk lamps on.

                         JOSH
              For I am a man of occasion.

                         DONNA
              I started working for you in February,
              this is April and you're an idiot.

                         JOSH
              Well you started working for me once in
              February, and then you stopped for a
              while.

                         DONNA
              Yes.

                         JOSH
              Then you started working for me again in
              April. That's the one I choose to
              celebrate, 'cause that's the only one
              where you started working for me and it
              wasn't followed by your <u>not</u> working but
              rather going back to your boyfriend. And
              how, in comparison to <u>that</u> and <u>him</u> you
              can call <u>me</u> mean is simply another in a
              long series of examples of how you--

                         DONNA
              Oh shut up. Honest to God, do you ever
              get tired of the sound of your own voice?

                         JOSH
              Noooo, no, no, no.

                                        (CONTINUED)

> DONNA
> Well, where are you going now?

> JOSH
> Sam and I are gonna punch up the thing
> for tomorrow. Hey, we need funny people.

> DONNA
> Yeah?

> JOSH
> You know any? See, right there was a
> joke. It's the oldest joke in the book.

> DONNA
> I'll say.

> JOSH
> You know what, Ado Annie? I sent you
> flowers. I think what you're trying to
> say is, Why thank you, Josh, they're
> beautiful, how very thoughtful of you.
> Not many bosses would've been that
> thoughtful.

> DONNA
> Really? 'Cause I think what I was trying
> to say was shove it.

> JOSH
> Okay, well then I guessed wrong.

> DONNA
> You want me to help with the thing?

> JOSH
> Yes I do, because you are such an
> hysterically funny person, did you notice
> how I used "an" there properly?

> DONNA
> Yes I did.

> JOSH
> You crack me up.

> DONNA
> You know, there are times?

> JOSH
> Yeah?

(CONTINUED)

14   CONTINUED: (2)   14

                    DONNA
         When, to put it quite simply, I hate your
         breathing guts.

                    JOSH
So the flowers really did the trick, huh?

                    DONNA
         Oh yeah.

And they walk out as we

                                CUT TO:

15   **INT. AINSLEY'S OFFICE - NIGHT**   15

AINSLEY's working at her desk in relaxed clothes. Sweatshirt,
jeans, maybe a baseball cap turned backwards.

There's a shout from upstairs in the hallway--

                    SAM (O.S.)
         Ainsley?!

AINSLEY doesn't even look up...

Finally SAM has made his way down to her office...

                    SAM
         Ainsley?!

AINSLEY ignores it...

                    SAM
         Ainsley?

                    AINSLEY
         Hello, Sam.

                    SAM
         Didn't you hear me shouting?

                    AINSLEY
         Yes I did.

                    SAM
         And?

                    AINSLEY
         I chose to ignore it.

                    SAM
         Because?

                          (CONTINUED)

15   CONTINUED:

                         AINSLEY
             You were shouting.

                          SAM
             You're adorable.

                         AINSLEY
             Yet ill-adored.

                          SAM
             Go figure.

                         AINSLEY
             Yeah.

                          SAM
             What are you doing?

                         AINSLEY
             I'm going up to Smith College tomorrow.

                          SAM
             Why?

                         AINSLEY
             It's my alma mater.

                          SAM
             Reunion?

                         AINSLEY
             No, the Women's Studies Department is
             having a panel on resurrecting the E.R.A.

                          SAM
             Who else is on the panel?

                         AINSLEY
             Rebecca Walker, Gloria Steinem, Ann
             Coulter, Naomi Wolf--

                          SAM
             You know something like 40 percent of all
             women oppose the E.R.A. and in my entire
             life I've never met one of them.

       AINSLEY looks at SAM a moment, then extends her hand--

                         AINSLEY
             Ainsley Hayes, nice to meet you.

                          SAM
             You're not.

                                          (CONTINUED)

15   CONTINUED: (2)   15

                        AINSLEY
          Yes.

                        SAM
          You're not.

                        AINSLEY
          Yes.

                        SAM
          You're not, you're not, you're not one of
          those people.

                        AINSLEY
          Sam, if by those people you're referring
          to Episcopalians--

                        SAM
          You're going back to Smith College, the
          cradle of feminism, to argue in
          opposition to the Equal Rights Amendment?

                        AINSLEY
          And get some decent pizza, yeah.

                        SAM
          They're gonna hate you.

                        AINSLEY
          Sam, I'm a straight Republican from North
          Carolina, you don't think they hated me
          the first time around?

                        SAM
          Yeah.

                        AINSLEY
          What are you doing?

                        SAM
          I want to punch up some of the jokes for
          the Correspondents' Dinner and I'm
          looking for people left in the building
          who are funny. I couldn't find any so I
          came to you.

                        AINSLEY
          I would think, Sam, with your infectious
          sense of humor, you would have no
          trouble--

                        SAM
          You want to help me or not.

                                              (CONTINUED)

15   CONTINUED: (3)   15

> > > AINSLEY
> > I need to do this.

> > > SAM
> > We've ordered Chinese food.

> > > AINSLEY
> > Okay.

AINSLEY gets up and we

CUT TO:

16   **INT. MRS. LANDINGHAM'S OFFICE - NIGHT**   16

TOBY and LEO sit and wait. After a moment...

> > > LEO
> > > (pause)
> > Did you see the draft for the
> > Correspondents' Dinner?

> > > TOBY
> > Yeah.

> > > LEO
> > It's not funny.

> > > TOBY
> > Sam's gonna work on it.

> > > LEO
> > > (pause)
> > Toby, take it easy in there, okay?

And before TOBY can respond, the Oval Office door opens from
the inside and CHARLIE steps out.

> > > CHARLIE
> > You can go in.

TOBY and LEO get up and walk into--

17   **INT. THE OVAL OFFICE - CONTINUOUS**   17

--where BARTLET is making himself a drink.

> > > TOBY
> > Good evening, Mr. President.

> > > BARTLET
> > Hey, Toby, you want a drink?

(CONTINUED)

17   CONTINUED:

                         TOBY
          No thank you, sir, I'm fine.

                         BARTLET
          Have a drink with me.

                         TOBY
          Sure.

                         BARTLET
          Bourbon, no ice?

                         TOBY
          Thank you.

                         BARTLET
          You know what I just found out recently?
          To be called bourbon it has to come from
          Kentucky. Otherwise it's called sour
          mash.

BARTLET hands TOBY his drink as well as a club soda to LEO. At
some point he'll go back and get his own drink.

                         BARTLET
          An Algerian-born terrorist named Reda
          Nessam was arrested at the Canadian
          border yesterday with a U-Haul containing
          10 two-ounce jars filled with
          nitroglycerine.

                         TOBY
          And they don't allow that kind of thing
          at Yosemite?

                         BARTLET
          No. Anyway, on advice from State and
          Intelligence, I closed the embassies in
          Tanzania and Brussels.

                         TOBY
          What about the FAA?

                         BARTLET
          They want me to order the airports to
          heightened security, but it's a holiday
          weekend. I don't know. Toby I gotta tell
          you something.

                         TOBY
          Does the FAA have to present evidence of
          a credible threat?

                                                          (CONTINUED)

17   CONTINUED: (2)

                              BARTLET
              Yeah.

                              TOBY
              How do they do that?

                              BARTLET
              I don't know, they do it.

                              TOBY
              Is there--Excuse me, sir--is there a time
              frame?

                              BARTLET
              About an hour. Toby, around ten years
              ago, for a period of a few months, I was
              feeling run down and had a pain in my
              leg. They both eventually subsided. But
              then eight years ago the pain came back.
              As well as numbness. My vision would be
              blurry sometimes and I'd get dizzy.
              During an eye exam, the doctor detected
              abnormal pupil responses and ordered an
              MRI. The radiologist found plaque on my
              brain and spine. I have a relapsing/
              remitting course of MS.

TOBY looks at BARTLET for the longest time...BARTLET's hanging
in there...

                              TOBY
                   (pause)
              I'm sorry, sir?

                              BARTLET
              I have Multiple Sclerosis, Toby.

And with this, BARTLET has come back to the chair and set the
bourbon bottle on the table as we

                                        FADE TO BLACK.

                         END OF ACT ONE

ACT TWO

FADE IN:

18   **INT. THE OVAL OFFICE - NIGHT**   18

BARTLET, LEO and TOBY are exactly where they were. They're
giving TOBY a moment to digest this.

It's gonna take more than a moment.

There's a long, tense silence before...

                         TOBY
                    (pause)
          What does relapsing/remitting mean?

                         BARTLET
          I'm sorry?

                         TOBY
          What does relapsing/remitting mean?

                         BARTLET
          It's--
              (beat)
          I don't know--It's the good kind of MS.

                         TOBY
          It's the good kind.

                         BARTLET
          Yeah. As opposed to secondary
          progressive.

                         TOBY
          Which is the bad kind.

                         BARTLET
          Yeah. MS is a chronic disease of the
          central nervous system. Symptoms can be
          as mild as numbness or as severe as
          paralysis.

                         TOBY
          And loss of vision.

                         BARTLET
          Yeah.

                         TOBY
          Cognitive function.

                                        (CONTINUED)

                         BARTLET
          Yeah.

                         TOBY
          Is it--I'm sorry--is it fatal?

                         BARTLET
          No. That's the good news. The bad news is
          there's no cure.

                         TOBY
          Yeah, that I knew. Does
          relapsing/remitting--

                         BARTLET
          --ever turn into secondary progressive?

                         TOBY
          Yeah.

                         BARTLET
          Sure.

                         TOBY
          Is there any way of telling if it's going
          to?

                         BARTLET
          No.

                         TOBY
          Okay.

TOBY gets out of his chair...no one says anything for a
moment. Then--

                         TOBY
          I'd like to stand up, can I stand?

                         BARTLET
          Yeah.

After a moment, CHARLIE enters...

                         TOBY
          I'm sorry, sir, I need to-- can I--
          'Scuse me.

And TOBY hustles for the portico door and goes outside...

BARTLET and LEO know that this isn't the moment to be
patronizing and so neither of them move to help.

                                        (CONTINUED)

18   CONTINUED: (2)   18

                          CHARLIE
              Mr. President?

                          BARTLET
              Yeah.

                          CHARLIE
              You wanted the call from Mr. Garreth at
              the FAA.

                          LEO
              Charlie, can you put it through to my
              office.

                          CHARLIE
              Yes sir.

CHARLIE exits.

                          LEO
                    (to BARTLET)
              Go take it in my office.

BARTLET waits a moment, then gets up and goes into Leo's
office. LEO's alone, looks out the window at TOBY, and we

                                              CUT TO:

19   **INT. ROOSEVELT ROOM - NIGHT**   19

Chinese food cartons are spread around the table, as well as
beer and soft drinks. JOSH, LARRY and ED are reading copies of
the speech. DONNA's making notes on a legal pad.

After a moment...

                          JOSH
              See?

                          ED
              Yeah.

                          JOSH
              Larry?

                          LARRY
              Yeah.

                          JOSH
              See the problem?

                          LARRY
              Well they didn't bring the funny, Josh.

                                              (CONTINUED)

19   CONTINUED: 19

                  JOSH
No they didn't.
    (to DONNA)
What are you doing?

                  DONNA
I'm jotting down some go-to's in case a
joke doesn't work. "I haven't seen an
audience this dead since--" that kinda
thing.

                  JOSH
You think the President's gonna get
heckled?

                  DONNA
No, but I've read the speech, and I think
you'd be wise to have some dead audience
metaphors in your pocket.

                  JOSH
Okay, here we go.
    (reading)
"Ladies and Gentlemen, I'm very happy to
be here and I want to thank the White
House Correspondents' Association for
inviting me. I expect I'll be stuck here
tonight with my fair share of verbal
harpoons, I don't mind, just don't stick
me with the dinner check." Wow.

                  DONNA
And then it says here *Allow for laughter.*

                  JOSH
Yeah, well unless we give that
instruction to the audience, I don't
think it's gonna be a problem.

SAM and AINSLEY enter--

                  SAM
Hey.

                  JOSH
I don't mind, just don't stick me with
the dinner check?

                  SAM
I know, it's like he's playin'
Grossingers.

                  (CONTINUED)

19   CONTINUED: (2)   19

                         DONNA
                      (reading)
          "I know some of you are troubled by my
          frequent use of Latin references, well
          all I can say is, 'No te preocupas.'"

                         ED
          And the joke there is that it's in
          Spanish.

                         LARRY
          It's that kind of Latin.

                         DONNA
          And that's probably why you'll want your
          first dead audience joke.

                         JOSH
          We're not gonna need a dead audience
          joke.

                         AINSLEY
          Donna, who gave you those beautiful
          flowers on your desk?

                         JOSH
          I did. Me. Those are from me.

                         AINSLEY
          What's the occasion?

                         DONNA
          Nothing.

                         JOSH
          Our anniversary.

                         DONNA
          Our not anniversary.

                         JOSH
          Donna doesn't like to talk about it.

                         DONNA
          I really don't.

                         AINSLEY
          Okay.

                                          (CONTINUED)

> SAM

A few years ago, Donna's boyfriend broke
up with her, so she started working for
Josh, but then the boyfriend told her to
come back and she did, and they broke up
and she came back to work.

SAM looks over to DONNA, who puts her hands out and shakes her
head as if to say "Did you <u>hear</u> what I just said?"

> SAM
>   (beat)

I thought you meant <u>you</u> didn't want to
talk about it.
>   (beat)

I'm a spokesman, it's in my blood.

> AINSLEY

Well they're nice flowers.

> LARRY

"I'd also like to thank our host, Bill
Maher"

> SAM

We're not making fun of the host.

> AINSLEY

Who are we making fun of?

> LARRY/ED/SAM/JOSH

Republicans.

> SAM

I only wish the Speaker were here
tonight, but he's held up in negotiations
on the Hill. He's demanding his latest
pre-nup include a line item veto.

> JOSH

There it is.

> SAM

All right, two groups. You guys over
there, we'll stay over here.

> AINSLEY

I want to be in the other group.

> SAM

Why?

(CONTINUED)

19   CONTINUED: (4)   19

                              AINSLEY
                    The Kung Pao Chicken.

                              SAM
                    Get the Kung Pao Chicken and come back
                    here. Let's go, in a half-hour, I want to
                    make Toby laugh.

                                                        CUT TO:

20   **EXT. PORTICO - NIGHT**   20

TOBY's standing next to one of the pillars. LEO steps out with
a fresh drink and hands it to TOBY.

                              LEO
                    So I found out about a year ago. Two
                    nights before the State of the Union he
                    had an attack.

                              TOBY
                         (pause)
                    He did?

                              LEO
                    When he passed out in the Oval Office?

                              TOBY
                    That was an attack.

                              LEO
                    Yeah.

                              TOBY
                    I thought it was the flu.

                              LEO
                    It wasn't.

LEO waits a moment, then walks inside. TOBY follows him into--

21   **INT. THE OVAL OFFICE - CONTINUOUS**   21

TOBY doesn't really know what to do with himself for a
moment...

                              TOBY
                    How is it poss--
                         (beat)
                    How is it possible that this was kept a
                    secret. First of all, who else knows?

                                                    (CONTINUED)

21   CONTINUED:

                          LEO
          You're the 16th person.

                          TOBY
          Who else?

                          LEO
          I'll tell you some of them, I won't tell
          you all of them.

                          TOBY
          Why not?

                          LEO
          'Cause it's not entirely my business, I'm
          not sure of my footing here, the
          President'll be off the phone in a minute
          and in the meantime you'll take what I
          give you.

                          TOBY
          It's not entirely your business?

                          LEO
          The First Lady. The doctor, the
          radiologist, the specialist, the kids--

                          TOBY
          Who else?

                          LEO
          That's it for now.

                          TOBY
          He took a physical. Those doctors were
          from eight years--he took a physical when
          he ran and disclosed the--

                          LEO
          It's in remission, it doesn't show up
          during a physical--

                          TOBY
          Leo--

                          LEO
          It's in remission, nobody lied.

                          TOBY
          Nobody lied?

                          LEO
          Nobody--

                                      (CONTINUED)

21   CONTINUED: (2)   21

                          TOBY
          Nobody lied? Is that what you've been
          saying to yourself over and over again
          for a year?

                          LEO
          Look--

                          TOBY
          Leo, a deception of <u>massive</u> propor-- I
          can't even--he gets a physical twice a
          year at Bethesda, his doctors are <u>Naval</u>
          officers, are you telling me <u>officers</u> are
          involved in this?

                          LEO
          Toby--

                          TOBY
          These guys are gonna be court-martialed!

                          LEO
          Nobody--listen to me--nobody lied, nobody
          was asked to lie.

                          TOBY
          Coercion--

                          LEO
          Nobody was asked to lie.

                          TOBY
          Officers, the First Lady, surgeons,
          Surgeon Generals for all I know--

BARTLET steps in from LEO's office.

                          BARTLET
          The plural of Surgeon General isn't
          Surgeon Generals, it's Surgeons General.
          Like Attorneys General. Or Courts
          Martial.
                (beat)
          Nobody was asked to lie.
                (pause)
          That was Garreth from the FAA. Upon
          interrogating Reda Nessam, they believe
          it's possible that another rental car
          crossed the border yesterday. They
          believe it's headed to a safe house in
          Paterson, New Jersey and the FBI thinks
          they can apprehend him in 24 hours.
                (MORE)

                                              (CONTINUED)

21   CONTINUED: (3)

> BARTLET (cont'd)
> Of course the only way all of this will
> happen is if Reda Nessam is telling the
> truth, so who wants odds? Anyway, they're
> still looking at forensic evidence so
> we're gonna talk again in a few minutes
> to decide if there's a credible threat.

BARTLET's got his back to TOBY.

> TOBY
> I'm sorry, sir, I didn't hear that.

> BARTLET
> I said we're gonna decide if there's a
> credible threat.
>   (smiles)
> Why, what are you guys talking about?

FADE TO BLACK

END OF ACT TWO

ACT THREE

FADE IN:

22   **INT. MRS. LANDINGHAM'S OFFICE - NIGHT**   22

CHARLIE's at his desk. JOSH comes in from the corridor.

                JOSH
Hey.

                CHARLIE
How you doin'.

                JOSH
You have any idea how much longer Toby's
gonna be?

                CHARLIE
I don't.

                JOSH
Lemme ask you, you think this joke's
funny? "I'm sorry the Speaker isn't here,
he's up on the Hill in last minute
negotiations. He's going over his pre-nup
and he wants a line item veto."

                CHARLIE
Well I think it's pretty funny, but--

                JOSH
What?

                CHARLIE
I wouldn't do it.

                JOSH
Why?

                CHARLIE
I think it's gonna call attention to the
First Lady not being there.

                JOSH
Where's Mrs. Bartlet gonna be?

                CHARLIE
She went back up to Manchester.

                JOSH
She's not coming to the Correspondents'
Dinner?

                        (CONTINUED)

22   CONTINUED: 22

                                   CHARLIE
Probably not.

                                   JOSH
Charlie, what's goin' on?

CHARLIE gives him a little look that says, "You know better
than to ask me stuff I'm not gonna tell you."

                                   JOSH
          (beat)
Sorry.
          (beat)
All right. You don't know when Toby's
out?

                                   CHARLIE
No.

                                   JOSH
Okay.

JOSH opens the door and goes into--

23   **INT. ROOSEVELT ROOM - CONTINUOUS**   23

--where DONNA, AINSLEY, ED and LARRY are in joke-writing mode.
They're scribbling on pads in various places and positions
around the room.

                                   JOSH
Alright, here we go.

SAM comes in from the corridor with an opened book--

                                   SAM
          (reading)
"Equality of Rights under the law shall
not be denied or abridged by the United
States or any state on account of sex."

                                   JOSH
What's the joke?

                                   SAM
It's not a joke.

                                   AINSLEY
It's the Equal Rights Amendment.

                                   JOSH
When did that come back?

                                       (CONTINUED)

23   CONTINUED:

                              DONNA
                        (re: ED and LARRY)
                   Read what these guys have.

JOSH takes the pad--

                              SAM
                        (to AINSLEY)
                   Shall not be abridged or denied on
                   account of sex. Very dangerous language.
                   This must be stopped. What could possibly
                   be your problem with the ERA?

                              AINSLEY
                   It's redundant.

                              JOSH
                   Why are we talking about the ERA?

                              SAM
                   She's doing a thing.

                              JOSH
                   Yeah, but it's not back or anything,
                   though, is it?

                              SAM
                   Certainly not if Phyllis Schlafly over
                   here has her way.

                              AINSLEY
                   Look--

                              SAM
                   It's redundant?

                              AINSLEY
                   I'm a low-maintenance lady, I got the
                   14th Amendment, I'm fine.

                              SAM
                   How 'bout--

                              AINSLEY
                   The 14th Amendment which says that a
                   citizen of the United States is anyone
                   that's born here, that's me, and that no
                   citizen can be denied due process. I'm
                   covered. Make a law for somebody else.

                                                     (CONTINUED)

                         JOSH
          Alright, here's a joke based on the
          premise that the party afterward is hard
          to get into...<u>and</u>, that the President is
          the Commander in Chief. "I hear the
          Bloomberg party's gonna be hard to get
          into this year. But I'm not worried. I'm
          going to the party with the 82nd
          Airborne."

                         DONNA
                   (pause)
          And then the President says, "Wow, I
          haven't heard a room this quiet since we
          lost the signal on Galileo."

                         JOSH
                   (pause)
          Or, "Wow, I haven't seen my staff update
          their resumes this quickly since *the last
          time I tanked at the Correspondents'
          Dinner*!"

                         DONNA
          Josh?

                         JOSH
          Yeah.

                         DONNA
          When you yell, you make it harder for
          people to find the funny.

                         JOSH
          Hey, who gave you those flowers on your
          desk?

                         DONNA
          A mean man who can't read a calendar.

                         JOSH
          Sam.

     JOSH calls SAM over to a private spot--

                         SAM
          We're doing fine, Toby's gonna come in
          here and nail it, this is his thing.

                         JOSH
          Yeah, cut the Speaker joke, okay, Mrs.
          Bartlet might not be there.

                                        (CONTINUED)

23   CONTINUED: (3)   23

> SAM
> (beat)
> Okay.

> JOSH
> All right, so we're gonna be fine here.

> SAM
> Yeah, we're doin' great.
> (to the GROUP)
> We're doin' great, everybody, right?

> ED
> Sam, we've got one here, but it involves a John Wayne impersonation and a sock puppet.

> SAM
> Yeah, we're eating it.

CUT TO:

24   **INT. THE OVAL OFFICE - NIGHT**   24

BARTLET and TOBY. LEO's gone for the moment.

> TOBY
> Leo said you had an attack last year.

> BARTLET
> Hm?

> TOBY
> Leo said you had an attack last year.

> BARTLET
> Yeah.

> TOBY
> A couple of nights before the State of the Union.

> BARTLET
> Yeah.

> TOBY
> Wasn't that also the night you saw satellite pictures of India moving on Kashmir?

> BARTLET
> Yeah.

(CONTINUED)

                         TOBY
          India and Pakistan were staring each
          other down, control of some nuclear
          weapons had been put in the field.

                         BARTLET
          Yeah.

                         TOBY
          So in the middle of a...I don't know what
          you call it--

                         BARTLET
          An episode.

                         TOBY
          You were in the Situation Room as
          Commander in Chief.

                         BARTLET
          I know, I can't believe we're all still
          here.

     TOBY is staring at BARTLET. "How the fuck can you make a joke
     about that?" BARTLET's staring right back at TOBY. "Yeah, I
     made the fuckin' joke, you got a problem I can help you with?"

                         TOBY
               (pause)
          Mr. President--

                         BARTLET
          The episode was over. Leo was with me,
          the Chairman of the Joint Chiefs was with
          me, as were the Secretaries of State and
          Defense.

                         TOBY
          Do you receive medication?

                         BARTLET
          I'm sorry?

                         TOBY
          Do you receive medication?

                         BARTLET
          I get injections of Betaseron.

                         TOBY
          From whom?

                                               (CONTINUED)

                    BARTLET
          From a doctor.

                    TOBY
          None of your current doctors are aware of
          your condition. Mr. President, is your
          wife medicating you?

                    BARTLET
          I think it would be best while
          temperatures are running a little high,
          that you refer to my wife as Mrs. Bartlet
          or the First Lady.

LEO comes in from his office...

                    TOBY
               (pause)
          Yes sir.

                    BARTLET
          Whatchya got, Leo?

                    LEO
          They'd like a few more minutes.

                    BARTLET
          The FAA?

                    LEO
          Yeah.

                    BARTLET
          Talk me through what heightened security
          means.

                    LEO
          Well they deploy more uniformed police
          and the dogs. They hand-search luggage--

                    BARTLET
          Discontinue--

                    LEO
          --curbside check-in, yeah, eliminate the
          first two rows of short term parking--

                    BARTLET
          Okay, they want a few minutes?

                    LEO
          Yeah.

                                        (CONTINUED)

24   CONTINUED: (3)

                    BARTLET
          Toby's concerned that the peaceful
          solution I brokered in Kashmir last year
          was the result of a drug-induced haze.

                    LEO
          I was there with him. So was Fitz. So was
          Cashman, Hutchinson, Berryhill--

                    TOBY
          Well that's *fantastic*!

                    LEO
          Toby--

                    TOBY
          None of you were elected!

                    BARTLET
          I was elected, they were appointed. Vice
          President was elected, has the
          Constitutional authority to assume my--

                    TOBY
          Not last May he didn't. He didn't last
          May when you were under general
          anesthesia.

                    BARTLET
          That's 'cause I never signed the letter
          and I don't think I got shot 'cause I got
          MS.

                    TOBY
          No, I don't think you did either, sir. I
          meant that during a night of extreme
          chaos and fear, when we didn't yet know
          if we'd been the victims of domestic or
          foreign terrorism, or even an act of war,
          there was uncertainty as to who was
          giving the national security orders, and
          it was because you never signed a letter.
          So I'm led to wonder, given your
          condition and its lack of predictability,
          why there isn't simply a signed letter
          sitting in a file someplace. And the
          answer of course is that if there was a
          signed letter sitting in a file
          someplace, somebody would ask why.
                    (pause)
          The Commander in Chief had just been
          attacked, he was under a general
          anesthetic.
                    (MORE)

                                                         (CONTINUED)

CONTINUED: (4)

> TOBY (cont'd)
> A fugitive was at large, the manhunt
> included every Federal, state and local
> law enforcement agency. The Virginia,
> Maryland, New Jersey, Pennsylvania and
> Delaware National Guard units were
> federalized. The KH-10s showed Republican
> Guard movement in Southern Iraq and
> twelve hours earlier an F-117 was shot
> down in the no-fly. And the Vice
> President's authority was murky at best.
> The National Security Advisor and the
> Secretary of State didn't know who they
> were taking their orders from. I wasn't
> in the Situation Room that night, but
> I'll bet all the money in my pockets
> against all the money in your pockets
> that it was Leo.
>> (beat)
> Who no one elected.
>> (beat)
> For ninety minutes that night there was a
> coup d'etat in this country.

BARTLET's silent for a moment. It's scary, until he busts
into--

> BARTLET
>> (singing)
> *"--and the walls came tumblin' down."*
>> (pause)
> I feel fine, by the way, thanks for
> asking.

> LEO
> Sir--

> BARTLET
> No, Leo, Toby's concern for my health is
> moving me in ways--

> TOBY
> Mr. President--

> BARTLET
> Shut up.
>> (beat)
> You know your indignation would be a lot
> more interesting to me if it weren't
> quite so covered in crap.

CHARLIE steps in--

> CHARLIE
> Sir?

(CONTINUED)

24   CONTINUED: (5)

> BARTLET
> Yeah.

> CHARLIE
> Mr. Garreth.

> BARTLET
> Thanks.

CHARLIE exits.

> BARTLET
> (to TOBY)
> Are you pissed 'cause I didn't say
> anything or are you pissed 'cause
> there were 15 people who knew before
> you did?
> (pause)
> I feel fine by the way, thanks for
> asking.

> LEO
> Take the call in here and we'll step
> outside for a minute.

TOBY and LEO exit onto the Portico.

BARTLET's left alone. He walks over to a couch, to try and
shake all this off somehow. He picks up the phone next to the
couch, hits a button and says--

> BARTLET
> (into phone)
> Yeah this is the President.

                                              FADE TO BLACK

                         <u>END OF ACT THREE</u>

ACT FOUR

FADE IN:

25   **EXT./EST. THE WHITE HOUSE - NIGHT**   25

                    SAM (V.O.)
          Self-deprecation.

                    ED (V.O.)
          Yes.

                                                    CUT TO:

26   **INT. THE ROOSEVELT ROOM - NIGHT**   26

                    SAM
          Self-deprecation is what we need.

                    LARRY
          Yes.

                    SAM
          Self-deprecation is the appetizer of
          charm.

                    ED
          We need jokes about the staff.

                    SAM
          We need jokes about the staff.

                    AINSLEY
          Let's start with you.

                    SAM
          Problem is there aren't many jokes you
          can make about me.

                    DONNA
          How 'bout this. Um. "Knock-Knock," "Who's
          there," "Sam and his prostitute friend."

                    SAM
               (beat)
          See, I think that was a bit of
          misdirected anger there.

                    DONNA
          I'm okay with that.

                                        (CONTINUED)

>   SAM
> Well in that case--Ainsley, you know why
> I got you flowers in April instead of
> February? 'Cause you ditched me the first
> time around to go back to the guy who
> ditched you the first time around, only
> to have him ditch you the second time
> around.

DONNA thinks a moment...then smacks JOSH in the back of the
head--

>   JOSH
> What the hell--that was <u>him</u>.

>   DONNA
> He was being <u>you</u>.

>   JOSH
> Well in fairness I think everybody should
> have a turn. Sam, is there anything we
> can pull, anything funny we can recycle?

>   SAM
> Yeah, pull something I wrote from October
> called Government-wide Accountability for
> Merit System Principles.

>   JOSH
>   (pause)
> That one was a barn burner was it?

JOSH exits.

>   DONNA
> Do you have any idea how much grief I
> took from him when I came back?

>   SAM
> How much?

>   DONNA
> None. I walked in the door, he said
> "Thank God. There's a pile of stuff on
> the desk." This is his way. He's just
> gonna snark me every April. Prince of
> passive/aggressive behavior.

>   SAM
> What does snark mean?

>   DONNA
> I don't know, but he's doing it.

>   (CONTINUED)

26   CONTINUED: (2)

                          SAM
          There coffee left?

                          ED
          In the mess.

                          SAM
          Anybody want anything?

                          AINSLEY
          Think they have cheesecake down there?

                          SAM
          It's quarter after midnight, the pastry
          chef usually stays on until dawn.

                          AINSLEY
          I'll go see what there is.

     SAM and AINSLEY exit into--

27   **INT. CORRIDOR - CONTINUOUS**   27

     --where they'll be making their way down to the mess. The
     corridors are unusually unpopulated.

                          SAM
          You know we should make a joke about
          women, 'cause there's no law against
          that, or paying them less money than men.

                          AINSLEY
          Well, there is a law against that, it's
          the Pay Equity Act, was passed in 1964
          when women were making 59 cents to the
          dollar.

                          SAM
          What are you making now?

                          AINSLEY
          79 cents.

                          SAM
          So everything's fine.

     They walk into--

28   **INT. CORRIDOR - CONTINUOUS**   28

> AINSLEY
> No, there are still some problems, but
> I'm not worried, 'cause the Federal
> Government's coming to the rescue.

> SAM
> Look--

> AINSLEY
> You think pay disparity is 'cause some
> sexist in human resources hired two
> people for equal positions and paid the
> man more.

> SAM
> Oftentimes women--

> AINSLEY
> And oftentimes women make less money over
> the course of their lifetime because they
> choose to.

> SAM
> Oh good night <u>nurse</u>, they don't <u>choose</u> to
> make less money, they are financially
> punished for having kids.

They start heading down--

29   **INT. STAIRWAY - NIGHT**   29

> AINSLEY
> They made a choice to have kids.

> SAM
> Not necessarily if you guys have your
> way, but that's a different can a tuna. I
> flat out guarantee you that if men were
> biologically responsible for procreation,
> there would be paid family leave in every
> Fortune 500.

They walk into--

30   **INT. MESS - NIGHT**   30

It's empty and dimly lit. SAM grabs a tray, some mugs and goes
to the coffee urn.

(CONTINUED)

30   CONTINUED: 30

> AINSLEY
> Sam, if men were biologically responsible
> for procreation they'd fall down and die
> at the first sonogram.

> SAM
> If the Amendment is redundant then what's
> your problem if it's passed or not?

> AINSLEY
> Because I'm a Republican, have we met? I
> believe that every time the Federal
> Government hands down a new law, it
> leaves, for the rest of us, a little less
> freedom. So I say let's just stick to the
> ones we absolutely need in order to have
> water come out of the faucet and our cars
> not stolen. That is my problem with
> passing a redundant law.
>   (pause)
> Sam?

> SAM
> Yeah.

> AINSLEY
> The all-night pastry chef, you were just
> kidding about that, right?

> SAM
>   (pause)
> Yeah.

SAM, AINSLEY and the coffee start upstairs as we

                                                CUT TO:

31   **EXT. PORTICO - NIGHT**   31

TOBY's sitting on the bench as LEO comes down the portico from
the residence.

He walks up to TOBY...

> LEO
> He's still on with State in the
> residence.

> TOBY
>   (pause)
> So Hoynes knows?

                                                (CONTINUED)

31   CONTINUED:

> LEO
> Hm?

> TOBY
> Hoynes is one of the 16?

> LEO
> Yeah.

> TOBY
> And he thinks the President won't run
> again.

> LEO
> He thinks there's a chance.

> TOBY
> Will he?

> LEO
> Will the President run?

> TOBY
> Where's the First Lady?

> LEO
> Up in Manchester.

> TOBY
> Why did she come to me after the State of
> the Union?

> LEO
> Toby--

> TOBY
> Why--why's she mad at the President? It's
> because the State of the Union set up the
> re-election run, and somehow she's under
> the impression that's not supposed to
> happen.

> LEO
> The First Lady--

> TOBY
> I have no kind of investigative mind.
> Zero. It took me six days and 23 minutes
> to figure it out.

> LEO
> He'll run.

(CONTINUED)

31   CONTINUED: (2)   31

> TOBY
> Yeah. Yeah, 'cause we stood in that
> office a couple months ago, you and I,
> and you said, "Take my hand. We just--"
> never mind.

> LEO
> He'll run.

> TOBY
> Hoynes was 14; who was 15?

> LEO
> Dr. David Lee, the anesthesiologist at
> G.W., he had to know about the Betaseron.
> Getting back to Hoynes--

> TOBY
> I'm sorry, Leo, but I need you to look at
> me right now and tell me the doctor's not
> under any kind of surveillance.

> LEO
> The doctor's free to talk to whomever he
> likes.

> TOBY
> Well I'm sure we're gonna find that out
> soon enough.

> LEO
> He's not gonna leak it.

> TOBY
> Someone will.

> LEO
> Toby--

> TOBY
> Leo, Hoynes left breadcrumbs, he <u>wanted</u>
> me to find out. A camping trip to
> Killington?

> LEO
> That was a jackass move.

> TOBY
> I don't think it was, I think he may be
> the only person around here acting
> responsibly.

(CONTINUED)

31   CONTINUED: (3)

                    LEO
To who?

                    TOBY
The Democratic Party. It's seven and a
half months till the Iowa caucus and no
one's been told the President might not
be the nominee?

                    LEO
He's gonna run.

                    TOBY
He may not have that option, Leo.

                    LEO
When the story breaks it'll be because we
broke it. And we'll control it and the
public will accept it. It's not like it's
unprecedented that a President conceal
health issues, what do you think is gonna
happen?
        (pause)
I mean it, what do you think is gonna
happen?

                    TOBY
        (pause)
I suppose... one of five things. The
President can decide not to run. He can
run and not win. He can run and win--

                    LEO
And what are the other two?

                    TOBY
Leo--

                    LEO
You think he's gonna need to resign?

                    TOBY
There's gonna be hearing upon hearing
upon hearing--

                    LEO
He hasn't broken a law.

CHARLIE steps out on the portico--

                    CHARLIE
The President's on his way back.

                                    (CONTINUED)

31   CONTINUED: (4)   31

                              LEO
                    Thanks.

CHARLIE goes back inside.

                              TOBY
                         (quietly)
                    Says you. And you don't have to break the
                    law to get served with Articles of
                    Impeachment.

                              LEO
                    Toby...it is never going to get that far.

TOBY looks down, smiles, shakes his head...

                              TOBY
                    Write down the exact date and time you
                    said that.

TOBY heads inside and we

                                                           CUT TO:

32   **INT. ROOSEVELT ROOM - NIGHT**   32

DONNA's got her legs up on a chair...

                              DONNA
                    See the thing about me, is that mine is a
                    <u>dry</u> wit.
                         (beat)
                    And a dry wit...like a fine martini, is
                    best enjoyed...

LARRY and ED are waiting for it...

                              LARRY
                    Uh-oh.

                              DONNA
                    Yeah, nowhere to go there.

SAM and AINSLEY come in with the coffee--

                              ED
                    What the hell took so long?

                              SAM
                    We got the coffee, but then I spilled it
                    coming up the stairs, you know, the first
                    couple of times. Where's Josh?

                                                        (CONTINUED)

32   CONTINUED: 32

                         DONNA
            You sent him to get the thing.

                         SAM
            For how long? I've had time to spill
            coffee, you know, a lot.

                         DONNA
            I'll find him.

DONNA exits.

                         SAM
            So. Guys.

                         ED
            Yeah.

                         SAM
            While I was downstairs I made a decision.
            I'm going to register with the Republican
            Party, and I'll tell you why if you're
            curious, it's because they are a freedom
            loving people.

                         AINSLEY
            We also like beef.

                         SAM
            You know you insist Government is
            depraved for not legislating against what
            we can see on a newsstand, or what we can
            see in an art exhibit, or what we can
            burn in protest, or which sex we're
            allowed to have sex with or a woman's
            right to choose, but don't you dare try
            and regulate this deadly weapon I have
            concealed on me, for that would encroach
            against my freedom.

                         AINSLEY
            Yeah and Democrats believe in free speech
            as long as it isn't prayer while you're
            standing in a school. You believe in the
            Freedom of Information Act except if you
            want to find out if your 14 year old
            daughter's had an abortion.

                         SAM
            We believe in the ERA.

                         AINSLEY
            Well go get 'em.

                                               (CONTINUED)

32   CONTINUED: (2)   32

                          SAM
          How can you have an objection to
          something that says--

                          AINSLEY
          Because it's humiliating. A new Amendment
          we vote on declaring that I'm equal under
          the law to a man? I am mortified to
          discover there's reason to believe I
          wasn't <u>before</u>. I am a citizen of this
          country, I am not a special sub-set in
          need of your protection, I do not have to
          have my rights handed down to me by a
          bunch of old, white, <u>men</u>.
                (beat)
          The same Article 14 that protects you
          protects me. And I went to law school
          just to make sure. And with that, I am
          going back down to the mess, because I
          thought I may have seen there, a peach.

AINSLEY turns and exits.

                          SAM
                (pause)
          I could've countered that, but I'd
          already moved on to other things in my
          head.

                                                   CUT TO:

33   **INT.JOSH'S OFFICE - NIGHT**   33

JOSH is standing on a step-ladder, trying to reach a binder
that's on top of a pile of binders on the top of the shelf.
He's trying to leverage it with a pencil as DONNA walks in--

                          DONNA
          Josh--

And the sound startles JOSH who makes a sudden movement which
sends piles and piles of folders and binders cascading and
crashing to the floor.

They look at the damage for a moment...

                          JOSH
          Oh, well that was predictable.

                          DONNA
          Yes.

                                              (CONTINUED)

33   CONTINUED:

                          JOSH
          I'm trying to find that speech Sam said.

                          DONNA
          You know we keep them on computer.

                          JOSH
          Well, yeah, sure, I suppose, but--

                          DONNA
          Except, you don't know how to use a
          computer.

                          JOSH
          Right.

                          DONNA
          Josh, Josh, Josh...

                          JOSH
          Yes.

                          DONNA
          Joshua, Josh, Josh...

                          JOSH
          What the hell is happening now.

                          DONNA
          You feel, I believe, because you're quite
          adle-minded, that this job was my second
          choice.

                          JOSH
          Hey I'm just grateful we were your last
          choice.

                          DONNA
          I'm going to give you a little gift right
          now which you don't deserve.

                          JOSH
               (beat)
          Donna, if you've got your old Catholic
          school uniform on under there, don't get
          me wrong, I applaud the thought, but--

                          DONNA
          'Kay, what I need is for you to stop
          being, like, <u>you</u> for a second.

                          JOSH
          Okay.

                                        (CONTINUED)

33   CONTINUED: (2)   33

                              DONNA
               When I came back, you remember I had a
               bandage on my ankle?

                              JOSH
               Yeah.

                              DONNA
               I told you I slipped on the ice on the
               front walk?

                              JOSH
               Yeah, and you know why? Because you
               didn't put down kitty litter.

                              DONNA
               I was actually in a car accident.

                              JOSH
               You were in a car accident?

                              DONNA
               It was--

                              JOSH
               Seriously, you were in an accident?

                              DONNA
               It was no big deal.

                              JOSH
               You told me it was a late thaw.

DONNA smiles for a moment at the sweetness of Josh having
bought that.

                              DONNA
                   (beat)
               Yes I did. Anyway, they took me to the
               hospital and I called him and he came
               down to get me, and on the way, he
               stopped and met some friends of his for a
               beer.

                              JOSH
                   (pause)
               He stopped on the way to the hospital for
               a beer?

                              DONNA
               Yes. And so I left him. Which was the
               point of my telling you this. I left him.
                   (beat)
                       (MORE)

                                                    (CONTINUED)

33   CONTINUED: (3)   33

> DONNA (cont'd)
> So stop remembering that. What I remember
> is that you took me back when you had
> absolutely no reason to trust me again.
> And you didn't make fun of me, or him,
> and you had every reason to.

> JOSH
> (pause)
> Donna--

> DONNA
> You're gonna make fun of him now, aren't
> you?

> JOSH
> No.

> DONNA
> 'Cause that's why I didn't tell you in
> the first place.

> JOSH
> I'm not gonna make fun of him.

> DONNA
> Good.

> JOSH
> But just what kind of a dumpkiss were
> you--

> DONNA
> He was supposed to meet his friends, he
> stopped on the way to tell them that he
> couldn't.

> JOSH
> And had a beer.

> DONNA
> Does this make you feel superior? Yes,
> you're better than my old boyfriend.

> JOSH
> I'm just saying if you were in an
> accident I wouldn't stop for a beer.

And JOSH is on his way out when he's stopped by--

> DONNA
> If you were in an accident I wouldn't
> stop for red lights.

JOSH looks at her...and as DONNA passes him on her way out--

(CONTINUED)

33   CONTINUED: (4)   33

                          DONNA
              Thanks for taking me back. Oh, and the
              flowers are beautiful.

DONNA exits as we

                                                        CUT TO:

34   **INT. THE OVAL OFFICE - NIGHT**   34

TOBY and LEO.

There's a long, long silence before...

                          TOBY
              Why <u>not</u> heighten security?

                          LEO
              Hm?

                          TOBY
              At the airports, why not heighten
              security, what's the downside?

BARTLET comes in from Landingham's office as LEO and TOBY
stand.

                          BARTLET
              Sorry about that.

                          LEO
              What's goin' on?

                          BARTLET
                  (calling)
              Charlie?
                  (to LEO)
              I gotta make the call.

                          CHARLIE
                  (entering)
              Yes sir.

                          BARTLET
              Let's get Garreth back.

                          LEO
              Toby was just asking what the downside of
              going to a security condition was.

                          BARTLET
              The scanners they use take an hour to
              search the luggage of 250 passengers.
                  (MORE)

                                                     (CONTINUED)

34   CONTINUED: 34

> BARTLET (cont'd)
> The condition requires two photo-I.D.s,
> most people only have one.
>   (beat)
> Delays. Delays are the downside.

CHARLIE steps in--

> CHARLIE
> Mr. Garreth.

> BARTLET
> That timed out well.
>   (punches a button and picks up
>   the phone)
> Hal, okay let's do it. I'm ordering the
> airports to a 2-condition, you'll have it
> in writing in about five minutes.
>   (beat)
> Thanks.

BARTLET hangs up...

> BARTLET
> I didn't know enough.

> TOBY
> I know the feeling.

> BARTLET
> I have no intention of apologizing to
> you, Toby.

> TOBY
> Would you mind if I ask why not?

> BARTLET
> 'Cause you're not the one with MS, a
> wife, three kids and airports to close.
> Not every part of me belongs to you. This
> was personal. I'm not willing to
> relinquish that right.

> TOBY
>   (pause)
> It will appear to many, if not most, as
> fraud. It will appear as if you denied
> the voters an opportunity to decide for
> themselves. They're generally not willing
> to relinquish that right, either.

> BARTLET
>   (pause)
> Yeah.

(CONTINUED)

57.

34   CONTINUED: (2)   34

>   TOBY
>   Mr. President, at some point in the near
>   future we're gonna have to speak to some
>   lawyers.

>   BARTLET
>   Well, that's what usually brings on the
>   episodes, but if you say so.

After a beat, TOBY cracks up... BARTLET smiles... then it all
subsides...

>   TOBY
>   It's 17 people by the way.

>   BARTLET
>   I'm sorry?

>   TOBY
>   You knew. We weren't counting you. It's
>   17 people.

>   BARTLET
>   I don't know, it may have been
>   unbelievably stupid.
>   (beat)
>   It may have been unthinkably
>   stupid, I don't know. I'm sorry,
>   I really am.

And TOBY's struck by the simple honesty of the apology...

>   TOBY
>   I've gotta go in the other room
>   and--

>   BARTLET
>   Yeah, I'll see you tomorrow,
>   thanks.

>   TOBY
>   Thank you, Mr. President.

TOBY exits out into--

35   **INT. CORRIDOR - CONTINUOUS**   35

--and walks into--

36   **INT. ROOSEVELT ROOM - CONTINUOUS**   36

--where he opens the door to shouting and laughing and cheers
of "Toby!," "Now we're in business," "Here we go," etc.

                                              (CONTINUED)

36   CONTINUED: 36

TOBY's making a brave attempt to cover that he's off-balance
and has just been shot from one world to another. The Oval
Office door is still open behind him.

                    ED (O.S.)
          I think that's a good one.

                    AINSLEY (O.S.)
          Toby!

                    JOSH (O.S.)
          What do you got?

                    ED (O.S.)
          Okay. So the President was asked to pick
          tonight's menu, and he says, just serve
          anything you want except lame duck.

                    SAM (O.S.)
          Toby listen to this.

                    TOBY
          Okay.

                    ED (O.S.)
          So the President says I know times are
          tough, the NASDAQ just filed for not-for-
          profit status.

                    JOSH (O.S.)
          Toby--

                    AINSLEY (O.S.)
          What about the one about the Pentagon?

                    JOSH (O.S.)
          Okay, you have to try to imagine that the
          President is saying it. Tell me if you
          think this is funny:

                                        FADE TO BLACK.

                    <u>END OF SHOW</u>

TWO CATHEDRALS

Directed by Thomas Schlamme

Tommy directing. St. Andrews in Delaware. The National Cathedral. The cigarette. The storm. The motorcade. The press conference. Mark Knoffler. And a fitting goodbye to Kathryn Joosten's wonderful Mrs. Landingham.

I've been having the time of my life. Thank you, Akiva.

Two Cathedrals

FADE IN:

1   **INT. LEO'S OFFICE - CONTINUOUS**   1

MARGARET knocks and enters, where Congressmen WADE and
WAKEFIELD are making an energetic case to LEO.

>   WAKEFIELD
>   Most of us are just hearing the news now.

>   WADE
>   A conference call.

>   LEO
>   Yes.

>   WAKEFIELD
>   There hasn't been a lot of time to digest
>   this.

MARGARET hands LEO a note, which he reads and puts down on his
desk.

>   WADE
>   But what we do know is it's the House
>   Democrats who are gonna take it in the
>   throat.

>   LEO
>   Yeah.

>   WADE
>   You might be able to get the voters to
>   accept MS in some of the suburban
>   districts, but the whole House is up for
>   re-election.

>   LEO
>   Yeah.

MARGARET quietly exits.

>   WAKEFIELD
>   It's not a matter of accepting M--There
>   was a cover--

                                              (CONTINUED)

1   CONTINUED: 1

> WADE
> The point is even if you could squeeze
> out an electoral--
>
> WAKEFIELD
> Even if you can squeeze out a win, this
> is what the campaign's gonna be about.
>
> WADE
> You're gonna have Democrats telling the
> President don't come to my district, I've
> got troubles enough, and your campaign
> never gets out of the Rose Garden.
>
> WAKEFIELD
> Yes, and we're running without a standard
> bearer. At a time when we've got policy
> cases against the Republicans on tax
> cuts, environment, education and this is
> what the campaign's gonna be about.
>
> WADE
> Now Leo, most of us are just hearing the
> news, and I don't like being the first
> one to say it, but I'm gonna: I think the
> President has got to strongly consider
> not running for re-election.

LEO stares at WADE, deadpan but disbelieving...

> LEO
>   (pause)
> You think you're the first one to say it?
>
> WADE
> Leo--
>
> LEO
> You are, at minimum, the 35th in the last
> two hours.
>
> WAKEFIELD
> I'm--
>
> WADE
> Well, we're the ones talking to you now
> and we're the ones that are asking. Is
> the President gonna run for re-election.

(CONTINUED)

1   CONTINUED: (2)   1

                           LEO
                       (pause)
                   Harry. Bill. There's gonna be a press
                   conference tonight. I'd watch.

                                                        SMASH CUT TO:

          MAIN TITLES

                           END OF TEASER

ACT ONE

FADE IN:

2   **INT. MURAL ROOM - DAY**   2

TOBY's meeting with some STAFFERS.

>   TOBY
>   He'll sit here with the First Lady on his
>   right.

>   LARRY
>   You don't want him in front of the
>   fireplace?

>   TOBY
>   The fireplace is too much, he'll sit
>   here. Which means they're gonna have to
>   light the room from outside the window,
>   do they know that?

>   ED
>   We'll let 'em know.

>   TOBY
>   Last time they didn't know. The President
>   taped an Easter message that looked like
>   it was lit by Ed Wood.

TOBY walks into--

3   **INT. CORRIDOR - CONTINUOUS**   3

--where SAM catches up to him.

>   SAM
>   Toby.

>   TOBY
>   A pitcher of water, but keep it
>   offscreen.

>   SAM
>   They know.

>   TOBY
>   They gotta light from outside the window.

>   SAM
>   Look--

(CONTINUED)

3   CONTINUED: 3

                              TOBY
                    If they don't light from outside the
                    window--

                              SAM
                    I don't care. Look. Toby. Has anyone
                    considered whether or not he's up for
                    this?

                              TOBY
                         (pause)
                    Up for this?

                              SAM
                    I mean some stuff has happened since--

                              TOBY
                    C.J. gave it to the network, we're pretty
                    much locked in, so--

                              SAM
                    When are we prepping with him?

                              TOBY
                    After the service.

                              SAM
                    There's gonna be time?

                              TOBY
                    We'll have the afternoon.

                              SAM
                    I think we should consider taking--

                              TOBY
                    There aren't any options left. We're
                    going on TV at eight.

     GINGER calls out--

                              GINGER
                    Toby.

     TOBY heads into--

4   **INT. COMMUNICATIONS BULLPEN - CONTINUOUS**   4

                              TOBY
                    Yeah.

(CONTINUED)

4   CONTINUED: 4

                    GINGER
          I'm sorry, but I had to put Greg
          Summerhays back on your schedule.

                    TOBY
          No, I took him off.

                    GINGER
          Leo's office had me put him back on.

They walk into--

5   **INT. CORRIDOR - DAY**   5

                    TOBY
          Why?

                    GINGER
          They want you to keep the appointment.

                    TOBY
          We've got her funeral today, we've got
          these...

                    GINGER
             (pause)
          I said four o'clock.

                    TOBY
          Yeah. All right.

TOBY continues down the corridor and we

                                          CUT TO:

6   **INT. C.J.'S OFFICE - DAY**   6

C.J.'s reading a file and walks up to CAROL at her desk.

                    C.J.
          Carol?

                    CAROL
          Yeah.

                    C.J.
          A.P. Reuters. Agence France. Something
          about seating on Air Force One.

C.J. hands CAROL the file.

                                          (CONTINUED)

                    CAROL
Seating arrangements?

                    C.J.
Seating arrangements on Air Force One.

JOSH comes in with a piece of paper.

                    JOSH
C.J.

                    C.J.
Listen, I was thinking since it's
probably gonna be a light day I'd
maybe blow off work, go shopping
or something.

JOSH smiles...

                    C.J.
What do you need?

                    JOSH
Can I give you a quick brief?

                    C.J.
Sure.

                    JOSH
The Justice Department's run out of money
in their suit against the tobacco
companies.

                    C.J.
The Justice Department's overmatched.

                    JOSH
Yeah, by hundreds of millions of dollars.
They're asking for 30 million and we
think they should have it.

                    C.J.
Who disagrees with us?

                    JOSH
8 of the 15 members of the sub-committee
that controls the budgets for Justice
and Commerce, including Kalmbach, who
has significant ties to tobacco, and
Warren and Rossitter, who do not.

C.J. puts on her coat.

                                  (CONTINUED)

6   CONTINUED: (2)   6

                                C.J.
                    We lost two Democrats?

                                JOSH
                    They have ideological objections.

                                C.J.
                    Yeah, it's just not a good time to
                    be losing Democrats.

        JOSH sighs--

                                JOSH
                    You haven't been in my office this
                    morning.

                                C.J.
                    We'll get 'em back.

                                JOSH
                    Anyway, Leo felt pretty strongly that
                    we should light a fire under it--

        They walk into--

7   **INT. PRESS BULLPEN - CONTINUOUS**   7

                                JOSH
                    --so I wrote up a pretty strongly worded
                    release.

        He hands her the paper--

                                C.J.
                        (reading)
                    "The White House... For Immediate
                    Release... Office of the Press..."

        They walk into--

8   **INT. CORRIDOR - CONTINUOUS**   8

                                C.J.
                        (reading)
                    "Today the President calls
                    on Congress... who deserve their day in
                    Court and this administration won't
                    sit on the bench while well-fed members
                    of the Appropriations Committee choke
                    off funding for a lawsuit aimed at
                                (MORE)

                                                              (CONTINUED)

CONTINUED:

                    C.J. (cont'd)
        perpetrators of hundreds of thousands of
        negligent homicides while filling their
        campaign war chests."

C.J. takes a moment to relish the release...

                    C.J.
        This is like the fire we used to throw
        in the early primaries.

                    JOSH
        Let Bartlet be Bartlet.

                    C.J.
        You gotta put it away for a while.

                    JOSH
        You think?

                    C.J.
        I'm going in there now to tell 'em a
        Landing Ship Helicopter Assault Team is
        steaming off Port-au Prince and then
        after that I'm bringing in A.P., Reuters
        and Agence France, nobody's gonna write
        about an appropriations bill. Haiti's
        gonna get bumped to the Lifestyle
        Section.

                    JOSH
        Yeah, I suppose.

C.J. begins to walk away.

                    JOSH
        Listen, have you seen him today?

C.J. turns around.

                    C.J.
        No, have you?

                    JOSH
        No.

                    C.J.
                (pause)
        All right, listen, I've gotta--

                    JOSH
        Yeah. Thanks.

                                    CUT TO:

9   **INT. ROOSEVELT ROOM - DAY**   9

SAM is in a meeting with Democratic Party strategists.

                   HANSON
Why are we assuming it's Hoynes?

                   PHILLIPS
Please.

                   HANSON
No, why are we assuming it's gotta be
Hoynes? You don't think Wedland's gonna
get into it? Hutchinson? Seth Gillette?

                   PHILLIPS
Please.

                   RENFRO
Gillette's lucky if he carries his
immediate family.

                   PHILLIPS
It's Hoynes.

                   GREENWAY
It's Hoynes.

                   PHILLIPS
Sam, you understand this conversation
isn't ruling out Bartlet as a candidate,
it's just a what-if. We're party
strategists, it's what we're paid for.

                   SAM
Yeah.

                   GREENWAY
Hoynes is the only one who put together
the money this fast.

                   PHILLIPS
He's the most successful fund-raiser
the party's ever had.

                   GREENWAY
Though obviously it'd be easier if Hoynes
is running as an incumbent.

                   SAM
Okay--

                   (CONTINUED)

9   CONTINUED: 9

> PHILLIPS
> Sam--

> SAM
> Thanks.

> PHILLIPS
> No, it was an inappropriate--

> SAM
> No, when I say okay, that's it, close
> your notebooks.
> (to GREENWAY)
> You don't talk like that here, I don't
> give a damn whose nephew you are.
> (to PHILLIPS)
> Tony, President Bartlet is not a
> candidate, he's the President.

SAM exits.

                                                  CUT TO:

10   **INT. SITUATION ROOM - DAY**   10

BARTLET, LEO, NANCY and a table full of people.

> LEO
> What are the conditions inside the
> embassy?

> NANCY
> They've still got running water, but the
> power's been cut. The emergency
> generator's got about 24 hours.

> LEO
> Any injuries?

> MOSLEY
> There aren't any injuries, but the Deputy
> Chief's a diabetic and he's running out
> of insulin.

> LEO
> The Red Cross can help us out there?

> MOSLEY
> Yes sir.

> LEO
> What's outside?

                                               (CONTINUED)

10   CONTINUED: 10

> NANCY
> About 1200 troops now with A-15s
> positioned outside the gates. They've got
> four 105 mm Howitzers--

We hear a BELL ringing as the sound becomes louder...

> LEO
> Which are trained at--?

> NANCY
> Our front door. Mr. President, we want to
> send Fitzwallace down there.

> BARTLET
> Why?

> NANCY
> There's a Haitian general named Francis
> St. Jacques. He trained with Fitz in
> Annapolis and--

DISSOLVE TO:

11   **EXT. A SMALL CHAPEL - DAY**   11

It sits on the campus of an exclusive New England boarding
school. A hundred or so teenage boys in blue jackets with the
school crest on the chest have just been let out of chapel
service and are standing around in clumps. Groups of faculty
members and administrators are off to the side.

> MAN (V.O.)
> Jed! Jed!

> BOY
> Jed. Jed, your father's calling you.

And JED, 17, hustles over to where his father, DR. BARTLET,
mid-40s, is standing. DR. BARTLET's with MR. SPENCE.

> DR. BARTLET
> Jed. Didn't you hear me calling you?

> JED
> No, sir, I didn't, I was--I didn't.

> DR. BARTLET
> Mr. Spence found this cigarette butt
> on the floor in the aisle of the chapel.

(CONTINUED)

11   CONTINUED:

> JED
> People shouldn't put their cigarettes out
> in the chapel, Mr. Spence.

> DR. BARTLET
> Well people shouldn't be smoking in the
> chapel I think was my point, Jed, do you
> understand what I'm saying?

> JED
> Yes sir.

> DR. BARTLET
> Could you tell your friends please?

> JED
> Yeah.

> DR. BARTLET
> Jed, hang on.

MR. SPENCE leaves.

> DR. BARTLET
> Now I want you to meet someone. She's
> gonna be taking over in my office for
> Mrs. Tillinghouse. Excuse me.

DR. BARTLET brings over a YOUNG WOMAN of 26 who's dressed for
church, complete with a hat we've seen once before.

> DR. BARTLET
> This is Delores Landingham. Mrs.
> Landingham, this is my eldest son, Jed.

                                              CUT BACK TO:

12   **INT. SITUATION ROOM - DAY**   12

BARTLET holds an unlit cigarette in his hand.

> LEO
> So what happens?

> NANCY
> Basically we can get St. Jacques to
> fracture Bazan's army.

> LEO
> So if we invade--

                                              (CONTINUED)

12   CONTINUED: 12

                              NANCY
                  It becomes peacekeeping.

BARTLET looks at LEO. LEO nods.

                              BARTLET
                  Okay, send Fitzwallace down. Anything
                  else?

                              NANCY
                  No sir.

BARTLET stands--

                              ALL
                  Thank you, Mr. President/Thank you,
                  sir/Thank you/etc.

BARTLET walks out the door into--

13   **INT. VESTIBULE - CONTINUOUS**   13

--where a MARINE GUARD comes to attention as he passes.
CHARLIE's waiting for him--

                              BARTLET
                  They've been in there 48 hours.

                              CHARLIE
                  Yes sir.

                              BARTLET
                  The guy's been President of his country
                  for two days, he's spent 'em both at
                  gunpoint.

                              CHARLIE
                  Yeah.

They start heading up--

14   **INT. STAIRWAY - CONTINUOUS**   14

                              BARTLET
                  What do you know about this storm?

                              CHARLIE
                  The one--

                              BARTLET
                  It's moving from Florida to South
                  Carolina.

                                                          (CONTINUED)

14   CONTINUED: 14

                         CHARLIE
             Yeah, it's supposed to be bad.

                         BARTLET
             It's a tropical storm.

                         CHARLIE
             Yes sir.

                         BARTLET
             No, I mean it's been designated a
             tropical storm, that means it has a
             surface wind speed of something.

        They walk out into--

15   **INT. CORRIDOR - CONTINUOUS**   15

                         CHARLIE
             Yes sir.

                         BARTLET
             Isn't it strange to have a tropical storm
             in May?

                         CHARLIE
             I'm not certain.

                         BARTLET
             I'm pretty sure there's a season and this
             isn't it.

                         CHARLIE
             I can have someone find out for you, Mr.
             President.

                         BARTLET
             I mean, it's not a big deal, it's just
             that I'm pretty sure it's strange.

                         CHARLIE
             The motorcade'll leave for the cathedral
             in an hour.

                         BARTLET
             You ever been to National Cathedral?

                         CHARLIE
             Yes sir.

                                                    (CONTINUED)

15   CONTINUED: 15

> BARTLET
> You know you can lay the Washington
> Monument down on its side in that church.

> CHARLIE
> I did actually.

They walk into--

16   **INT. MRS. LANDINGHAM'S OFFICE - CONTINUOUS**   16

> BARTLET
> We should try it.

> CHARLIE
> You only have two meetings between now
> and then, is there anything else you
> need, sir?

> BARTLET
> I need pallbearers.

> CHARLIE
> Yes sir.

BARTLET walks into the Oval Office but we stay in Mrs.
Landingham's, seeing something on the coat tree that Bartlet
was looking at...a soft black hat.

                                               FADE TO BLACK

<u>END OF ACT ONE</u>

ACT TWO

FADE IN:

17   **INT. PRESS BRIEFING ROOM - DAY**   17

C.J.'s at the podium.

>   C.J.
> Also in the combat radius will be six
> J-Socs out of McDill and a Battalion
> Landing Team, they'll cover that at the
> Pentagon briefing. Yes.

>   REPORTER
> Does the fact that the OAS has passed a
> resolution allowing you to explore
> military options mean you've exhausted
> the diplomatic ones.

>   C.J.
> Of course it doesn't, but it should
> underline the consequences for Bazan
> should he decide to enter our embassy
> and/or arrest the democratically elected
> President of Haiti. That's all I have for
> now, thank you.

C.J. exits and CAROL steps to the podium--

>   CAROL
> Before you all go, C.J. needs to see
> A.P., Reuters, and Agence France in the
> office, she needs to discuss seating
> arrangements on Air Force One.

                                       CUT TO:

18   **INT. CORRIDOR - DAY**   18

SAM catches up with C.J. as she walks.

>   SAM
> C.J.

>   C.J.
> Yeah.

>   SAM
> We've got a problem.

                                 (CONTINUED)

18   CONTINUED:

> C.J.
> That's pretty hard to believe.

> SAM
> We can't have the press conference in the
> East Room.

> C.J.
> What are you talking about?

> SAM
> I just got off with Brian Coburn and we
> can't have it in the East Room.

> C.J.
> Why not?

> SAM
> They've been pulling the wiring and they
> found asbestos and they have to seal it
> off.

> C.J.
>   (pause)
> There's been asbestos in the East Room
> this whole time?

> SAM
> Yeah. So I'm going to make a list--

> C.J.
> Put together--okay--

> SAM
> Yeah.

> C.J.
> Put together a list of alternatives.

SAM heads off as CAROL comes along with three REPORTERS--

> C.J.
> Come on in.

> REPORTER #1
> C.J., I don't have any problem with my
> seat on the plane.

> C.J.
>   (smiles)
> Get inside.

(CONTINUED)

18   CONTINUED: (2)   18

They go into--

19   **INT. C.J.'S OFFICE - CONTINUOUS**   19

                         REPORTER #1
              Seriously, I complained that one time
              'cause I don't know, I was in a bad mood.

                         C.J.
              This isn't about seating arrangements.
              Notebooks, no tape recorders, the story's
              embargoed for an hour and you'll identify
              me as a senior White House official.

C.J. closes the door as we

                                                         CUT TO:

20   **INT. OVAL OFFICE - DAY**   20

Where LEO's meeting with two economic ADVISORS. BARTLET's just
barely on the outskirts of it.

                         LEO
              Are we talking about the opening bell?

                         ADVISOR #1
              That depends, when's it gonna leak?

                         LEO
              I'm sorry?

                         ADVISOR #1
              When are we leaking the story.

                         LEO
              C.J.'s doing it right now.

                         ADVISOR #1
              Wall Street'll have it in an hour, in two
              hours, sellers will outnumber buyers.

BARTLET notices that the door to the portico has swung open...

                         BARTLET
              Excuse me, keep going.

                         LEO
              In what sectors?

                                                         (CONTINUED)

20   CONTINUED:

> ADVISOR #2
> In all sectors of the...

BARTLET's gotten up and walked out into--

21   **INT. MRS. LANDINGHAM'S OFFICE - CONTINUOUS**   21

> BARTLET
> Charlie.

> CHARLIE
> Yes sir.

> BARTLET
> Do you have any idea why the door to the
> portico keeps swinging open, it's a
> little annoying.

> CHARLIE
> They're replacing the latch, it's
> swinging open from the wind.

> BARTLET
> But the door opens <u>out</u>.

> CHARLIE
> When the right sequence of doors are open
> in the building there's a wind tunnel
> into the Oval Office.

> BARTLET
> No kidding.

BARTLET walks back into--

22   **INT. THE OVAL OFFICE - CONTINUOUS**   22

> ADVISOR #1
> Well Japan's gonna be up and trading by
> the time we go on TV.

BARTLET closes the door.

> BARTLET
> Charlie says there's a wind tunnel
> created by...something...they're fixing
> the latch.

MARGARET steps in--

> MARGARET
> Mr. President?

(CONTINUED)

> BARTLET
> Yeah.

> LEO
> Is the motorcade ready?

> MARGARET
> Yes sir.

> BARTLET
> Okay. Well. We've gotta go. I don't know
> what to say. Leo's pretty rich, maybe he
> can buy some tech stocks, and jack-up the
> price.

> LEO
> Keep me posted on the bellwethers, okay.

> ADVISOR #1
> Yeah.

> ADVISOR #2
> Thank you, Mr. President.

The ADVISORS exit....

> LEO
> (to MARGARET)
> Is the First Lady meeting us in the car?

> MARGARET
> Yes. It's a non-denominational service.

> BARTLET
> What'd she say?

> LEO
> She said the First Lady's meeting us in
> the car.

CUT TO:

23   **INT. DR. BARTLET'S OFFICE - DAY**   23

DELORES is typing at her desk as JED sorts files.

> JED
> It wasn't a non-denominational service.

> DELORES
> Of course it was.

(CONTINUED)

23   CONTINUED: 23

> JED
> It wouldn't have felt non-denominational
> if you were Jewish.

> DELORES
> It was a non-denominational Christian
> service.

> JED
> Attendance at Chapel is required for
> every--

> DELORES
> It was a non-denominational service.

> JED
> "Our Father" is not non-denominational.

> DELORES
> Everyone says Our Father.

> JED
> Catholics don't. Catholics don't say "For
> thine is the kingdom and the power and
> the glory forever and ever." You know,
> I'm just saying.

They walk into--

24   **INT. CORRIDOR - DAY**   24

> DELORES
> Why do you work here?

> JED
> I'm sorry?

> DELORES
> Why do you work here after classes? I
> can't imagine anyone in your family is on
> work-study.

> JED
> No, I get free tuition. So, you know, I
> guess it's a good idea to give something
> back.

> DELORES
> Why do you call your father sir?

(CONTINUED)

24   CONTINUED: 24

                          JED
          Is this gonna be a whole afternoon of
          questions?

                          DELORES
          Well actually, you've been talking for
          quite some time.

                          JED
          I'm sorry, am I boring you, Delores?

                          DELORES
          Mrs. Landingham, please.

                          JED
          My father's the Headmaster.

                          DELORES
          Yeah, but before he was your Headmaster,
          he was your father, right?

                          JED
          I don't want to make the other guys feel
          uncomfortable.

                          DELORES
          So you call him sir.

                          JED
          Yeah.

                          DELORES
          Oh.

                                                      CUT TO:

25   **EXT. MOTORCADE - DAY**   25

      A motorcycle escort leads the MOTORCADE.

                                                      CUT TO:

26   **INT. BARTLET'S LIMO - DAY**   26

      We HEAR sirens as BARTLET and ABBEY ride in back.

                          ABBEY
          You know they released the girl from the
          hospital this morning.

                          BARTLET
          The driver?

                                                      (CONTINUED)

26   CONTINUED: 26

                          ABBEY
              Yeah, she fractured her wrist, some
              stitches over her eye and the other two
              have some scrapes and bruises. It looks
              like they're going to charge her with
              vehicular manslaughter.

There's a long silence...

                          ABBEY
                    (pause)
              Frank Mitchel, Joanna, Bill Carney, they
              told me they're in meetings all morning.

                          BARTLET
              Yeah.

                          ABBEY
              Consensus seems to be that if you step
              back, put your support behind Hoynes,
              there's a decent chance the Democrats'd
              keep the White House.

                          BARTLET
              The world'll rest easier. We're here.

The car's pulled to a stop and the door is opened from the
outside. BARTLET and ABBEY step out onto--

27   **EXT. NATIONAL CATHEDRAL - CONTINUOUS**   27

The steps leading to one of the country's most spectacular
churches are a sea of men and women in black. There's a heavy
police and Secret Service presence. There's a whir of camera
activity aimed at BARTLET and ABBEY.

                                              CUT TO:

28   **INT. NATIONAL CATHEDRAL - DAY**   28

Music summons the gravity of the occasion as about 150
mourners are milling around and taking their seats. A closed
casket sits at the front.

The organ music ends and ABBEY and BARTLET have taken their
places. Anyone sitting stands up as MONOHAN, a man who's
clearly very high up in the clergy, steps out to the pulpit in
full robes. The room stays standing for the invocation.

                                              (CONTINUED)

28   CONTINUED: 28

And during this we see that all of our friends are here. LEO,
SAM, TOBY, C.J., DONNA, JOSH, BONNIE, GINGER, MARGARET,
CAROL...with everything that's been going on, this is going to
serve as a sacred 90 minutes. They obviously never had the
relationship with her that Bartlet or even Leo did, but she
was a friend of theirs and they worked in a foxhole and this
is probably the only time they're given to come to terms that
she's in that box.

> MONOHAN
> I am the Resurrection and I am life says
> the Lord. Whoever believes in me shall
> live, even though he die. God of Mercy,
> you are the hope of sinners, the joy of
> saints. We pray for our sister, Delores,
> whose body we honor with Christian
> burial. Give her happiness with your
> saints, and raise up her body with the
> saints of the last day to be in your
> presence forever. As for me, I know that
> my redeemer lives, and that at the last
> he will stand upon the earth. After my
> awaking, he will raise me up--

> DELORES (O.S.)
> ‚Ted.

> MONOHAN
> --and in my body I shall see God.

> DELORES (O.S.)
> Jed!

> MONOHAN
> I myself shall see and my eyes behold
> him.

DISSOLVE TO:

29   **EXT. DEERFORTH SCHOOL - DAY**   29

JED, in khakis and a shirt with the sleeves rolled up, is
watering some BOATS (SCULLS) used in rowing. Delores walks up
from behind.

> DELORES
> Jed. Jed.

JED looks up.

(CONTINUED)

                    JED
        I'm trying to get through an honest day's
        work, Mrs. Landingham.

                    DELORES
        You missed a spot.

                    JED
        I didn't miss it, I just haven't gotten
        to it yet.

                    DELORES
        Okay.

                    JED
        You have a habit of doing that, you know.

                    DELORES
        What's that.

                    JED
        Telling me I'm doing something wrong
        before I've had a chance to do it
        at all.

                    DELORES
        Well, that must be a little annoying.

                    JED
        Yeah.

                    DELORES
        I got a project for you.

                    JED
        Really.

                    DELORES
        You can show the courage, and the
        intellect, and the leadership skills
        everyone talks about.

                    JED
        I'm a little busy right now hosing down
        the boats.

                    DELORES
        You know the women who work at
        this school are paid less money than
        the men?

                                            (CONTINUED)

29   CONTINUED: (2)   29

                         JED
            Sorry?

                         DELORES
            The women are paid less money than the
            men.

                         JED
            No, I didn't know that.

                         DELORES
            You think your father does?

                                              CUT BACK TO:

30   **INT. NATIONAL CATHEDRAL - DAY**   30

                         MONOHAN (O.S.)
            First reading will be from Mr. Charles
            Young from the Book of Wisdom, Chapter
            III.

            And CHARLIE makes his way to the podium as we

                                              CUT TO:

31   **EXT. DEERFORTH LIBRARY - DAY**   31

            DELORES is sitting on the stoop and waiting. After a moment,
            JED comes out.

                         DELORES
            I'd like an opportunity to make my case.

                         JED
            What are you doing here?

                         DELORES
            I'm raising an issue.

                         JED
            You've been raising this issue for a week
            now.

                         DELORES
            I can tell it's had quite an effect on
            you.

                         JED
            Don't you have a husband?

                                              (CONTINUED)

31   CONTINUED: 31

>   DELORES
>   What does that have to do with anything?
>
>   JED
>   I'm saying shouldn't you maybe go home
>   when you're done with work?
>
>   DELORES
>   Shouldn't you be minding your own
>   business?
>
>   JED
>   I just thought since you were minding
>   everybody else's, you know--
>
>   DELORES
>   Now what's that supposed to mean?
>
>   JED
>   In my family we don't talk about money.
>
>   DELORES
>   That's because you <u>have</u> money.
>
>   JED
>   Numbers, Mrs. Landingham.
>
>   DELORES
>   Excuse me?
>
>   JED
>   If you want to convince me of something,
>   show me numbers.

JED heads off and we

>   CUT BACK TO:

32   **INT. NATIONAL CATHEDRAL - DAY**   32

CHARLIE's at the podium.

>   CHARLIE
>   (reading)
>   "But the souls of the virtuous are in the
>   hands of God, no torment shall ever touch
>   them. In the eyes of the unwise, they did
>   appear to die, but they are at peace.
>   (MORE)

>   (CONTINUED)

32   CONTINUED: 32
                              CHARLIE (cont'd)
                  But though in the sight of others they
                  were punished, their hope is full of
                  immortality."

                                                  FADE TO BLACK

                              <u>END OF ACT TWO</u>

ACT THREE

FADE IN:

33   **EXT. CAMPUS - DAY**   33

JED is trying to start his car. He's not having much success. One try. Two.

The window is rolled down and DELORES leans in.

>DELORES
>Your car won't start.

>JED
>Yes.

>DELORES
>What's wrong with it?

>JED
>It's possibly the starter motor or the fan belt.

>DELORES
>Do you know anything about cars?

>JED
>No.

>DELORES
>Then why do you know--

>JED
>'Cause those are the two things I've heard of.

JED opens the door and gets out--

>DELORES
>You fix your car and pretend you're not listening, I'm just gonna stand here and talk to you 'cause I know you are.

JED opens the hood--

>JED
>What could you possibly want?

>DELORES
>I've got numbers.

(CONTINUED)

33   CONTINUED: 33

>   JED
>   There's something abnormal about you.
>
>   DELORES
>   Florence Chadwick in the English
>   Department has been here 13 years, she
>   makes $5900 a year, Mr. Hopkins in the
>   English Department's been here four years
>   fewer and makes $7100 a year.
>
>   JED
>   Is this really the best time for this?
>
>   DELORES
>   You don't seem to be going anywhere. A
>   female cook makes $3200, compared to a
>   male electrician who makes $3900.

                                                                       CUT TO:

34   **INT. NATIONAL CATHEDRAL - DAY**   34

--where the MOURNERS are on their feet reciting in unison.

>   MOURNERS
>   "--channel of your peace. Where there is
>   hatred, let us show love--"

During this, an OFFICIAL USHER off to the side will make eye
contact with SAM, who'll make similar eye contact with JOSH.
It's a cue.

>   MOURNERS
>   "Where there is injury, harmony. And
>   where there is doubt, let there be faith
>   in you. Amen."

And the *Mozart Requiem* begins as TOBY, JOSH, SAM and CHARLIE
take their places with two other pallbearers at the casket and
lift it to their shoulders. A PRIEST and ALTAR BOYS lead them
up the aisle and out the door.

>   DELORES (V.O.)
>   The Chaplain makes forty-one hundred--

                                                                       CUT TO:

35   **EXT. CAMPUS - DAY**   35

JED's trying to start the car.

                                                                    (CONTINUED)

35   CONTINUED:

                    DELORES
--the nurse makes thirty-one hundred.
Miss Mueller gets paid an additional two-
hundred dollars a year to conduct the
choir and band, while Mr. Ryan gets paid
an additional <u>four</u>-hundred dollars a year
to coach the rowing team.

                    JED
Crew.

                    DELORES
What?

                    JED
It's not rowing, it's crew. And Florence
Chadwick is a married woman with no
dependants and Mr. Hopkins has a family
of four to support.

                    DELORES
If we paid people according to how many
children they had to support then Malcolm
Bundy the groundskeeper would get triple
what the Headmaster gets.

                    JED
Mrs. Landingham--

                    DELORES
You know I'm right.

                    JED
   (beat)
Look--

                    DELORES
You know I'm right. You've known it since
I brought it up, you've known it since
before that.

                    JED
What do you want me to do about it?

                    DELORES
I want you to bring it up with your
father.

                    JED
See, I'm not a woman and I don't work
here.

                    (CONTINUED)

35   CONTINUED: (2)   35

                              DELORES
               The women who do are afraid for their
               jobs. If they bring it up. They're afraid
               for their jobs. What is it <u>you're</u> afraid
               of?

                              JED
               Why do you talk to me like this?

                              DELORES
               'Cause you never had a big sister and you
               need one.
                    (pause)
               Look at you. You're a boy king.
                    (beat)
               You're a foot smarter than the smartest
               kids in the class, you're blessed with
               inspiration you must know this by now,
               you must've sensed it.
                    (pause)
               Look, if you think we're wrong, if you
               think Mr. Hopkins should honestly get
               paid more than Mrs. Chadwick, then I
               respect that. But if you think we're
               right and you won't speak up 'cause you
               can't be bothered, then God, Jed, I don't
               even want to know you.
                    (beat)
               Come inside. I'll call Triple-A.

       JED stands there for a moment...

                              JED
               Miss Mueller only gets half as much to
               teach music as Mr. Ryan gets to coach
               crew?

                              DELORES
                    (pause)
               You're gonna do it.

                              JED
               No, I didn't say that.

                              DELORES
               Yes you did.

                              JED
               When?

                                                          (CONTINUED)

>   DELORES
>   Just then. You stuck your hands in your
>   pockets, you looked away and smiled. That
>   means you made up your mind.

>   JED
>   That doesn't mean anything.

>   DELORES
>   Oh yes it does.

>   JED
>   I stuck my hands in my pockets.

>   DELORES
>   And looked away and smiled. We're in.

                                              CUT BACK TO:

36   **INT. NATIONAL CATHEDRAL - DAY**   36

The place has pretty much emptied out. LEO comes and slides in
next to BARTLET...

>   LEO
>   (pause)
>   It was a beautiful service. I thought.
>   (beat)
>   I thought it was a beautiful service.

>   BARTLET
>   Yeah.

>   LEO
>   She was a real dame, old friend. A real
>   broad.

>   BARTLET
>   Yeah.

>   LEO
>   (pause)
>   We've gotta go back to the office now,
>   sir.

>   BARTLET
>   Yeah.

>   LEO
>   We've got some decisions to make now.

                                                 (CONTINUED)

36   CONTINUED: 36

> BARTLET
> Leo, would you do me a favor?

> LEO
> Yeah.

> BARTLET
> Would you ask the agents to seal the
> cathedral for a minute.

> LEO
> Yeah.

And LEO gets up and walks to the back of the cathedral,
whispering something to one of the agents at the door.

BARTLET stands alone. After a moment he hears the sound off-
screen of heavy doors slamming closed.

When the final door is slammed closed, he says simply--

> BARTLET
> You're a sonofabitch, you know that? She
> bought her first new car and you hit her
> with a drunk driver, what, was that
> supposed to be funny?

BARTLET walks up the aisle...

> BARTLET
> (pause)
> "You can't conceive, nor can I, the
> appalling strangeness of the mercy of
> God," says Graham Greene. I don't know
> whose ass he was kissing there, 'cause I
> think you're just vindictive. What was
> Josh Lyman, a warning shot? *That was my
> son!*
> (beat)
> What did I ever do to yours but praise
> His glory and praise His name?
> (beat)
> There's a tropical storm that's gaining
> speed and power. They say we haven't had
> a storm this bad since you took out that
> tender ship of mine in the North Atlantic
> last year. 68 crew. You know what a
> tender ship does? Fixes the other ships.
> It doesn't even carry guns. It just goes
> around and fixes the other ships and
> delivers the mail, that's all it can do.
> Gratias tibi ago, domine.
> (MORE)

(CONTINUED)

36   CONTINUED: (2)   36
                          BARTLET (cont'd)
                     (pause)
            Yes, I lied, it was a sin, I've committed
            many sins, have I displeased you, you
            feckless thug?
                     (beat)
            3.8 million new jobs, that wasn't good?
            Bailed out Mexico, increased foreign
            trade, 30 million new acres of land for
            conservation, put Mendoza on the bench,
            we're not fighting a war, I've raised
            three children, that's not enough to buy
            me out of the doghouse? Haec credam a deo
            pio? A deo iusto, a deo scito? Cruciatus
            in crucem. Trus in terra servus, nuntuis
            fui. Officum perfeci. Cruciatus in
            crucem. Eas in crucem.

And BARTLET takes a cigarette out, lights it, takes a drag,
blows out a long stream of smoke, tosses the cigarette on the
floor beneath him and stubs it out with his foot.

                          BARTLET
            You get Hoynes.

And BARTLET turns and makes the long walk up the aisle and out
of the church.

                                                   CUT TO:

37   **EXT./EST. THE WHITE HOUSE - DAY**   37

                                                   CUT TO:

38   **INT. TOBY'S OFFICE - DAY**   38

TOBY, SAM, JOSH and C.J. are sitting in a quiet state of
limbo. The work they had to do is done. Now they're just
waiting.

After a moment...

                          C.J.
                     (pause)
            We'll call them Answer "A" and Answer
            "B."

                          JOSH
            Yeah.

                          C.J.
            "Mr. President, does this mean you won't
            be seeking a second term."
                     (beat)
                          (MORE)

                                                   (CONTINUED)

CONTINUED:

                        C.J. (cont'd)
          Answer "A" is You Bet. I will absolutely
          be seeking a second term, I'm looking
          forward to the campaign, there is great
          work that is yet to be done.

                        JOSH
               (pause)
          Yes.

                        C.J.
          Answer "B"--

                        JOSH
          "Are you out of your mind. I can't
          possibly win re-election. I lied about a
          degenerative illness, I'm the target of a
          Grand Jury investigation and Congress is
          about to take me out to lunch. I'd sooner
          have my family take their clothes off and
          dance the tarentella on the Truman
          Balcony, than go through a campaign with
          this around my neck."
               (pause)
          Think that's too on the nose?

                        C.J.
          I do.

There's another long silence...then--

                        SAM
          I want to bring it up again.

                        C.J.
          Why?

                        SAM
          'Cause I got shouted down the first three
          times and I work here just like you do,
          can I help you?

There's a lot of misplaced anxiety today.

                        C.J.
               (beat)
          Sorry.

                        SAM
          I think we have to explore ways of
          calling this off.

                        TOBY
          Sam--

                                              (CONTINUED)

38   CONTINUED: (2)

> SAM
> I think it might be a mistake to send him
> on in a moment when we're trying to
> demonstrate--
>
> TOBY
> Listen--
>
> SAM
> We don't know what the hell they're
> talking about in there, Toby, we don't
> know whether he's running or not. I think
> we have to have--
>
> TOBY
> There are no ways. The story is leaked,
> it's out there, we're doing this. Don't
> worry. It's gonna be fine. They're
> lighting him from outside the window.

GINGER's stuck her head in--

> GINGER
> Toby?
>
> TOBY
> I have a meeting, believe it or not, with
> Greg Summerhays, for reasons passing
> understanding.

JOSH, SAM, and C.J. exit as GREG SUMMERHAYS enters.

> TOBY
> Hello.
>
> GREG
> Toby, it's good to see you.
>
> TOBY
> How are you, Greg.
>
> GREG
> I was sorry about the, uh, President's
> secretary.
>
> TOBY
> Thank you.
>
> GREG
> Did you know her well?

(CONTINUED)

38   CONTINUED: (3)   38

                          TOBY
              Yeah.

                          GREG
              Let me get to why I'm here. I want to--

                          TOBY
              You want to buy Atlantic Intermedia.

                          GREG
              Yeah.

                          TOBY
              Greg, there's a reason the FCC--

                          GREG
              I'm not here about the FCC.

                          TOBY
              Why are you here?

                          GREG
              I'm launching a 24 hour cable news
              channel and I'm building it to compete.
              And I'd like you to be the news director.

                          TOBY
              Okay. Thanks for coming in. Excuse me.

        TOBY gets up and walks out as we

                                                              CUT TO:

39   **INT. JOSH'S OFFICE - DAY**   39

        JOSH is at his desk. DONNA steps in...

                          DONNA
              It was a nice service, don't you think?

                          JOSH
              Yeah. Yeah, it was.

                          DONNA
                    (beat)
              I'm gonna run across the street to the
              OEOB for a minute. The President's still
              after information on the storm, I'm not
              sure why he's got it in his teeth.

                          JOSH
              Yeah.

                                                              (CONTINUED)

39   CONTINUED: 39

> DONNA
> Josh, can this really be how it works? We
> have no idea if he's gonna run again,
> he's in a room with Leo making a
> decision? Two people, in a matter of
> minutes? This is how it works?

The phone rings...

> JOSH
> This is how it works today.

DONNA picks up the phone--

> DONNA
> Josh Lyman.
>   (to JOSH)
> It's Leo.

                                                        CUT TO:

40   **INT. JOSH'S BULLPEN - DAY**   40

As TOBY fumes down the corridor toward Josh's office--

> BONNIE
>   (calling out)
> Hey, Toby.

> TOBY
> Don't anybody talk to me right now.

TOBY walks into--

41   **INT. JOSH'S OFFICE - CONTINUOUS**   41

--where JOSH is hanging up the phone.

> TOBY
> Josh. Greg Summerhays was here to offer
> me a job. Leo got me a lifeboat. I'm
> gonna rip his arms off and beat him with
> his own--

> JOSH
> Toby, that was Leo. He wants us over
> there. It's answer "B."

                                                    (CONTINUED)

41   CONTINUED: 41

JOSH waits a moment, then heads out.   TOBY and DONNA follow.

                                              FADE TO BLACK

                        <u>END OF ACT THREE</u>

ACT FOUR

FADE IN:

42   **EXT./EST. THE WHITE HOUSE - NIGHT**   42

And the storm has come. Rain, wind, lightning, the works.
Nothing like what it's gonna be, but it's pretty bad.

>   ANCHOR (V.O.)
>   ...with the President and First Lady
>   having just concluded the interview.
>   President Bartlet is expected to be--

                                                    CUT TO:

43   **INT. CORRIDOR - NIGHT**   43

LEO is walking BARTLET from the Mural Room to his office as we
see and hear the coverage playing on monitors in the Roosevelt
Room where staffers have just finished watching the interview.

>   ANCHOR (ON TV)
>   --arriving at the State Department for
>   a press conference. Typically, a press
>   conference particularly of this size
>   would be held in the East Room of the
>   White House, but we're told there are
>   some repairs going on there and so the
>   change of venue.

They walk into--

44   **INT. LEO'S OFFICE - CONTINUOUS**   44

>   ANCHOR (V.O.)
>   Chris Watson, can you tell us what we
>   might expect to hear from the President
>   in a few minutes. Wait. Alright. Our
>   apologies. We'll have Chris in a moment.
>   Let's go to--

>   LEO
>   Why don't you sit here for a few minutes.

>   BARTLET
>   Yeah.

>   LEO
>   I'm gonna get C.J., you two do a last
>   minute review.

                                              (CONTINUED)

44   CONTINUED: 44

                           BARTLET
          I'm fine.

                           LEO
          I'm gonna get C.J.

                           BARTLET
          Yeah.

                           LEO
          Sit here. Close your eyes a few minutes.
          Charlie'll get you when we're ready.

                           BARTLET
          Yeah.

                           BARTLET (FROM TV) (V.O.)
          A couple of years ago I began
          experiencing blurred vision and numbness
          in my legs. Two years and many tests
          later--

LEO exits and closes the door behind him as we

                                                          CUT TO:

45   **INT. TOBY'S OFFICE - NIGHT**   45

BARTLET's interview from a few minutes ago is on the monitor
as TOBY watches--

                           BARTLET (FROM TV)
          --I was diagnosed with a course of
          relapsing/remitting Multiple Sclerosis.

                           ANCHOR (V.O.)
          That startling admission made just
          moments ago from--

LEO steps in--

                           LEO
          Toby.

                           TOBY
          Yeah.

                           LEO
          Where's C.J.?

                                                          (CONTINUED)

45   CONTINUED:

                         TOBY
          She ran back to her office.

                         ANCHOR (V.O.)
          The President has this to say--

                         TOBY
          They're gonna run this clip forever.

                         LEO
          No, we're about to give 'em clips to
          beat it.

                         TOBY
          Leo, you got me a lifeboat?

                         LEO
          Greg Summerhays?

                         TOBY
          Yeah.

                         LEO
          Yeah, I got you a lifeboat.

                         TOBY
          Did you imagine that there were any
          circumstances under which I would use it?

                         LEO
          No.

                         TOBY
          Then why--

                         LEO
          To show him that.
               (beat)
          C.J.'s in her office?

          TOBY's turned his attention to the screen...

                         TOBY
               (beat)
          You think he's gonna change his mind,
          don't you.

                         LEO
          Hm?

                                              (CONTINUED)

45 CONTINUED: (2)

                    TOBY
          You think he's gonna run.

                    LEO
               (pause)
          C.J.'s in her office?

                    TOBY
               (pause)
          Yeah.

LEO exits.

                                        CUT TO:

46 **INT. LEO'S OFFICE - NIGHT**   46

BARTLET stands behind a desk. There's a knock on the door.

                    BARTLET
          Yeah.

MARGARET opens the door--

                    MARGARET
          Mr. President, you wanted to see Donna
          Moss?

                    BARTLET
          Yeah.

DONNA steps in.

                    DONNA
          Good evening, sir.

                    BARTLET
          How are you.

                    DONNA
          Fine, thank you, sir. We all thought
          you did very well.

                    BARTLET
          That was the easy part.

                    DONNA
          It didn't look that easy.

                    BARTLET
          Talk about the weather.

                                        (CONTINUED)

46   CONTINUED: 46

>   DONNA
> A tropical storm is a cyclone in which
> the maximum sustained surface speed of
> the wind is 34 nautical miles per hour.

>   BARTLET
> And there's a tropical storm season,
> right?

>   DONNA
> Yes sir. It's June 1st to November 30th.

>   BARTLET
> Okay, and how many times, say in the last
> hundred years, has a tropical storm come
> up the Atlantic seaboard to Washington in
> the middle of May?

>   DONNA
> According to the National Oceanic and
> Atmospheric Administration, it hasn't
> happened in the last century.

>   BARTLET
> At all.

>   DONNA
> No sir.

There's a KNOCK on the door--

>   BARTLET
>   (calling)
> Yeah.

C.J. enters.

>   C.J.
> Excuse me, sir.

>   BARTLET
> Yeah, thanks, Donna.

>   DONNA
> Thank you, Mr. President.

DONNA exits.

>   BARTLET
> According to the NOAA, the storm is a non-
> recurring phenomenon.
>   (MORE)

(CONTINUED)

46   CONTINUED: (2)

                    BARTLET (cont'd)
        Which is science's term for "We don't
        know <u>what</u> in the world is going
        on but we're stocking up on canned
        goods."

                    C.J.
        I just wanted to review a few things.

                    BARTLET
        Is this stuff that you don't think I
        remember from an hour ago?

                    C.J.
        You'll want to take the first question
        from Lawrence Altman, the *Times* chief
        medical correspondent.

                    BARTLET
        Why?

                    C.J.
        Because if you call on anyone else,
        the first question'll be about re-
        election. Calling Altman it'll be a
        medical question and he'll have two or
        three follow-ups. It'll allow you to feel
        comfortable a little before you start
        with the political mess.

                    BARTLET
        Okay.

                    C.J.
        Altman will be in the front row, first
        seat on your right.

                    BARTLET
        Okay.

                    C.J.
            (pause)
        Mr. President?

                    BARTLET
        Yeah.

                    C.J.
        Where's Altman gonna be?

                    BARTLET
        C.J.--

                                        (CONTINUED)

46   CONTINUED: (3)   46

> C.J.
> Mr. President, I'm going there right now.
> This is the last time I'm gonna see you
> before you step up, please, where--

> BARTLET
> Front row, first seat on the right.

> C.J.
> Whose right?

> BARTLET
> My right.

> C.J.
> Thank you, sir.

C.J. exits. BARTLET's alone in the room for a moment. Then
there's--

KNOCK KNOCK KNOCK

BARTLET doesn't say anything...

KNOCK KNOCK KNOCK

BARTLET doesn't say anything...

                                                    CUT TO:

47   **INT. DR. BARTLET'S OFFICE - DAY**   47

--where JED is knocking on the office door. He's wearing his
school coat and tie.

> DR. BARTLET (O.S.)
> Come in.

JED opens the door and walks into the office. DR. BARTLET is
behind his desk with a copy of the school newspaper.

> DR. BARTLET
> (reading)
> "If you hide your ignorance, no one will
> hit you, and you'll never learn." Is this
> your quote?

> JED
> (pause)
> Dad, I wanted to mention something to you
> that maybe you weren't aware of regarding
> salary equity.

                                              (CONTINUED)

> DR. BARTLET
> Is this your quote? "If you hide your
> ignorance, no one will hit you, and
> you'll never learn."

> JED
> It's actually Ray Bradbury.

> DR. BARTLET
> And you quoted Ray Bradbury.

> JED
> Yes.

> DR. BARTLET
> In an article you and your friends wrote
> condemning Professor Loomis.

> JED
> For banning certain books from the
> library, yes.

> DR. BARTLET
> He's a professor of literature.

> JED
> He banned Henry Miller, he banned
> D.H. Lawrence.

> DR. BARTLET
> Jed--

> JED
> *Giovanni's Room* 'cause it's too
> homosexual.

> DR. BARTLET
> Stop it right now, you're a guest
> at this school.

> JED
> I'm a student at this school.

> DR. BARTLET
> Jed--

> JED
> He banned *Fahrenheit 451* which is
> about banning books.

(CONTINUED)

> DR. BARTLET
> Was that supposed to be funny?
>   (beat)
> That word play that you just did
> there, was that meant to be funny?

> JED
>   (beat)
> That was supposed--

CRACK! DR. BARTLET smacks him across the face. It's not the
first time that's happened but JED wasn't expecting it.

> DR. BARTLET
>   (pause)
> Was there anything else?

> JED
>   (long pause - evenly)
> It's not a non-denominational service.

> DR. BARTLET
> Don't start with this.

> JED
> Catholics <u>don't</u> believe that man is saved
> through faith alone, Catholics believe
> that faith has to be joined with good
> works.

> DR. BARTLET
> You're the only one who seems to mind
> the service.

> JED
> I'm the only one who's Catholic.

> DR. BARTLET
> You're Catholic because your mother is.
> And you're at this school because I'm the
> Headmaster. How's that for clever with
> words.
>   (beat)
> Now what was it you came in here to talk
> to me about.

> JED
>   (pause)
> Nothing.

> DR. BARTLET
> Please close the door behind you.

(CONTINUED)

47   CONTINUED: (3)   47

And JED walks out and we

                                                    CUT TO:

48   **INT. THE OVAL OFFICE - NIGHT**   48

As BARTLET closes the door from LEO's office behind him. **The**
room is empty and he stands right there for a moment.

He goes to the desk. After a moment the door to the portico
swings open with a loud *WHACK*!

                          BARTLET
          Ah...*dammit*--
              (shouting without thinking)
          Mrs. Landingham!

And then BARTLET realizes he's shouted for someone who's been
dead two days. And no sooner does he realize that than his
head is turned by the door from the outer office opening
quickly. MRS. LANDINGHAM enters.

                     MRS. LANDINGHAM
          I really wish you wouldn't shout, Mr.
          President.

                          BARTLET
              (pause)
          The door keeps blowing open.

                     MRS. LANDINGHAM
          Yes, but there's an intercom, and you
          could use it to call me at my desk.

                          BARTLET
          I was--

                     MRS. LANDINGHAM
          You don't know how to use the intercom.

                          BARTLET
          It's not that I don't know how to use it,
          it's just that I haven't learned yet.

They smile at each other...

                          BARTLET
              (pause)
          I have MS and I didn't tell anybody.

                                          (CONTINUED)

48   CONTINUED:

                    MRS. LANDINGHAM
Yeah.
     (pause)
So you're having a little bit of a day.

                    BARTLET
You gonna make jokes?

                    MRS. LANDINGHAM
God doesn't make cars crash and you know
it. Stop using me as an excuse.

                    BARTLET
The party's not gonna want me to run.

                    MRS. LANDINGHAM
The party'll come back, you'll get 'em
back.

                    BARTLET
I've got a secret for you, Mrs.
Landingham. I've never been the most
popular guy in the Democratic Party.

                    MRS. LANDINGHAM
I've got a secret for you, Mr. President.
Your father was a prick who could never
get over the fact that he wasn't as smart
as his brothers. Are you in a tough spot?
Yes. Do I feel sorry for you? I do not.
Why? Because there are people way worse
off then you.

                    BARTLET
Give me numbers.

                    MRS. LANDINGHAM
I don't know numbers, you give them to
me.

                    BARTLET
How 'bout a child born in this minute has
a one in five chance of being born into
poverty.

                    MRS. LANDINGHAM
How many Americans don't have health
insurance?

                    BARTLET
44 million.

                                  (CONTINUED)

> MRS. LANDINGHAM
> What's the number one cause of death
> for black men under 35?

> BARTLET
> Homicide.

> MRS. LANDINGHAM
> How many Americans are behind bars?

> BARTLET
> 3 million.

> MRS. LANDINGHAM
> How many Americans are drug addicts?

> BARTLET
> Five million.

> MRS. LANDINGHAM
> And one in five kids in poverty?

> BARTLET
> It's 13 million American children. Three
> and a half million kids go to schools
> that are literally falling apart, we need
> 127 billion in school construction, and
> we need it today.

> MRS. LANDINGHAM
> To say nothing of 53 people trapped in
> an embassy.

> BARTLET
> Yes.

> MRS. LANDINGHAM
> You know if you don't want to run again,
> I respect that. But if you don't run
> because you think it's gonna be too
> hard...or you think you're gonna lose...
>   (pause)
> ...well, God, Jed, I don't even want to
> know you.

And BARTLET looks away. There wasn't a puff of smoke or
anything, but when BARTLET looks back, she's gone. That's
okay, he knew she would be.

BARTLET looks over at the open door. The storm is in full
force out there.

(CONTINUED)

48   CONTINUED: (3)

He stands in the doorway to the portico. The wind is making the rain spray in and we hear rumbling thunder and some lightning.

BARTLET steps out onto--

49   **EXT. PORTICO - CONTINUOUS**   49

The rain and wind knock him in the face. He stands there not flinching. He wants it.

We hear Mark Knopfler's aching guitar and the sound of thunder turns into the intro to *Brothers in Arms*. As the song begins, everything else is MOS.

And CHARLIE steps out on the portico from MRS. LANDINGHAM's office. It's time to go. He's holding a coat out for BARTLET but BARTLET doesn't want it.

                              CHARLIE
          Mr. President. Mr. President. It's time.

BARTLET heads inside.

                              LYRIC
                    These mist covered mountains
                    Are home now to me
                    But my home is the loneliness
                    And always will be
                    Someday you'll return to
                    Your valleys and your farms
                    And you'll no longer yearn to be
                    Brothers in Arms

CHARLIE stands there a moment, and as CHARLIE follows him in, he takes off his coat and throws it on a chair and continues on as the dirge-like quality of the song now picks up some tempo and determination.

We begin a SERIES OF SHOTS--

50   **INT. CORRIDOR - NIGHT**   50

The BARTLET entourage picking up momentum--

                                                        CUT TO:

51   **INT. STATE DEPARTMENT AUDITORIUM - NIGHT**   51

Jam packed. C.J.'s already taking questions.

                                                  (CONTINUED)

51   CONTINUED: 51

                         C.J.
          And he'll be speaking to that just as
          soon as he gets here. Uh, Frank, then
          Leslie.

                         LYRIC
          Through these fields of destruction
          Baptisms of fire.

                                                            CUT TO:

52   **EXT. DRIVEWAY - NIGHT**   52

We see the red and blue flashing lights of the motorcade as
people fight the rain and wind.

                         LYRIC
          I've witnessed your suffering
          As the battles raged higher

                                                            CUT TO:

53   **INT. STATE DEPARTMENT AUDITORIUM - NIGHT**   53

                         REPORTER #2
          Has there been any discussion of a
          Special Prosecutor?

                         C.J.
          Tomorrow morning the President will
          direct the Attorney General to appoint a
          Special Prosecutor, yes. I can't see,
          Joan?

                         LYRIC
          And they did hurt so bad
          In the fear and alarm
          You did not desert me
          My Brothers in Arms

54   **INT. BARTLET'S LIMO - NIGHT**   54

The sky is exploding from the storm. BARTLET and LEO are
staring straight ahead.

                                                            CUT TO:

55   **INT. STATE DEPARTMENT AUDITORIUM - NIGHT**   55

                         C.J.
          A list of three prosecutors is given to a
          three judge panel.
                         (MORE)

                                                            (CONTINUED)

55   CONTINUED: 55

                         C.J. (cont'd)
             The prosecutors as well as the judges
             were all appointed by Republican
             Presidents. Please. I can only answer 14
             or 15 questions at once. Hal--

DONNA and MARGARET take their places in the back of the room,
surrounded by REPORTERS.

                                                    CUT TO:

56   **INT. NATIONAL CATHEDRAL - NIGHT**   56

It's empty except for some CUSTODIANS sweeping up in the
aisles. The front door is open and the storm can be seen
outside in the night.

A CUSTODIAN sees something on the ground. He bends down and
picks up a cigarette butt. And out the front doors we suddenly
see the flashing lights of Bartlet's motorcade go by. The
music continues as we

                                                    CUT TO:

57   **INT. STATE DEPARTMENT AUDITORIUM - NIGHT**   57

                         C.J.
             --I can't comment on a witness list that
             doesn't exist, but I imagine subpoenas
             will be issued to most senior White House
             staff including myself.

                                                    CUT TO:

58   **EXT. STATE DEPARTMENT AUDITORIUM - NIGHT**   58

A motorcycle escort breaks off as BARTLET's LIMO pulls up to
the front and BARTLET et al step out into the rain.

                                                    CUT TO:

59   **INT. STATE DEPARTMENT CORRIDOR - NIGHT**   59

As BARTLET et al come in. BARTLET's handed a towel which he
uses to quickly wipe his face while he's walking and hands it
back as we--

                                                    CUT TO:

60   **INT. STATE DEPARTMENT AUDITORIUM - NIGHT**   60

As we see through glass doors BARTLET et al approaching, CAROL
nods to C.J.

                                              (CONTINUED)

60   CONTINUED:

> C.J.
> Again, I can't comment on what kind of
> hearings Congress has in mind, I'm sure
> there'll be one, but you'd have to talk
> to Congress. Okay, here now, the
> President of the United States.

BARTLET steps up on stage and everyone comes to their feet. He
makes eye-contact with C.J.

> C.J.
> (to BARTLET)
> Front row on your right.

BARTLET takes his place at the podium, looks at the guy, then
looks to the middle of the crowd and calls on someone at
random. Uh-oh.

> BARTLET
> Yes. Sandy.

> REPORTER (SANDY)
> Mr. President, can you tell us right
> now if you'll be seeking a second
> term?

And BARTLET doesn't answer... the staff is getting curious...

> BARTLET
> (pause)
> I'm sorry, Sandy, there was a bit of
> noise there, could you repeat the
> question.

The staff is thinking "Please, God, come to me papa..."

> SANDY
> Can you tell us right now if you'll be
> seeking a second term?

Again BARTLET is silent...

LEO and TOBY watch from a TV monitor that is broadcasting the
press conference. LEO turns his attention from the TV monitor
to the front of the room...

> LEO
> (to TOBY)
> Watch this.

(CONTINUED)

60   CONTINUED: (2)   60

And BARTLET thinks... looks away... sticks his left hand in
his pocket... and just as he smiles we

                                                      FADE TO BLACK

                            <u>END OF SHOW</u>

The weekly cast and crew table-read in the Roosevelt Room

ABOUT THE AUTHOR

Aaron Sorkin (Creator/Executive Producer) graduated from Syracuse University in 1983 with a bachelor of fine arts degree in theatre. In 1989, he received the Outer Critics Circle award as Outstanding American Playwright for *A Few Good Men* and followed that with the off-Broadway comedy *Making Movies*. His screen adaptation of *A Few Good Men* was nominated for four Academy Awards° and five Golden Globe Awards, including Best Picture and Best Screenplay.

Sorkin received his second Golden Globe nomination for *The American President*, and his screenplay for *Malice* was nominated for the Edgar Allen Poe Award by the Mystery Writer's Association of America. He is a founding member of the Playwrights Unit of Playwrights Horizons.

Sorkin was also creator and executive producer of the award-winning television series *Sports Night* which aired on ABC for two seasons (1998-99, 1999-2000). Sorkin's work on *Sports Night* earned the TCA Award for Best Comedy Series, The Viewers for Quality Television Award for Best New Comedy Series, The Directors Guild of America Award, The Humanitas Prize, the Genesis Award, and two Emmy Awards°. In 1999, Sorkin was also rewarded with his first Emmy Award° nomination for his critically acclaimed writing on the show.

To date, Sorkin's work on *The West Wing* has garnered 17 Emmys° including Outstanding Writing For a Drama Series. In 2001, *The West Wing* won its second consecutive Emmy° for Outstanding Drama Series. These wins make it the all-time leader with the most Emmys° won by a series not only in its first season, but also the most Emmys° won by any series in one season. *The West Wing* has also won a

Golden Globe Award for Best Television Drama Series, two consecutive Peabody Awards for Broadcast and Cable Excellence, and the Humanitas Prize, as well as TCA Awards for Best Drama Series, New Program of the Year, and Program of the Year.

Sorkin was also the recipient of the Producers Guild Award, in addition to the People for the American Way's Spirit of Liberty Award.